Recent Research in Psychology

Laurence B. Brown

Editor

Religion, Personality, and Mental Health

Springer-Verlag

New York Berlin Heidelberg London Paris
Tokyo Hong Kong Barcelona Budapest

Dr. Laurence B. Brown, Alister Hardy Research Centre, Westminster College, Oxford OX2 9AT, United Kingdom

With 3 Illustrations.

Library of Congress Cataloging-in-Publication Data
Religion, personality, and mental health / [edited by] Laurence B.
  Brown, Ph.D.
      p. cm.—(Recent research in psychology)
    Includes bibliographical references and indexes.
    ISBN 0-387-97773-2
    1. Mental health—Religious aspects. 2. Psychology, Religious.
  3. Personality—Religious aspects. I. Brown, Laurence Binet, 1927–
  . II. Series.
  BL65.M45R47 1993
  200'.1'9—dc20   93-15258

Printed on acid-free paper.

Production coordinated by Chernow Editorial Services, Inc., and managed by Francine McNeill; manufacturing supervised by Jacqui Ashri.
Typeset by Best-set Typesetter Ltd., Hong Kong.
Printed and bound by Braun-Brumfield, Inc., Ann Arbor, MI.
Printed in the United States of America.

9 8 7 6 5 4 3 2 1

ISBN 0-387-97773-2 Springer-Verlag New York Berlin Heidelberg
ISBN 3-540-97773-2 Springer-Verlag Berlin Heidelberg New York

Acknowledgments

Meetings held in Sydney at the time of the XXIV International Congress of Psychology enabled a core of the group whose papers are presented here to discuss them, both before and after they had been read at that Congress. This group was drawn from Europe, North and South America, and Australia. The meetings were not only agreeable social occasions, but they allowed an exchange of ideas and experience, which emphasized that friendship with others working in the same field is an important feature of good scientific communication. Those who were unable to attend those meetings but whose papers are included here have, however, broadened the scope of this set of papers. They are to be thanked for that. Another outcome of those meetings in Sydney has been the establishment of the *International Journal for the Psychology of Religion*, edited by L.B. Brown and H. Newton Malony, Volume 1, Number 1, of which appeared early in 1991.

Many arrangements for the meetings in Sydney were made by the late Louise Kahabka. The final preparation of the manuscripts was most capably done by Maxine Mackellar.

Contents

Contributors

Valerie Amos, B.A., Department of Psychology, Royal Holloway and Bedford New College, University of London, Egham, Surrey TW20 0EX, United Kingdom

Allen E. Bergin, Ph.D., Department of Psychology, Brigham Young University, Provo, UT 84602, USA

Laurence B. Brown, Ph.D., Alister Hardy Research Centre, Westminster College, Oxford OX2 9AT, United Kingdom

Jocelyn Delbridge, B.A., Deceased

Leslie J. Francis, Ph.D., Trinity College, Carmarthen, Dyfed SA31 3EP, United Kingdom

Vivienne Goldblatt, B.A., Department of Psychology, Royal Holloway and Bedford New College, University of London, Egham, Surrey TW20 0EX, United Kingdom

Bruce Headey, Ph.D., Department of Political Science, University of Melbourne, Parkville VIC 3052, Australia

Nils G. Holm, Ph.D., Department of Comparative Religion, Abo Akademi, 20500 Abo, Finland

Kate Loewenthal, Ph.D., Department of Psychology, Royal Holloway and Bedford New College, University of London, Egham, Surrey TW20 0EX, United Kingdom

H. Newton Malony, Ph.D., Graduate School of Psychology, Fuller Theological Seminary, Pasadena, CA 91182, USA

Sean Mullarkey, B.A., Department of Psychology, Royal Holloway and Bedford New College, University of London, Egham, Surrey TW20 0EX, United Kingdom

Kathleen V. O'Connor, Ph.D., University Counselling Service, University of Sydney NSW 2006, Sydney, Australia

Thorleif Pettersson, Ph.D., Department of Social Sciences of Religion, Faculty of Theology, Uppsala University, Uppsala, Sweden

Carole A. Rayburn, Ph.D., 1200 Morningside Drive, Silver Spring, MD 20904, USA

Clelia Maria Nascimento Schulze, Ph.D., Federal University of Santa Catarina, Universitario-Trinidad-Caixa Campus, Postal 476, Cep. 88049-Florianopolis, Santa Catarina, Brazil

Lee J. Richmond, Ph.D., Education Department, Loyola College in Maryland, Baltimore, MD 21210, USA

Lynn Rogers, M.A., Department of Counseling and Education, Johns Hopkins University, Baltimore, MD 21218, USA

Emma Shackle, Plater College, Oxford, United Kingdom

Hans Stifoss-Hanssen, Ph.D., Institute of Behavioral Medicine and Psychiatry, Ostmarka Psychiatric Hospital, Trondheim, Norway

Alexander J. Wearing, Ph.D., Department of Psychology, University of Melbourne, Parkville VIC 3052, Australia

Owe Wikstrom, Ph.D., Faculty of Theology, Uppsala University, Uppsala, Sweden

1
Introduction

Laurence B. Brown

Nearly all the papers in this collection were prepared initially by a group of psychologists interested in the social scientific study of religion. They included some working with the mentally ill in medical, religious, or secular contexts, as well as teachers and researchers in psychology or theology. Their papers aim to test, or to reflect on, common prejudices about the links between mental health and religion, especially when they are thought to be mediated by personality characteristics. All the papers have been revised for this collection.

A clear consensus emerged that religion has many positive effects, despite Wulff's (1991, p. 307) unguarded assertion that, "without question the mentally disturbed are frequently attracted by religion."

Any assumption that religion is necessarily a "danger" to health, or closely related to mental illness, is not supported by the evidence from carefully controlled studies that follow a social science perspective. Malony's paper, page 16 in this collection, therefore emphasizes that we must take account of the ways in which anyone's religion is integrated into their life, the functions it serves for them and their acceptance by other members of the religious and other groups to which they belong. Each of those factors must be considered before any conclusion about a person's immaturity, or mental state, can be reached; it is not enough to refer only to their religious stance. That is so because interactions between any individual and their environment are so close that it is unusual for religious beliefs and practices to express inner states or psychological traits directly, if only because competent members of a social group will be constrained by the demands imposed on them by others in that group.

The next paper, by Wikstrom (page 29), argues that any approach to the psychology of religion must be built from a social perspective on both religion and psychology. It is only when support from a particular tradition, culture, or social group is lacking that a person's religious claims might signify or help to diagnose a "mental illness."

Psychiatry and Religion

There is a continuing dance between psychiatry and religion, with the DSM-III-R (American Psychiatric Association, 1987) using religious examples to illustrate such psychiatric categories as catatonic posturing, delusions, and depression. But in *Psychiatry and Religion*, Robinson (1986) stresses the therapeutic value of religion, noting that "healing and religion have been separated for only a few centuries" (p. ix). Wide differences in the public and private expressions of religion, and in its overt and covert alignments, make it hard to know how much of a person's hidden religious beliefs or practices conform to an accepted orthodoxy.

Single case studies, such as Holm's (page 42) biographical account of the Swedish-Finnish writer Joel Pettersson, do not overcome those problems, nor do they show that a psychiatric illness alone destroys a person's religion. Furthermore, such psychobiographies as Erikson's (1958) analysis of *Young man Luther*, which was built to support his theory of psychosocial development, and the varied interpretations of St. Augustine's *Confessions* (1991) gathered by Capps and Dittes (1990), set out the uneasy balance between the sociopolitical pressures and personal needs or goals that are so often identified with a religious perspective.

Any conclusions about individuals do not easily generalize to other people, and when the results are averaged across individuals they inevitably obscure their specific characteristics. Figure 1.1 shows this eloquently with reference to recordings of cortical evoked potentials. When closed response categories are used to gather the data from groups of individuals, details of the responses of individuals are further obscured. Idiosyncratic responses from the members of any social or religious group are therefore located behind the forms of expression that are judged appropriate for particular settings or activities, except among those who are specially recognized for their creativity, insight, or leadership.

Idiosyncratic constructions of religious meaning are illustrated in the paper by Delbridge, Headey, and Wearing (page 50), who interviewed 20 people selected by their answers to a social survey, to contrast the reactions of satisfied and dissatisfied religious or nonreligious people. Those interviews show some of the detailed opinions and explanations that are concealed behind the consensus that social surveys aim for.

Religious Belief and Practice

Like a grammar, most of our social knowledge is taken for granted. Talking to others about religion could therefore be more a matter of getting the linguistic "register" correct, than of making factual remarks or disclosures about oneself. In that sense, Kroll and Sheehan's (1989)

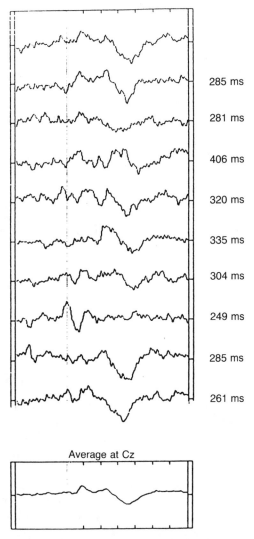

285 ms

281 ms

406 ms

320 ms

335 ms

304 ms

249 ms

285 ms

261 ms

Average at Cz

FIGURE 1.1. Single trial cortical evoked response potentials to auditory stimuli (oddball paradigm) with the largest stimulus identified within trains of background stimuli. Their mean is at the bottom and reaction times are on the right-hand side (Courtesy of Dr. Evian Gordon, Neuroscience Unit, Westmead Hospital, Sydney, Australia).

study of the religious beliefs, practices, and experiences of 52 psychiatric patients, which found that the opinions of those patients were in accord with national public opinion poll results, supports the social reasonableness of an "accepted" religious stance that might, nevertheless, be easily criticized from some other theological or philosophical perspective.

Bergin's (page 69) innovative longitudinal study of 60 young Mormons over 3 years focuses systematically on their religious development, adjustment, and experiences. He stresses the variability in their adaptation to a religious life-style and shows that while arguments about the links between religion and poor mental health are often designed to discredit religion, all the people he studied were coping well. To question the psychological validity rather than the epistemological status of a person's religion involves an ill-informed emphasis. Questions about religion and mental health therefore continue to be debated with little reference to the values and prejudices that are concealed behind exaggerated claims about the pathological character of some religious attachments. But religious attachments themselves may be less of a problem than religious instability, in the sense of switching allegiance, which Shaver, Lenauer, and Sadd (1980), and Witztum, Greenberg, and Dasberg (1990) found can indicate a degree of maladjustment. Witztum et al. noted, however, that increased religious observance following such a switch can be followed by a reemergence of chronic problems. Bergin (1991), on the other hand, points to other studies that have shown the adaptive value of a religious conversion.

Religion and Personality

Personality has been the topic most frequently investigated by psychologists and sociologists interested in religion, reflecting an assumption that they are closely related, or that religious attachments themselves have powerful effects on one's character. So religious items are found in many measures of personality and of values (e.g., Allport, Vernon, & Lindzey, 1960; Heist et al., 1968), although the 11 religious items in the Minnesota Multiphasic Personality Inventory (MMPI) that form a coherent factor (Johnson et al., 1984) are not separately scored. Despite that, Francis's (page 94) review of Eysenck's measures of personality shows that there are no close links between religiousness and neuroticism. His major finding is that although introverts are more religious than extraverts, that finding depends on their lack of impulsivity, which could implicate a broadly biological factor, following Eysenck's theory of personality, or the effects of a religious socialization.

While Diener (1984) noted that the personality factors that have been related to a sense of subjective well-being include high self-esteem, internality, extraversion, sensation-seeking, and sociability, he says that "religious faith, the importance of religion and religious traditionalism generally relate positively to subjective well-being," although others have held that "religiosity (is) correlated inversely with positive moods." Nevertheless, "because people are in general more sociable when they are happier" (ibid.), links between religiousness and subjective well-

Research reviewed by Taylor and Brown (1988) therefore suggests that "happy people are more likely to have positive conceptions of themselves, a belief in their ability to control what goes on around them, and optimism about the future" (p. 200). Others have argued that, because the world is an uncertain and frightening place, we create positive and life-affirming illusions to help us cope with the existential terrors of failure, chaos, and underlying disorder (cf. Becker, 1973). This contrast of optimism against pessimism supports the psychological validity of religion, despite the criticism of it as deliberately manipulated and socially sanctioned sets of illusions that draw in the weak or oppressed, offering them "pie in the sky." Expecting those who are "mature" to have no need of God as an explanatory "hypothesis" is, however, more moralistic than data-based, since it introduces other constructions of the meaning of religious doctrines and practices for individuals.

The large number of trade books offering self-help advice, holistic treatments, and carefree "religious" solutions to personal and social problems shows the extent to which religions and quasi-religions are accepted as instrumentally useful, and not simply as expressions of belief about life itself or the purpose of the world. To assume that religious people accept all the doctrines and practices of their "faith," or that they are all exploited by what their critics regard as an unreal dependence on wished-for truths, disregards the major finding that most religious systems (except those that are closed or authoritarian) tolerate, and might even foster, different orientations or attitudes (cf. Allport, 1960).

The obscure connections between personality and religion are illustrated by Bergin's (1983) meta-analysis of the relationships between religion, mental illness, and psychopathology in 24 separate studies, which found no support for direct links between those variables. This is not surprising, however, granted the lack of agreement about how religion should be defined. As Bergin put the problem, "one researcher views a worshipful lifestyle positively in terms of reverence, humility, and constructive obedience, as universal moral laws, whereas another researcher views the same lifestyle negatively as self-abasing, unprogressive, and blindly conforming." To control for this lack of agreement, Bergin restricted his meta-analysis to studies with at least one broadly religious measure and an independent measure of "pathology," disregarding conventional traits such as dominance, altruism, and introversion.

Mental Health and Religion

This field continues to suffer from the wide range of theories that are either not well-defined, or tested with nonstandard measures applied to samples of convenience, with little firm agreement about what it is that

If adherence to a religious regimen has implications for health status, then should this relationship not be manifest in differential rates of physician and hospital visits: (a) between the formally attached and unattached (i.e., between the churched and unchurched); (b) between adherents of various belief systems (i.e., denominations) which differ in their degrees of rigor in regard to health-related demands; (c) by the extent to which fellowship is experienced (e.g., by the frequency of religious attendance); and (d) by one's status within or commitment to one's particular religious institution (e.g., by whether one is or is not a church officer)?

Similar points can be made about the lack of agreement about how religious affiliation or the frequency of religious attendance is to be validly (and consistently) operationalized, especially in relation to the effects that an investigator's (often unstated) values have on the ways they might want to break up religious phenomena when identifying any links between religion and personality. Following Bem and Funder (1978), we must recognize that religious contexts, doctrines, and rituals themselves presuppose an ideal person who, as a Christian, can be expected to achieve salvation or solace in time of trouble (accepting Rokeach's [1969] analysis of religious values). It is, however, important to distinguish the coherence of self-report measures of underlying predispositions from an account of a person's specific actions, which are likely to depend on their context, and do not allow for sound measures of general tendencies or habits about church-going or prayer, for example (cf. Fishbein & Ajzen, 1974, p. 335f).

The breadth of the early work on religion and mental health is shown by the U.S. National Institute of Health's bibliography, with 1,835 entries (Summerlin, 1980). A review by Koenig, Smiley, and Gonzales (1988) that focused on religion, general health, and aging emphasizes the benefits that religious alignments can provide. Yet pervasive contrasts between the uses and misuses of a religion that retains the interest of many people are hard to resolve without an open-minded attitude to religion and a pluralistic approach to mental and physical health, that separates biological and psychosocial factors from their existential or moral parameters.

Jahoda's (1958) influential review of the criteria for mental health included positive attitudes to the self through an ability to "self-actualize," a sense of autonomy, and social or environmental mastery. Jourard and Landsman's (1980, p. 131) comparable analysis identified such characteristics as positive self-regard; realistic self-perceptions; creativity; and an ability to care about others and the natural world, to do productive work, to have an openness to new ideas and people, and to love. None of these socially desirable features carries a necessary link with religious involvement or detachment. Judgments about someone's "religious health" are therefore likely to refer to a set of secular criteria, unless a disapproved form of religion is at issue or a positive stance towards it has been adopted. Bergin (1991) describes another empirical consensus about mental health values or "themes," which includes the expression of feelings, autonomy and responsibility, integrative coping, self-awareness and growth, forgiveness, and "spirituality/religiosity."

Although mental health is identified with a sense of subjective well-being and control, the term is also applied negatively to mental "illness," where it involves an unhealthy adaptation to the environmental, economic, political, and cultural pressures on (or from) everyday life that implicate biological as well as social links between any individual, their world, and their future. Religious feelings and attitudes involved there have less to do with "spirituality" than with maintaining the psychological balance between what Allport and Ross (1967) identified as extrinsic (or instrumental) and intrinsic religious orientations. Contrasting an opportunistic or adaptive use of religion against an intrinsic commitment to religious goals (Donahue, 1985) has, however, become a major tool for many psychologists of religion (cf. Gorsuch, 1988).

While a religion can assist someone's adjustment through the beliefs it offers, or the support it makes available, it is no more ambiguous than any therapeutic technique that can sustain a sense of self, or facilitate involvement with others or with their natural environment (although that last perspective has been neglected). The optimism that underestimates our vulnerability to cancer or overestimates the chances of winning a lottery helps us cope. Self-mastery allows us to stop smoking, change our diet, and alter other risks to health. Whether such deliberate changes are to be justified on religious, ascetic, scientific, or other grounds is unlikely to alter their efficacy, even if they draw criticism because of the source.

Batson and Ventis (1982, p. 221f) listed the findings from 57 different studies that provide empirical evidence concerning correlations between the amount of religious involvement (rather than its form) and mental health. In their careful analysis, with "line scores" for seven conceptions of mental health (covering the absence of illness, appropriate social behavior, freedom from worry and guilt, personal competence and control, self-acceptance and self-actualization, unification and organization, open-mindedness and flexibility, on p. 231) they emphasize that the "apparently contradictory conclusions that others have drawn" (p. 232) may depend on a lack of agreement about what could be involved. Their broad conclusion is that "except among clergy, religious involvement is positively correlated with absence of mental illness. But it is negatively correlated with personal competence and control, self-actualization, open-mindedness and flexibility, and freedom from worry and guilt (except among the elderly)" (p. 233).

For Batson and Ventis, the effects of religion on mental health, and the "apparently contradictory conclusions drawn by Becker, Dittes, and (by) Sanua (1969)" (p. 232) depend on differences in the conceptions of mental health and on how to be "religious." But as they say, "an extrinsic, means orientation appears to have a rather pervasive negative relationship to mental health, regardless of how mental health is conceived. But both the intrinsic and the quest orientations have positive relationships with at least some conceptions of mental health" (p. 249). Batson and Ventis's (1982) meta-analysis "underscores the need for further research," not least because "the evidence for a given relationship is (often) limited to one or two findings" (p. 250), which are inevitably generalized from diverse approaches to data collection and analysis.

Although meta-analyses cannot give the confidence we need to predict individuals' reactions, they help to generate further testable hypotheses. Nevertheless, whether or not "religion is a force for mental health or selfishness . . . depends on the particular orientation to religion and the particular conception of mental health in question" (Batson & Ventis, 1982, pp. 250–251). There are also enormous individual differences in the desire for a "spiritual dimension" in life, and in what those needing it might be likely to find in "some of the heavens and some of the hells to which different ways of being religious are likely to lead" (Batson & Ventis, p. 311).

Personality and Religion

Despite different uses of terms such as "personality" and "mental health" (cf. Hall & Lindzey, 1978, p. 4), they both imply a functional orientation to the "whole person," giving motivation a crucial role in understanding belief and action, and expecting stable or consistent traits to "explain" why particular people might act differently from others in comparable situations. Theologians, philosophers, and sociologists seem to have accepted those assumptions, although Lamiell (1987, p. 179) argued that we will only make progress in the study of personality if we replace our search for the "correlates of individual differences" by exposing the "grounds on, and the reasoning processes by which individuals frame personal knowledge and extend it into action."

The attitudes of those professionally involved with mental health have an important place there; Bergin (1991) found that psychiatrists and psychologists are the least actively religious of the four groups of professionals in the United States that were surveyed, although one third of them did say that they regularly attend religious services. Perhaps a part of the problem stems from a mismatch between the way religion is misunderstood by a client and their therapist, although it is hazardous to question that. Since only 20% of those in Bergin's study rated a "religious content" as important in the treatment of "all or many clients," social scientists are not immune to similar effects when discussing their research.

While religion can occupy a central and integrative role in the development of a life-style and the "character" that is associated with it, since religions constrain some actions and facilitate others, the relationships between personality and religion have been interpreted through a variety of theories (cf. Wulff, 1991), with a primary disagreement about whether religion is a unitary phenomenon, or involves a group of separate attitudes (cf. Dittes, 1969), and has positive or negative consequences (Spilka & Werme, 1971).

When Dittes (1969, p. 637) examined the evidence for a relationship between religious attitudes and personality variables, he noted that religion is taken to be a single variable by asking, "Who is, and who is not, religious?" He also stressed that that approach had not properly addressed the possibility, raised consistently by William James and Freud, as the best-known theorists in this field, that particular doctrines or practices and types of religion may be differentially associated with personality characteristics. Dittes therefore concluded that

The psychological research reflects an overwhelming consensus that religion (at least as measured in the research, usually by institutional affiliation or adherence to conservative traditional doctrines) is associated with awareness of personal inadequacies, either generally or in response to particular crisis or threat situations; with objective evidence of inadequacy, such as low intelligence; with a strong responsiveness to the suggestions of other persons or other external influences; and with an array of what may be called desperate and generally unadaptive manoeuvres. Here, perhaps, are the sick souls and divided selves, two types of religious predispositions described by William James (1902), and with which he felt particularly sympathetic. (Dittes, 1986, p. 636; although Smith, 1985, p. xxixf, argues that many commentators have oversimplified this contrast.)

Those popular assumptions have not really changed, despite the finding that being trained into a religious stance is an essentially social process, and that negative traits such as conformity, rigidity, suggestibility, and defensiveness are often assigned to religious people by their critics. This does not, however, necessarily make such people in any sense "mentally ill." Furthermore, accepting or giving up a religion typically involves reacting against social rather than psychopathological pressures (Hunsberger & Brown, 1984).

Perspectives on Religion

Dittes (1969, p. 606) also noted that the outsiders to any religious system can be expected to take it as a coherent and unitary phenomenon while its insiders draw subtle distinctions between traditions, doctrines, institutions, groups, and religious individuals. Shackle and Brown's (page 119) comparison of the practice of prayer among a group of secondary school girls and women in a church-based prayer group shows their very different attitudes, and emphasizes the need for detailed information if we would understand how religious practices become self-sustaining. Another paper at that phenomenological level is Schulze's (page 130) hospital-based South American study of different attitudes towards death, which shows that they depend on the role-based relationships that are involved there.

It is now realized, however, that many interpretive theories depend on an observer's perspective, similar to that found in the lay or common-sense analyses that are used to predict others' behavior (Heider, 1958), which disregard each actor's perspective on the causes or reasons for their own actions (Hampson, 1989). This contrast, which has profoundly influenced recent studies of personality, has had little effect on psychologists of religion, beyond a few appeals to religious attributions (cf. Proudfoot & Shaver, 1975; Spilka, Hood, & Gorsuch, 1985), and to a developing interest in the functional uses of religion in coping (Pargament et al., 1988), which is likely to help replace the early reliance on structural theories of religion.

The level of interpretation of any data necessarily constrains the validity of the conclusions that particular studies can support. Interpretations that refer to habits, traits, or roles, and to beliefs rather than to "personality," depend on interpretive judgments based on observation or on individuals' self-reports. When social support, strong commitment, and even a lack of insight allow religious fantasies and illusions to be expressed in public, it is important to know if they are being offered seriously, or as playful disclosures. Just as children must learn to distinguish their fantasy from reality, being able to recognize that difference is a crucial feature of good mental health, especially since inappropriate religious claims are easily misunderstood. Any interpretation of what is said or done in the name of religion must recognize this, and keep a "distance" to avoid being misunderstood.

Some of the prejudices associated with these contrasting religious orientations are discussed in the next five papers. Stifoss-Hanssen (page 138) compared the rigidity of religious attitudes among patients against the greater flexibility of the hospital's staff. O'Connor (page 144) contrasted the effects of social or contextual factors on loneliness and on well-being in two groups of College "freshers." She found that those in an explicitly religious institution felt less alienated than those in a secular university. Loewenthal and her colleagues (page 154) examined the tensions that arise from religious sanctions within a group of Anglo-Jewish women in London, England, while Rayburn and her collaborators (page 167) looked at the stresses experienced by groups of women who are religious professionals in the United States. Despite those social pressures, that being "religious" remains an important cultural marker is shown by Pettersson's (page 174) comparative study of values across the predominantly Protestant and Catholic countries in Europe.

Social prejudices about the positive or negative effects of particular religious traditions on mental health, or on a sense of well-being, often neglect the extent to which many appeals to religion are accepted, and may help to resolve life crises. Conflicts between what is expected in religion, and what it is possible to "get away with" were recognized by Hartshorne and May (1928), although their findings have only recently been given the attention they deserve through an awareness of the situated nature of the pressures from religion itself towards conformity and doctrinal orthodoxy (Deconchy, 1991). The practice of religion (except in strictly defined "religious contexts") can, nevertheless, be hard to maintain, unless one retreats from "the world," has strong social support, or an ideological commitment. But even then, insiders to a religious life are easily criticized by the outsiders who fail to understand the meanings it can carry for them.

Cultural and Traditional Differences

Being "religious" entails the match of a template of imposed demands against preferred or acceptable beliefs and actions, to find a symmetry between one's own characteristics or reactions and a plausible religious context within which it is possible to display a religious orientation. When those contexts enable sympathy, social support, and friendship they mediate a religious ethic, although religious demands themselves are more likely to produce changes in their adherents than it is possible for those demands to be changed. Furthermore, the templates about church-going, for example, are different for "theologically liberal Congregationalists and charismatic members of fundamental sects" (Schiller & Levin, 1988). But the members of those latter groups are more likely to be identified as "Protestant" than "Catholic" or "Jewish," and the beliefs and attitudes of people within those traditions will reflect their religious training or experience more clearly than any predisposing, or even consequential personality-based processes.

The need for achievement, for social support, hope, positive moods, or an improved quality of life are in no sense specifically religious goals. To find that religion activates "hardiness" or helps to construe illness as a challenge emphasizes that religious attitudes must be understood with reference to base-response rates, and to stereotypes about the effects of an alignment with any health-related beliefs and practices.

These essays aim to exemplify some of those effects, and they show that there are no consistent relationships between religion, personality, and mental health. While Batson and Ventis (1982, p. 234ff) concluded that some links were proven, they noted that strong contradictions reflect prior theoretical assumptions, and conjectured that if "young Francis of Assissi" had consulted leading psychotherapists, "Freud would almost certainly have diagnosed sickness; Boisen might have said that Francis was sick but on his way to health, and Jung and Allport would likely have contended that Francis's religion was an important source of mental health. We, if not Francis, would have been left very confused" (ibid. p. 250).

Other problematic features of the relationships between religion and mental health include the restricted Christian and Western perspectives that have been pursued. Investigations within other traditions are needed for that to change, unless the problematic relationship between religion and mental health is a peculiarly "modern," and so Western, phenomenon.

Although debates about bioethics and the implications of holistic perspectives on health care have not yet been touched by psychologists of religion, to align religion with health could itself be a relic of the healing properties that early religious rites possessed, even if only for the cleanliness they encouraged, or for pragmatic answers to those who asked, "Why did I become ill?" A religious commitment can help to sustain such coping efforts, and Lazarus and Folkman (1984, pp. 74–88) stressed that "existential beliefs" not only answer those questions, but could themselves activate positive values and meanings when circumstances seem to be completely overwhelming. A religious conversion could then "change the way they appraise their relationship to the world at every level of being" (ibid., p. 65).

Any attempt to assign personality characteristics to religious "types" assumes more freedom in choosing a religion than is usually exercised, although religious systems can themselves shape their members, which begs the question. That a strong tradition supports these analyses is shown by Immanuel Kant who said (in 1797), when "throwing out some opinions at random," that "some people think that in religion the choleric temperament is orthodox, the sanguine is latitudinarian, the melancholic is fanatical, the phlegmatic is indifferent" (Gregor, 1974, p. 166).

No psychological perspective allows us to claim that one religious experience, tradition, or perspective is necessarily superior to another, beyond prejudiced or cultural and other expectations. Although claims on religious healing can lead to traumatic disappointment, or reported successes, an heroic resignation to illness is usually judged virtuous. But since it is easier to look where the light is brightest, the effects of age, sex, ethnicity, and denominational alignments on health or religiousness have been more readily identified than has the place of asceticism, mystery, prophecy, or enthusiasm. While the language of religion is performative (when "we give thanks") or figurative (and "we await your coming"), to interpret it concretely provides another source of misunderstanding.

Disagreements can be expected about the papers in this collection, whether because they have examined the "wrong" things, or because particular theories and analyses, like those relying on Jungian principles or on the "structuring power of the contents of a Christian (or Eastern) tradition" (Fowler, 1981) have been disregarded. Such holistic approaches are more readily accepted by "religious psychologists" than by academics, who prefer to rely on analytic and empirical methods. Despite barriers between those groups, an interest in religion was kept alive by religious psychologists, especially during the 1930s when psychology was dominated by Behaviorism.

The studies reported here all help to develop a consensus about what it is that religion can contribute to mental health. Extending these and other findings should produce stronger hypotheses about the benefits for mental health of particular religious alignments, independently of the mediation of any personality variables.

References

Allport, G.W. (1960). *Religion and prejudice in personality and social encounter.* Boston: Beacon Press.

Allport, G.W. & Ross, J.M. (1967). Personal religious orientations and prejudice. *Journal of Personality and Social Psychology, 5*(4), 432–443.

Allport, G.W., Vernon, P.E., & Lindzey, G. (1960). *Study of values* (3rd ed.). Boston: Houghton-Mifflin.

American Psychiatric Association. (1987). *Diagnostic and statistical manual of mental disorders* (3rd ed., rev. [DSM-III-R]). Washington DC: Author.

Batson, C.D. & Ventis, W.L. (1982). *The religious experience: A social-psychological perspective.* New York: Oxford University Press.

Becker, E. (1973). *The denial of death.* New York: Free Press.

Bem, D.J. & Funder, D.C. (1978). Predicting more of the people more of the time. *Psychological Review, 85,* 485–501.

Bergin, A.E. (1983). Religiosity and mental health: A critical reevaluation and meta-analysis. *Professional Psychology: Research and Practice, 14*(2), 170–184.

Bergin, A.E. (1991). Values and religious issues in psychotherapy and mental health. *American Psychologist, 46*(4), 394–403.

Capps, D. & Dittes, J.E. (1990). *The hunger of the heart: Reflections on the Confessions of Augustine.* Society for the Scientific Study of Religion, Monograph Series, Number 8.

Deconchy, J.-P. (1991). Religious belief systems: Their ideological representations and practical constraints. *International Journal for the Psychology of Religion, 1*(1), 5–21.

Diener, E. (1984). Subjective well-being. *Psychological Bulletin, 95*(3), 542–575.

Dittes, J.E. (1969). Psychology of religion. In G. Lindzey & E. Aronson (Eds.), *The handbook of social psychology* (2nd ed.), (vol. 5, pp. 602–659). Reading MA: Addison-Wesley.

Donahue, M.J. (1985). Intrinsic and extrinsic religiousness: Review and meta-analysis. *Journal of Personality and Social Psychology, 48*(2), 400–419.

Erikson, E. (1958). *Young man Luther: A study in psychoanalysis and history.* New York: Norton.

Fishbein, M. & Ajzen, I. (1975). *Belief, attitude, intention and behaviour: An introduction to theory and research.* Reading, MA: Addison-Wesley.

Fowler, J.W. (1981). *Stages of faith.* San Francisco: Harper and Row.

Gorsuch, R.L. (1988). Psychology of religion. *Annual Review of Psychology, 39,* 201–221.

Gregor, M.J. (1974). *Immanuel Kant: Anthropology from a pragmatic point of view*. The Hague: Mouton.

Hall, C.S. & Lindzey, G. (1978). *Theories of personality*. New York: John Wiley.

Hampson, S.E. (1989). *The construction of personality: An introduction* (2nd ed.). London: Routledge.

Hartshorne, H. & May, M.A. (1928). *Studies in deceit*. New York: Macmillan.

Heider, F. (1958). *The psychology of interpersonal relations*. New York: Wiley.

Heist, P.A., Youge, G., McConnell, T.R., & Webster, H. (1968). *Omnibus personality inventory*. New York: The Psychological Corporation.

Hunsberger, B. & Brown, L.B. (1984). Religious socialisation, apostasy and the impact of family background. *Journal for the Scientific Study of Religion, 23*(3), 239–251.

Jahoda, M. (1958). *Current concepts of positive mental health*. New York: Basic Books.

James, W. (1902). *The varieties of religious experience*. New York: Collier. Reprinted in Smith, J.E. (ed., 1985).

The Works of William James (Vol. 15). Cambridge, MA: Harvard University Press.

Johnson, J.H., Null, C., Butcher, J.N., & Johnson, K.N. (1984). Replicated item level factor analysis of the full MMPI. *Journal of Personality and Social Psychology, 47*(1), 105–114.

Jourard, S.M. & Landsman, T. (1980). *Healthy personality: An approach from the viewpoint of humanistic psychology* (4th ed.). New York: Macmillan.

Koenig, H.G., Smiley, M., & Gonzales, J.A.P. (1988). *Religion, health, and aging: Review and theoretical integration*. New York: Greenwood Press.

Kroll, J. & Sheehan, W. (1989). Religious beliefs and practices among 52 psychiatric inpatients in Minnesota. *American Journal of Psychiatry, 146*(1), 67–72.

Lamiell, J.T. (1987). *The psychology of personality: An epistemological enquiry*. New York: Columbia University Press.

Lazarus, R.S. & Folkman, S. (1987). Transactional theory and research on emotions and coping. *European Journal of Personality, 1*(3), 141–169.

Pargament, K.I., Kennell, J., Hathaway, W., Grevengoed, N., et al. (sic) (1988). Religion and the problem-solving process: Three styles of coping. *Journal for the Scientific Study of Religion, 27*(1), 90–104.

Proudfoot, W. & Shaver, P. (1975). Interrelations of religious and ethnic attitudes in selected Southern populations. *Journal for the Scientific Study of Religion, 14*, 317–330.

Robinson, L.H. (Ed.). (1986). *Psychiatry and religion: Overlapping concerns*. Washington DC: American Psychiatric Press.

Rokeach, M. (1969). Value systems in religion. *Review of Religious Research, 11*(1), 3–39.

St. Augustine (1991). *Saint Augustine: Confessions*. Translated with an introduction and notes by Henry Chadwick. Oxford: Oxford University Press.

Sanua, J.D. (1969). Religion, mental health, and personality: A review of empirical studies. *American Journal of Psychiatry, 123*, 1203–1213.

Schiller, P.L. & Levin, J.S. (1988). Is there a religious factor in health care utilization?: A review. *Social Science and Medicine, 27*(12), 1369–1379.

Shaver, P., Lenauer, M., & Sadd, S. (1980). Religiousness, conversion, and subjective well-being: The "healthy-minded" religion of modern American women. *American Journal of Psychiatry, 137*(12), 1563–1568.

Smith, J.E. (1985). Introduction to William James, *The varieties of religious experience*. Cambridge, MA: Harvard University Press.

Spilka, B., Hood, R.W., Jr., & Gorsuch, R.L. (1985). *The psychology of religion: An empirical approach*. Englewood Cliffs, NJ: Prentice Hall.

Spilka, B. & Werme, P.H. (1971). Religion and mental disorder: A research perspective. In M. Strommen (Ed.), *Research on religious development: A comprehensive handbook* (pp. 161–181). New York: Hawthorn.

Summerlin, F.A. (1980). *Religion and mental health: A bibliography*. Rockville, MD: U.S. Department of Health and Human Services.

Taylor, S.E. & Brown, J.D. (1988). Illusion and well-being: A social psychological perspective on mental health. *Psychological Bulletin, 103*(2), 193–210.

Witztum, E., Greenberg, D., & Dasberg, H. (1990). Mental illness and religious change. *British Journal of Medical Psychology, 63*, 33–41.

Wulff, D.M. (1991). *Psychology of religion: Classic and contemporary views*. New York: John Wiley and Sons.

---

* A 164-item bibliography concerning the relationship between mental health and religious variables can be found in Batson, C.D., Schoenrade, P., & Ventis, W.L. (1993). *Religion and the individual: A social-psychological perspective*. New York: Oxford University Press, pp. 241–254.

2
The Uses of Religious Assessment in Counseling

H. NEWTON MALONY

Increasingly, it is becoming apparent that religion plays a part in mental health as well as in mental illness (cf. McPherson, 1988). What people believe about transcendent reality and how they act on those beliefs have been found to be intricately involved in their life adjustment and effectiveness (Atkinson, 1986). This essay considers some of the ways in which an assessment of how individuals are using religion in their daily lives can be employed in the counseling process, with *counseling* defined as intentional efforts to help persons adjust more effectively to the culture in which they choose to live and *religion* defined as the beliefs and practices of a group of persons who have bonded themselves together around a transcendent belief about the nature of reality and of life. *Religious assessment* is defined in terms of judgments about the extent to which persons are applying the tenets of their religious tradition to their daily lives.

The Structural Phases of Counseling

In considering the relations among these constructs, the first issue concerns the structural phases in counseling within which a religious assessment might be appropriate. Three structural phases are identified, the first and second phases being descriptive, while the third is prescriptive.

The first phase of counseling involves *diagnosis*, with the presenting symptoms or problems described under some diagnostic label. In the second phase *mental status* or the underlying personality structure of the individual is described. These two phases are synonymous with Axes 1 and 2 of *The Diagnostic and Statistical Manual of Mental Disorders, 3rd Edition, Revised* (DSM-III-R, American Psychiatric Association, 1987).

The third, prescriptive phase involves *treatment*, when the counselor purposefully attempts to interact with clients in an effort to restore them to a more satisfying and effective social adjustment. A religious assessment is appropriate and important in each of these phases (cf. Malony, 1987).

Diagnosis

Religion can be present or absent in the problems presented to a counselor. While the DSM-III-R does not label religion as pathological, there has been a consistent tendency in the history of abnormal psychology for it to be viewed as a negatively confounding factor in mental health. The cases reported in Milton Rokeach's *The Three Christs of Ypsilanti* (1964) are examples of this tendency. In this nonfictional account, 3 men at the state mental hospital at Ypsilanti, Michigan, thought they were Jesus Christ. After 6 months of meeting with each other they were still convinced of their identities and were so disturbed that they would not have been able to maintain themselves outside the hospital environment.

Religion can, however, function negatively in less extreme ways when, for example, people have an excessive need to repeatedly confess their errors to God, or engage in compulsive acts to atone for their guilt. It should also be said that the behavior of many of the world's religious leaders, for example Jesus, Buddha, and Mohammed, would probably have been diagnosed as pathological because of their religious preoccupations, had they ever gone to counselors for help. As far as is known, however, they did not seek such counsel, although Kazanzakis's novel *The Last Temptation of Christ* (1960) pictures one or more of Jesus' friends as thinking he was mad.

On the other hand, religion can function *positively* in the problems presented to counselors, because of a subtle and often ignored relationship between the violation of ethical or moral values and real guilt, psychosomatic displacement, and anxiety. In these situations, religion may well be the source of such concern, although not all guilt is pathological, nor is all anxiety detrimental, in spite of what some theorists have presumed (cf. Ellis, 1976). Guilt and anxiety might serve positive and corrective roles, as Mowrer (1961), Finch (1983), and others have noted. The symptoms which provoke someone to seek counseling may themselves be the result of a constructive, rather than a destructive, religious faith. For example, if a man's anxiety is overtly related to marital infidelity or the sexual abuse of his daughter, it may be that his religious faith is provoking this guilt and concern. Suffice it to say that the chief diagnostic questions to be asked in the first structural phase of counseling are:

— is religion present or absent in the presenting problem, and
— if present, is religion functioning positively or negatively?

The assertion that religion can serve a negative or positive function in the problems brought to counselors leads naturally into the second structural phase of counseling, with judgments about religion's place in the mental status or personality of the client.

Mental Status

It is helpful to think of a person's mental status as the underlying personality-based "precondition" for the emergence of the problem which is diagnosed in Phase 1 of counseling. Mental status is like the soil in which a tree is planted. It is a necessary, but not automatically a sufficient cause of the problem. Whenever counselors judge a person's religion to be playing a constructive or destructive role in their symptoms, they have subtly moved over into this second phase, having determined that religion is an underlying personality strength, or a personality weakness.

For example, if an individual is overcome with religious guilt and anxiety when they confess to having molested a child, we might judge this to be a reflection of character strength and a positive personality trait. If, however, a person reports that God told them to molest this child, we would not hesitate to judge their religion to be distorted, and a negative personality trait.

In personality structure, religion functions as one among many attitudes, or predispositions to respond in certain ways to the environment. As such, any person's religion can vary as to whether it is (a) important or unimportant, (b) active or inactive, (c) good or bad, and finally (d) helpful or harmful in their adjustment. Since the goal of counseling is readjustment to the culture in which one chooses to live, and personality can be understood as the style through which that adjustment is achieved, all the other religious dimensions (such as important-unimportant, active-inactive, good-bad) interact and contribute to the primary helpful-harmful criterion.

The "importance" dimension here refers to the significance which persons attribute to religion in their lives, and unless religion is judged to be important it will not contribute significantly to adjustment or maladjustment. The "activity" dimension refers to the amount of energy persons put into their religious thought and action. Again, where there is little activity, adjustment will be unaffected by religion. The "goodness" dimension then refers to the correctness of an individual's religion as seen from the viewpoint of that person's given religious tradition. Where a person's religion is ill-formed or partially developed it will either have less total impact on adjustment, or function in an uneven, and potentially harmful, manner.

All the major world religions have well thought out theories about how faith should function to facilitate adjustment. The more a person's religion functions in accord with these tenets, the more likely will their religion contribute constructively to their total adjustment. Each religious tradition should therefore provide counselors with a systematic way to make this good/bad assessment. The *Religious Status Interview* (RSI, Malony, 1987), to be discussed later, is an example of such a measure from the Christian point of view.

It should be noted that a somewhat limited, but fairly typical, definition of the goal of counseling is being used here, as "effective readjustment to the culture in which one chooses to live." Tradition-based religions help people make this adjustment. As Milton Yinger (1970) suggests, religion is the way in which people handle life's basic enigmas, tragedies, and mysteries. Enigmas are the incongruities and the injustices that result from breakdowns in this give-and-take of the social contract. Tragedies are unexpected disruptions, losses, injuries, and deaths that occur prematurely in life. Mysteries are the ultimate imponderables about purpose, meaning, and destiny that plague the human consciousness.

In a more pragmatic sense, tradition-based religions handle these enigmas, tragedies, and mysteries by giving a worldview, a sense of identity, comfort or challenge, encouragement and companionship. A religious worldview includes an understanding of ultimate reality, the meaning of history, and the ideal purpose of individual existence. This view of the world provides individuals with a sense of identity that supersedes the ebb and flow of their daily life. Religion puts failures and tragedies within a context that gives comfort. It also challenges believers to live life in terms of their ideals, and encourages them to persist when they would otherwise give up. Finally, religion provides companionship with others who are like-minded, through worship and involvement with other religious organizations.

Each religious tradition accomplishes these functions in different ways. The unique characteristics of the Christian tradition, for example, are that it is theistic, historical, transactional, interpersonal, redemptive, and corporate. As contrasted with traditions which do not believe in God, the Christian tradition affirms a divinity who is transcendent yet personal. It is historical in that it affirms that this God acted in space and time to create the world. Furthermore, the Christian God acted in history by sending the prophets and His Son to reveal His intent for life. The Christian faith is also transactional in the sense that the will of its God is to be fulfilled through the actions of human beings during their lifetime. The primary way in which the Christian God's will is to be accomplished is through each person's interactions with other persons. Thus, it is interpersonal. The Christian faith also provides for redemption in realizing that humans fail in their attempts to live godly lives and need ways to be forgiven and try again. Finally, the Christian faith is corporate because it recognizes each person's need for support and fellowship in their attempts to fulfil the will of God in history. So the church is an essential part of the Christian faith.

The Religious Status Interview (RSI, Malony, 1987) attempts to measure these uniquely Christian characteristics, as they help people to make an adequate adjustment to life. Whether a person's religious functioning is good or bad from a particular point of view is inextricably tied up with the theology of tradition.

Some combination of the importance, activity, and goodness of one's religion determines whether it functions as a personality strength or weakness. At the very least, it can be asserted that if persons profess to be religious, an assessment of the extent to which their intentions and behaviors approximate their tradition's religious ideal is a measure of their adaptation to its cultural norms. Apart from any evaluation of the absolute validity of a given society's religions, identification with the norms of some viable tradition, and even with a particular religion, is a legitimate, albeit minimal, criterion for mental health.

It is noteworthy that, while most counselors readily recognize this criterion in cross-cultural research, they have been less willing to apply the same type of evaluation to their own cultures. For example, it has seemingly been easier for some social or behavioral scientists to judge as abnormal those New Guinea tribespeople who do not participate in their culture's religious ceremonies, than to apply the same rules of thumb in their own society to people who have disaffiliated from a conservative religious upbringing. They have, in fact, often made the opposite judgment when applauding such counter-cultural actions as indications of mental health (cf. Ellis, 1976).

Nevertheless, one caution should be noted in judging conformity with a religious tradition as *prima facie* evidence for adjustment to a given culture. This is the caution of presuming that "the more religion the better." That this is not necessarily true can be seen in the assessment of an "involvement in organized religion" (cf. the RSI, Malony, 1987) by asking whether daily worship at church is automatically judged better than weekly worship. Would attendance at religious committee meetings every night of the week therefore always be judged as more ideal than attending such meetings once every two weeks?

The same issue can be seen in questions which assess one's dependence on God for making daily decisions and taking care of daily needs. Would a person's religion be judged as "more helpful" if they depended entirely on God, without assuming that we have any personal responsibility for our behavior? The same dilemma can be seen in dealing with forgiveness and accountability. Would a complete reliance on God to forgive sin be better than a concern to avoid wrongdoing?

In each of these instances the answer is "No!," since in Christian traditions the ideal is to balance one's own responsibility for behavior against dependency upon the leadership and direction of God. Ideally, Christians should live as if God has a will for their lives and as if they had the responsibility to use their best judgment to act upon it. Christians should affirm that God forgives their wrongdoing but that they are obligated to correct their errors and attempt to change themselves for the better.

The solution to the dilemma of whether "more religion is better religion" is, therefore, "in moderation." According to the Christian ideal, religious faith should have an important place in life, but it should not take the place of responsible action, since Aristotle's golden mean is an implicit value in Christianity. As Thomas Aquinas and others have asserted, a prime index of God's image in human beings is reason, so that people are never to replace their own ability to make decisions with a pseudo-pious dependence on God.

But this is a complex issue, as William James noted in his distinction between the "saint" and the "fanatic" (James 1902/1958). There is a fine line between them, and James's comments still have merit so many years after he first made them. Where an all-encompassing religious preoccupation comes out of concern for others and a conscious intent to do good, sainthood and personality integration are possible. Where such a preoccupation becomes compulsive or guilt ridden and results in a tangential or narcissistic withdrawal from life, fanaticism and personality disintegration are possible.

That the distinction between sainthood and fanaticism is not always easy to make is shown by the following examples. A psychiatrist sought a consultation about a nun who was hospitalized, to know if being a nun required a person to engage in prayers of penitence every hour on the hour. Since the nun was not cloistered but belonged to a socially active order, a judgment was made that hourly prayers of penitence were compulsive defenses. It was then found that she had been hospitalized for obsessional fears of impending disaster and guilt over her own apostasy, and that her prayers were a desperate effort to maintain emotional and mental control. They could have been religious behaviors which kept her from getting worse, but it would be difficult to describe her faith as a "personality strength." Her religious practice was an exaggeration of more appropriate behavior, and indicated fanaticism rather than sainthood.

Another example involves a young woman who had been deprogrammed by her devoutly Catholic family after she had become a member of the Unification Church. She left college and joined others in selling flowers on the street corners of Washington, DC, 7 days of each week. Selling these flowers was an act of devotion leading to heavenly credit, according to her Moonie theology. While at home for her sister's wedding, she was spirited away to a strange cabin and exposed to a week of intense pressure to leave the group and return home. She acquiesced and went back to the small midwestern town where she grew up.

She did not, however, return to Catholicism but began to attend a Protestant church, because part of her conversion to the Unification Church had been based on disillusionment with her Catholic upbringing.

She desired a religious experience that was more demanding, and to be involved in a more cohesive fellowship than she had found in her own family tradition. Both of these she had experienced in the Moonies, and even after she was deprogrammed, she still remained dissatisfied with Catholicism.

She said that her parents were willing for religion to be part of her life but they were not willing for it to be all of her life. When she had returned home, they told her that she would have to worship at the Catholic church, or to leave, as they were embarrassed for the neighbors to see her going to a Protestant church. She chose to leave home, and returned to college in a nearby city. Her desire for a more engrossing experience of faith than she had had at home was probably an indication of healthy individuation, and not a sign of pathology or fanaticism. If anything, it tended toward sainthood, so that her religious behavior was a personality strength rather than a weakness.

These observations lead naturally to the third phase of the counseling process, namely, treatment. Here the question is, "How can the assessment of religious functioning assist in the amelioration of the problems which provoke persons to seek counseling?"

Treatment

As noted earlier, treatment is prescriptive rather than descriptive, and we are concerned here with how religious assessments can be used to help persons effectively readjust to their environment. In treatment planning, counselors no longer ask the diagnostic question of *whether* religion is involved in the symptom pattern or in the mental status of an individual. They are interested in knowing how an understanding of the diagnostic information can be used to help people readjust to life.

That attention to religious issues in this treatment phase of counseling is by no means a new idea is indicated by Ellis in his treatise, *The Case against Religion* (1976), by Propst in her volume, *Psychotherapy in a Religious Framework* (1988), and by Lovinger in his book, *Working with Religious Issues in Therapy* (1984).

There appear to be at least five counselor options for utilizing the assessment of religion in this treatment phase of counseling, as they disregard, annihilate, correct, reinstate, or encourage it.

To take the *disregard* option would assume that a person's functional religion is so weak or ill-formed that it is having no impact, and cannot be used in treatment. To take the *annihilate* option would assume that the person's functional religion was completely destructive and needed obliterating because, as part of the pathology, it would impede treatment. To take the *correct* option would assume that parts of the functional religion were weak or erroneous, and should be changed, or else they would handicap treatment. The *reinstate* option assumes that while the

functional religion was potentially helpful it was not consciously operative, and should be made explicit, self-conscious, and intentional. The
encourage option would imply that the person's functional religion was
adequate, active, and a definite strength to be supported and enhanced.

In any or all of these options, counseling requires an active role from
the counselor, since the root meaning of the word "counseling" is "to
give advice." So the idea that the treatment phase of counseling should
include didactic, intentional, and directive advice on the part of the
counselor is explicit and essential. While almost all counseling theories
recognize this role for the counselor *implicitly*, the possibility of explicitly
using religious assessment in counseling is most similar to that of the
cognitive-behavioral and rational-emotive schools (Kendall & Hollen,
1979). Furthermore, it should be emphasized that the most nondirective
and client-centered approaches accept that counseling involves at least
two discrete phases, in understanding and in change. In the change
or treatment phase, therefore, the counselor actively offers recommendations, explores alternatives, and encourages commitment to other
forms of action. In every approach, that directive or interpretive phase
involves sensitive skill, so that a religious assessment in treatment does
not imply approval for overly authoritarian, dogmatic, or unskilled counseling. Recognizing that all counseling involves direction is not a license
for the unbridled imposition of religion on to another's problems.

One of the dangers in suggesting that religious assessments should
become part of the treatment phase of counseling is that counselors will
impose their own religious values on their counselees. When counselors
counsel, they must share their own values (cf. Bergin, 1980), including
their personal and professional evaluations of the value of religion in
general, of given religious traditions, and of various beliefs within that
specific tradition.

The use of a standard *pro forma* like the Religious Status Interview
(Malony, 1988) is intended as a corrective to this temptation for counselors to impose their own religious values inappropriately in the counseling
process. This Interview therefore gives an empirically based standard
against which to compare the functional Christianity of individuals, and a
firm base for checking the tendency counselors might have to contaminate
their counseling with their own religious convictions, rather than adopting
a neutral, pragmatic approach to other traditions. Whether a given
counselor agrees with the tenets of these scales or not, their use allows
the judgment that where a client's functional religion meets the prescrip-
tions of a particular tradition, the counselor can use it, and where it does
not, the counselor can disregard or annihilate it. Making that judgment
must be separated from personal opinions about the validity of a given
religious tradition.

Turning to these options in more detail, let us first consider the option
to disregard information gathered from the assessment of functional re-

ligion in a given individual. As noted above, such an alternative is based on a judgment that while someone might profess to be religious, their identification with Christianity is nominal and there is no confounding of religion with their symptoms. So their faith is nonfunctional and benign, and neither a personality strength nor a personality weakness.

Disregarding the client's religion is not unique, in the sense that all counselors must decide which parts of the person's experience they will emphasize. While it might be possible to reconstruct a viable faith in a person, deciding to disregard the client's religion is typically based on a counselor's decision that to deal with other parts of the client's experience is more constructive and economical of time and energy.

The option to annihilate the client's religion is the most radical of the treatment options. As noted earlier, deciding to destroy a client's religion should not be based on a counselor's personal opinions. Any efforts to annihilate their client's faith should be grounded in the results of a standard assessment, as is the conclusion that a client's functional religion is so far from the norm that it is either a major part of the pathology, a significant personality weakness, or both.

The importance of making the decision to confront and destroy a client's religion on the basis of ratings predetermined and agreed by professionals in a given religion cannot be overemphasized. Albert Ellis, in his book, *The Case against Religion* (1976), made the mistake of evaluating Christianity through criteria gleaned from his own negative experiences. Freud made the same mistake in *The Future of an Illusion* (1964). While Ellis's and Freud's criteria for mental health are acceptable, their judgments about Christianity are not. In an article entitled, "The Case for Religion: A Counter to Albert Ellis" (1985), I noted that he compared good psychology with bad religion and that many of his criticisms of bad religions would be shared by professional religious scholars. But when Ellis recommended efforts to do away with a client's religion, he did so on the basis of ill-informed judgments about good religion. Suffice it to repeat that the decision to confront a client's faith should be based on standardized and "ideal" ratings of their religious tradition which are not contaminated by a counselor's prejudgments.

The next option for the use of religious assessment in the treatment phase of counseling is to correct the religion of the client. This also should be done on the basis of standardized ratings, and not on biased judgments. In fact, if counselors assume a simply pragmatic view of the value of religion, a client's functional religion can be corrected regardless of whether the counselors are themselves religious or not. Although religion may not play a significant role in the life of the counselor, it can be utilized in treatment alongside the other interests and values in the client's life with which counselors may not identify, but which they should respect and bring into treatment.

Correcting functional religion aims to assist clients to conform more effectively to the norms of their faith, with the assumption that that will lead to higher personal satisfaction, less internal conflict, greater social approval, and a better adjustment. Attempts to correct must, however, be grounded in a functional evaluation of the client's religious tradition, and not on its absolute validity.

The Religions Status Inventory (RSI) (Malony, 1987) can show that a client's functional religion is deficient in one or more dimensions. The counselor may then, through sensitive suggestions, raise the possibility of the client changing in those areas, so that, for example, they might increase their involvement in organized religion by participating more in their church's worship, service, and study opportunities. They might also become more trusting

— in their awareness of God, and more aware of issues of social justice;
— in their acceptance of God's grace and steadfast love, and less judgmental and more forgiving of themselves;
— in experiencing fellowship, becoming less suspicious of and less pre-judgmental toward others.

These are but a few examples of how counselors can use deficiencies (or exaggerations) as treatment recommendations, when they judge that a client's functional religion is part of their problem and that they are capable of constructively altering their behavior.

Counselors may also aim to reinstate their client's functioning religion, although there is a subtle difference between that and giving encouragement. Reinstatement implies that the client's religion is adequate but needs reactivating, while encouragement implies that the client's religion is adequate and effective but requires support and reassurance. In a sense, this distinction is between making a dormant faith operative and making a working faith more applicable.

In reinstating a client's faith, the intention is to make it functional by tying the adjustment problems directly to faith affirmation. The client could be reminded with "if-then" statements that, since they affirm certain beliefs, they should be able to relate those beliefs to the specific difficulties they are experiencing.

Giving clients encouragement is like using bellows to fan a fire into white-hot coals; it must be assumed that someone is trying to make an adequate faith work in their adjustment efforts. They also need support and encouragement to "keep up the effort," and to "keep trying—it should work" as typical ways in which encouragement and support can be used.

Conclusion

This essay has considered the uses of a religious assessment in counseling, that is seen to involve three structural phases: in diagnosis, an evaluation of mental state, and then in treatment. In the diagnostic phase, religion can be present or absent, negative or positive. In an evaluation of the mental state it is necessary to assess religion with a standardized procedure and to determine thereby whether a functional religion is important or unimportant, active or inactive, good or bad, and therefore helpful or harmful to the personality. In the treatment phase, that assessment might be used by counselors to disregard, annihilate, correct, reinstate, or encourage their clients' religious functioning.

Appendix

This description of the Religious State Inventory (RSI) (Malony, 1987) shows how one religious tradition might provide counselors with a standardized measure of that tradition's understanding of an optimal religious functioning. In its complete form it involves a 33-question interview that is based on eight theological categories that were suggested for this purpose in *The Minister as Diagnostician*, by Paul Pruyser (1976). Those categories, with their descriptions of optimal Christian functioning are:

Awareness of God—Christians for whom their faith is functioning optimally are aware that they have been created by God and made in His image. While recognizing their own capabilities, they recognize their dependence on God for strength. They have a realistic awareness of their own limitations but do not deny their responsibility to utilize their abilities in fulfilling God's will. They worship God as an expression of their reverence and love for Him. They pray as a means of communing with God and expressing their concerns honestly to Him.

Acceptance of God's Grace and Steadfast Love—Christians for whom their faith is functioning optimally know God loves them unconditionally. They accept God's love and forgiveness as an impetus for new life and responsible action. God's love gives them the ability to find meaning in the suffering and difficulties of their lives. They trust the goodness of God.

Being Repentant and Responsible—Christians for whom their faith is functioning optimally take responsibility for their own feelings and actions. They do not deny, however, the influence of other factors, such as the environment and the power of others, on the personal difficulties they may face or the sins they commit. They accept their inner impulses as part of their humanity, yet realize a proclivity toward evil. They are able to request and accept forgiveness from others without feeling threatened or self-deprecating. They forgive others without continuing to experience resentment towards them.

Knowing God's Leadership and Direction—Christians for whom their faith is functioning optimally trust in God's leadership yet accept their own role in the process of making decisions. They express an optimistic yet realistic hope in God's control of life. They have a strong sense of their own place in making the will of God come to pass. This identity as God's steward gives deep meaning to their lives.

Involvement in Organized Religion—Christians for whom their faith is functioning optimally engage in regular and systematic involvement with other Christians in worship, prayer, study, and service. By their behavior, they evidence commitment to organized religion. They know the value of group identity and involvement. They join with others in trying to grow in their spiritual understanding and faithful behavior.

Experiencing Fellowship—Christians for whom their faith is functioning optimally experience fellowship at various levels of intimacy and involvement with other believers. They identify themselves with other members of the family of God in local communities, and throughout the world. They rejoice with others in knowing themselves as those who have accepted God's invitation to try to live as followers of Christ, and have a sense of fellowship with Christians everywhere. They see the world and all people in it as part of God's good creation, to be respected, honored, and loved.

Being Ethical—Christians for whom their faith is functioning optimally follow their ethical principles in a flexible, but committed, manner. Religious faith underlies their total behavior, with religious life being the moral life. They show a concern for peace, love, and justice in both the personal and social areas of their life. They are concerned for individual responsibility and social justice, with the sense that they are serving God through their vocations.

Affirming Openness in Faith—Christians for whom their faith is functioning optimally experience their religion as the prime directive for their lives. They spend a significant amount of time discussing, reading, and thinking about their faith. They attempt to grow in, and increase their understanding of their faith. While expressing confidence in and commitment to the Christian faith, they nevertheless are tolerant of others' points of view and willing to examine others' beliefs in an honest manner. They are open to critiques of Christianity, so that their faith is complex.

It is obvious from these descriptions of the dimensions of the RSI that this interview schedule takes the content of faith seriously while it attempts to avoid the common error of assessing only religious beliefs or motives. As a measure of "functional theology" that may not correlate well with successful adjustment to a given culture, it should, nevertheless, accurately assess who is living by the standards of their chosen religion. It is assumed that a judgment of such good or bad religious functioning interacts in a positive manner with self-esteem and personality strength, and should therefore relate to evaluations of mental status. High scores on this interview have been found to be related to judgments of religious maturity made by pastors, to not being hospitalized for an emotional disturbance or in counseling, and to possessing positive personality traits. The full interview has also been found to have both test-retest and interrater reliability. While the Religious Status Interview has not yet been related to the counseling process it offers an example of how such a standardized scale can assist in the assessment of whether persons' religion is a strength or weakness for them.

References

American Psychiatric Association. (1987). *Diagnostic and statistical manual of mental disorders* (3rd ed., rev. [DSM-III-R]). Washington DC: Author.

Atkinson, B.E. (1986). *Religious maturity and psychological distress among older Christian women.* Unpublished doctoral dissertation, Graduate School of Psychology, Fuller Theological Seminary, Pasadena, CA.

Bergin, A.E. (1980). Psychotherapy and religious values. *Journal of Consulting and Clinical Psychology, 48,* 95–105.

Ellis, A. (1976). *The case against religion: A psychotherapist's view.* New York: Institute for Rational Living.

Finch, J.G. (1983). *Nishkamakarma.* Pasadena, CA: Integration Press.

Freud, S. (1964). *The future of an illusion.* Garden City, NY: Doubleday.

James, W. (1958). *The varieties of religious experience.* New York: Mentor Books. (Original work published 1902)

Kazantzakis, N. (1960). *The last temptation of Christ.* New York: Simon & Schuster.

Kendall, P.C. & Hollen, S.D. (Eds.). (1979). *Cognitive-behavioral interventions.* New York: Academic Press.

Lovinger, R.J. (1984). *Working with religious issues in therapy.* New York: Aronson.

Malony, H.N. (1985). *The case for religion: A counter to Albert Ellis.* Unpublished document, Graduate School of Psychology, Fuller Theological Seminary, Pasadena, CA.

Malony, H.N. (1987). The clinical assessment of optimal religious functioning. *Review of Religious Research, 30*(1), 3–17.

McPherson, S.E. (1988). *Concurrent validation of the religious status interview with personality traits, religious orientation, and spiritual maturity.* Unpublished doctoral dissertation, Graduate School of Psychology, Fuller Theological Seminary, Pasadena, CA.

Mowrer, O.H. (1961). *The crisis in psychiatry and religion.* New York: Van Nostrand.

Propst, L.R. (1988). *Psychotherapy in a religious framework: Spirituality in the emotional healing process.* New York: Human Sciences Press.

Pruyser, P.W. (1976). *The minister as diagnostician.* Philadelphia: Westminster Press.

Rokeach, M. (1964). *The three Christs of Ypsilanti.* New York: Knopf.

Yinger, J.M. (1970). *The scientific study of religion.* New York: Macmillan.

3
Psychology in the Phenomenology of Religion: A Critical Essay

Owe Wikstrom

I would like to make a few critical remarks on a topic which, in my opinion, is seldom examined. That is the psychological implications of disciplines that border on the psychology of religion, especially in the history of religions and comparative religion. I wish to stress the importance of researchers in the field of religious studies, or *Religionswissenschaft*, taking into account the individual's religious experience as it has been described and analyzed by sociologists or psychologists of religion, by systematic and practical theologians, and by philosophers of religion. I hope that my remarks on a recent multivolume encyclopedia (Eliade, 1987) will show why I am doing this. But first, a general observation.

In my opinion, it is essential for the future of the Psychology of Religion that researchers do not lean only towards the main lines and concepts, as well as the methods and questions raised by the paradigms of social psychology, cognitive psychology, psychoanalytically oriented psychology, and so forth. That side represents one of the "legs" that the body of our field will continue to walk on, as a necessary, but not a sufficient condition.

If the topic of our research claims to be a real field for scientific inquiry on its own merit, and not an appendix to general psychology or a form of applied Christian theology, I think it is essential to underline the importance for scientific work to describe and partly explain religious experience within the field that used to be called Religious Studies. That must be the other "leg" of the Psychology of Religion. Of course, historians, anthropologists, or phenomenologists of religion do not claim to have access to the batteries of measuring instruments and statistical procedures, or to the specialized language systems of psychology when we talk in terms of neopsychoanalytical theories or social psychology. Nevertheless, their interest is directed not only to collective cultural artifacts, descriptions of myths, rituals, or organizations and their change over time, but also to a transcultural and transhistorical understanding of "religious man." The basic focus there must be an individual's religious experience as such.

Let us, for example, listen to Professor Wilfred Cantwell Smith, one of the most distinguished scholars and the former head of the Department of Comparative Religion at Harvard University. In his excellent book *Faith and Belief* (1979), we can clearly see the ethnoscientific perspectives he adopted at the very outset of his study. As he says,

Our question is to understand faith as a characteristic quality or potentiality of human life; that propensity of man that across the centuries and across the world has given rise to and been nurtured by a prodigious variety of religious forms and yet has remained elusive and personal, prior and beyond the forms. What kind of being are we, that throughout history, we have created great systems of religious patterns and programmes, ideas and dances, images and institutions, and then have lived our life in terms of them, in ways both grotesque and sublime? (1979, p. 4)

Professor Smith's question can just as well be understood in terms of psychology, as in terms of cultural anthropology.

It should be important for psychologists to communicate with other scholars, who are working seriously in the field by taking notes, tape recording, observing, or interviewing, and in libraries analyzing and structuring texts and paintings, music and dances, to compare and understand the complexity and the varieties of religious experience. I think of those experiences in terms of phenomena like prayers, demon possession, glossolalia, visions, or meditation, and in different religions, geographic areas, climates, and layers of history.

In the history of the scientific study of religion in Scandinavia, especially in Uppsala (and also in Nijmegen, Holland) there is an old connection between phenomenological and psychological interests in religious experience. In Sweden a line runs from Nathan Soderblom, who specialized in Iranian religion, through to Tor Andrae, whose main interest was Muslim mysticism, to Hjalmar Sundén, the first to occupy a chair in the psychology of religion in Sweden. They all tried not to fall out but to keep the two legs of the psychology of religion together (Wikström, 1993).

If we look upon the "real" old-timers like Wilhelm Wundt, William James, and James Bisset Pratt, we can see that they also tried not to be absorbed totally into the academic society of psychologists. While they "translated" religious behaviors and experiences into the terms of psychological theories, they argued for and respected the specific qualities of religious people.

We can of course question the postulate of a religious "a priori." My point, however, is not to agree or disagree with the claims of any ontological genesis or structure for this "a priori religion," or for philosophical discussions of the beliefs of researchers in the field of religion. I would, instead, stress the fact that psychologists of religion ought to listen, learn, and maintain a critical conversation with those in departments of religious studies.

"Religious Experience" in Comparative Religion

The late Mircea Eliade's great overview, *The Encyclopedia of Religion*, was published in 16 volumes in 1987. Basic topics in history, phenomenology and comparative religion are described there. While I have not scrutinized every single entry, my aim is to discuss the role of *psychology* in these volumes. In bringing some order to the many perspectives to be found in this Encyclopedia I will raise three questions:

1. What kind of religious phenomena do these scholars of religion observe and discuss in psychological terms?
2. Which are the main psychological theories and concepts used, and applied to these phenomena?
3. How are these theories used?

As I scrutinize that Encyclopedia I will not keep those questions apart. A short overview, however, provides us with seven different clusters of terms in which psychological questions are discussed from the perspective of comparative religion. These are:

1. General concepts, such as religious experience, sacred and profane, ritual, myth, rites of passage, archetypes, and tradition.
2. Experientially oriented concepts, including conversion, dreams, ecstasy, glossolalia, meditation, mysticism, healing, states of consciousness, attention, spiritual discipline.
3. Concepts bordering on religious experiences, such as chance, fate, magic, divination, superstition, astrology, psychedelic drugs.
4. Intense religious experiences, such as possession, affliction, cursing, demons, exorcism, voodoo, shamanism, witchcraft.
5. Biographies of William James, James Bisset Pratt, Sigmund Freud, Carl Jung, Mircea Eliade, Rudolph Otto, Wilhelm Wundt, and Nathan Soderblom.
6. The history of science, psychology of religion, psychology and religious movements, psychotherapy and religion, comparative religion, phenomenology of religion, and the study of religion.

Let me start by saying that I intend to concentrate on the entries other than those in (5) and (6) that deal directly with psychology or the psychology of religion.

Explicitly Psychodynamic and Implicit Social Psychology

In these entries, psychology is mentioned explicitly either by remarks on theory (Oedipus complex, perception, projection, etc.) or with reference to theorists like Jung, Pratt, Erikson, Piaget, and Freud; and implicitly where psychological problems of the structure, genesis, and function of religious experience are discussed indirectly.

I have found it interesting to scrutinize the two "levels" of explicit and implicit psychological analysis. The perceptual, psychoanalytic, and Jungian traditions are overwhelmingly dominant at the explicit level, depending on the kind of problem under discussion. Carl Jung on the role of symbols, the theories in Eliade, and the phenomenological tradition from Schleiermacher and Rudolph Otto to the later Eranos circle are emphasised.

But it is more interesting that sociology especially, as well as social psychology, are elaborated in an implicit and therefore less sophisticated way. It seems as if perceptual and pharmacological approaches (especially when dealing with intense experiences) and dynamic psychological concepts and models of man (in discussions of spirit possession, shamanism, cursing, healing, etc.) are used more frequently to explain religious experience, than are the traditions of social psychology, the sociology of knowledge, or the interactionist tradition that derives from Mead. Psychoanalytic theory has also been applied more thoroughly to comparative religion than has social psychology. This is especially interesting, because these social psychological approaches have had an immense impact on the scholarly thinking of psychologists of religion.

In considering the psychological theories that have been used, let me start by looking closely at two entries on "experientially oriented concepts." The main content in the *Dream* entry is a description of patterns in the perception of dreams, reflected in dream classifications, attitudes towards dreams, and the behavior that dreams may influence, determine, or explain. The author of that entry, Benjamin Kilmore, starts with "The royal Message and apocalyptic dream" in the Old Testament and in Ancient Mesopotamia, in Greece and Rome, and in the New Testament, and points to a difference between pure "psychological dreams" and "revelatory dreams." In the latter, one used divinatory techniques of interpretation, especially in the sleeping temple in Askleipios, to understand the future, the past, and/or to detect and determine guilt. The opinions of the Greek Church-fathers about the psychological and religious role of dreams, especially in the classic text of Artemidoros Oneirocritica (used by Sigmund Freud (1991) in his first chapter of "The Interpretation of Dreams" (1900)), are scrutinized.

It is important that Kilmore does not stop there, but describes the role of dreams in non-Western religions such as Siberian shamanism, North American Indian religions and those in the Pacific. He ends with a few remarks on the role of jinns in the Muslim world, where the dreamer awakens from a seduction experienced in a dream, "possessed" by the seductive spirit. Cases of hysteria (both individual and collective) together with various forms of *bouffe deliriant* (as an acute, delusional psychosis) are assumed to focus around sexual anxieties and wishes in these cultures. In fact, the union of demon and human is sometimes expressed by the idea of a marriage between a jinn and a possessed individual. Hundreds of Morrocans make yearly pilgrimages to sanctuaries where they await the dream that is believed will cure them—a belief akin to that of the Askleipian tradition.

When Kilmore uses psychological theories and thoughts to bring his phenomenological observations into a "known" body of knowledge, he moves from intrapsychological models to interpersonal or collective structures. He uses ideas from social psychology indirectly or implicitly, but employs ideas from classical Freudian psychoanalysis explicitly. At the beginning of one paragraph he says, "To grasp cultural theories of dreams as theories of thinking, it is necessary to analyze patterns in the perception of dreams. These social and cultural patterns are of course perceived by individuals who make them meaningful in terms of their own psychodynamics."

In the article on *spirit possession* Vincent Crapanzano says, "The interpretation of dissociation, trance, ritual trance and other altered states of consciousness as spirit possession is a cultural construct that varies with the belief system in a culture."

We find a similar tendency in the entry on *Attention*, where Philip Novak stresses the importance of attention in different religious traditions, especially in the practice of meditation and contemplation. Even when he describes techniques provided by a particular religious community and discusses them in terms of the psychology of perception, but especially the old experiment of Deikmann on deautomatization, and the theories of Robert Ornstein, he stresses the importance of the interpreting myth. In other words, the cognitive framework of a particular religion, or of a subgroup in a religious tradition, is decisive, not only in the interpretation but in the genesis of religious experience. As he says, "The accoutrements of a spiritual tradition provide a protective and constructive framework within which the focus on attention is supported and legitimated."

In the dream article, Kilmore writes that "we project inner feelings onto the external world just as we internalize the natural and social world." Especially in a homogeneous culture, dream incubation, dream content, and interpretation are functions of its theory of knowledge, so that the dreams are as relevant or real in this context as is the natural world.

To summarize, these articles underline the importance of three kinds of psychological processes:

1. The role of the cognitive content in a specific religious tradition, its myths, theories of knowledge, anthropological assumptions, and cosmological worldviews, which can, in an elaborated theoretical perspective, become the psychological worldview.
2. The intrapsychic emotional dynamics of the individual, which depend on his personal history and his role in group-dynamic interactions. In our terms, this involves the classical insights of psychoanalysis. The main impression one has is that the authors avoid a "nothing-but" fallacy of reductionism and "either-or" arguments, promoting multidimensional psychological descriptions instead.
3. In this multidimensional understanding, these authors try to keep the intrapsychic emotional dynamics and the cognitive frameworks of the religious traditions that correspond to and interact with these "inner emotions" together. The religious experience (whether it is conversion, healing, spirit possession, or glossolalia) can thus be described as a mutual interaction of (a) emotional and (b) cognitive processes that are, in their turn, embedded in individuals with (c) socialization into their traditions and (d) the situational processes of their immediate context.

Is a priori Religiousness a Psychological Explanation?

If we turn to the entry on *Ecstasy*, we find that the material is ordered differently. After the usual philological analysis, the author of this entry (Arvind Sharma) provides us with an historical, anthropological, and phenomenological overview, and concludes with a few sociological and psychological questions. The sociology of ecstasy there follows the old notions of Durkheim and Weber, who drew attention to the socially integrative function of shamans. The Sufis in Islam, for example, and their experience of collective *dihkr* led in the beginning to a break within the religious tradition, instead of integrating it. The classical approach is, however, that ecstasy—on a social level—is a solution to deprivation and that secret possessional cults may flourish, particularly among women or dispossessed groups, in patriarchal or authoritarian societies.

Coming to a psychological understanding, Sharma says, "one must distinguish clearly among certain approaches within the Psychology of Religion; the Psychoanalytical, the Pharmacological and the Mystical approach (sic)."

If we look closely into his psychoanalytic way of understanding ecstasy we find a mini-review of the old discussion between Freud and Romain Rolland on the "oceanic feeling" as a kind of regression. But of course, modern "self-psychology" and theories like that of Heinz Kohut are not mentioned, although there are a few remarks on the toxic effects of the hallucinogen drugs used in the Hindu tradition, in Native American churches, and privately in Huxley's and Koestler's classic experiments. One of the difficulties with the efforts to describe the psychological conditions behind ecstasy depends on the fact that shamanistic ecstasy (which is "longed for" and collectively legitimized and supported) is mixed with the intense experiences of individual mystics like St. Bridget or St. Therese.

It is, however, typical that "the mystical approach" there is placed under a heading, "psychological explanations." With this, Sharma seems to propose that the claims of ecstatics that they have reached the realms of, or union with God or an Ultimate ontological identity, are to be accepted as a psychological explanation. This proposal clearly demonstrates another way of using a "psychological explanation" from that employed in psychology or in the psychology of religion itself. If "participation in God or Unio mystica" is a scientific effort to understand an experience itself, this is not an explanation or understanding, but a phenomenological description. For a psychologist, this kind of "explanation" involves a vicious circle, where the explanans is not distinguished from the explanandum. From the perspective of a believer's own theory of knowledge, this is of course relevant as a kind of "religious psychology," that must be distingushed from the psychology of religion.

It is quite another thing to say that an ecstatic experience in a particular context, or as a result of socialization into and interiorization of a (religious) worldview, is both explained, described, and experienced as a mystical vision. In another context someone may feel that the "I/Thou" distinction is broken, and that *samadhi*, or the Muslims' loss of Self into God in the process of *fana'* and *tahwid* is reached. A secular positivist student in a situation of sensory deprivation can interpret his feelings of deautomation as an interesting free-floating ego-loss; or if he knows a neoanalytical theory he can say that he feels total regression, or experiences primary processes. Any interpretation depends on the motivation, context, and especially the worldview of the participants.

From a social psychological perspective, especially on the basis of theories about the sociology of knowledge, it is possible to separate the border between the religious claims to truth in a mystical experience, and the psychological function of those claims. This problem is elaborated in Katz's (1983) *Mysticism and Religious Traditions* (see also Wikstrom, 1987, p. 394).

As regards the boundary between a scientific and psychological understanding and religious engagement, it is important to make a distinction between the necessity of a methodological reduction in the social sciences on one hand, and an ontological reduction on the other. The latter is not at all a consequence of the obligation of a researcher to follow the "rules" of social science or psychological methods. If, however, psychological models and concepts are reified and "filled" with ontological or transcendent meaning (instead of being provisional concepts, ready to be left when they no longer have an explanatory value), then psychology is not a science, but a belief: no longer psychology but psychologism. This entry on Ecstasy demonstrates the problems in not making explicit the basic rules of methodological reduction, and their philosophical implications. As I see it, one cannot use "mystical" descriptions as psychological explanations.

Existential Questions as Dynamic Factors in Religion

Let us look even more closely at the article on *Ritual* by Leach. It starts with a long introduction on the difficulties in defining rituals as culturally specified sets of behavior, and on the symbolic dimensions of human behavior regardless of its social, religious, or other content. The main focus for the author is that ritual is a form of social communication or a code, to be treated as a cognitive category carrying other meaning beyond its religious contexts.

A quite different connotation of ritual is met when scholars define it in relation to psychopathology. The psychiatric, mainly psychoanalytic approach, understands ritual as a kind of obsessive-compulsive behavior that covers hidden emotional or developmental conflicts. Psychoanalytically oriented social anthropologists have similarly proposed that the manifest religious content of ritual masks its basic or "latent" social or psychosexual goals.

Anthropologists like Victor Turner and Clifford Geertz are, however, interested in the explicit religious meaning of a ritual's symbolism. They point out that ritual acts endow culturally important cosmological conceptions and values with a persuasive emotional force, unifying individual participants into a genuine community. From this perspective, rituals are seen in terms of their own claims, for their existential or spiritual importance, rather than in terms of some hidden cognitive grammar, psychodynamic force, or for their social references.

In this sense, Geertz and Turner are close to phenomenologists of religion such as Otto and Eliade, who think that rituals arise from and celebrate an encounter with the "numinous" or "sacred." That takes us back to the researchers who claim both the specific character of religious experience and the transcendent genesis and structure of these experiences. But when Leach finally produces his own definition, he chooses to exclude psychiatric or psychopathological associations, defining ritual as "those conscious and voluntary, repetitious and stylized symbolic bodily actions that are centered on cosmic structures and/or presence" (Eliade, 1987). He says that not only the body, but the body's social and cultural identity has a relation to, and feels in contact with, transcendental realms.

If we "translate" this definition into the language of the Psychology of Religion, we come close to those who maintain the importance of the cognitive content, worldview, or symbolic universe in any religious tradition. This means that functional descriptions of rituals do not depend solely on intrapsychological forces, as Freud maintained in 1907. Instead, the myths accompanying the ritual "sculpt," and even generate, the experiences they are describing, since "rituals cluster around those primary realities (such as sexuality, birth, death, strife and failure) that force us to face our personal limits and our merely relative existence."

This view is close to that of those trying to combine functional or deprivational categories with humanistic or existentialist psychological terms. Let us remember that Batson and Ventis (1982) stress an extremely wide and functional definition of religion as "whatever we as individuals do to come to grip personally with the questions that confront us because we are aware that we and others like us are alive and that we will die. Such questions we shall call existential questions" (p. 7).

This in turn seems to fit with Yinger's (1977) sociological perspective, which tried to understand the genesis of religious myths, rites, and experiences in terms of basic existential threats such as meaning, suffering, and death. In that sense, the descriptions of phenomenologists' views of the function of ritual come close to the argument Jan van der Lans (1987) presented at a Scandinavian conference on The Psychology of Religion on "meaning-giving behavior—a neglected but urgent research task for the psychology of religion." If rituals are seen historically as a kind of existentially provocative and "existentially draining behavior," one can search for other symbols, concepts, and behaviors having the same function, and even try to understand not only the ontogenesis of ritualization (like Erikson), but its social and societal correspondences. A functional description of the role of ritual in classical religions can contribute to and may even deepen the research that is needed into "secular" behaviors which give transcendent meaning.

Experience as a Kind of Perception

Fate, Chance, Magic, and Divination are four entries which provide new and widening perspectives for psychologists. Hjalmar Sunden stresses the importance of two quite different ways of understanding reality, and claims that we have either interpreted reality mechanistically, as a deterministic process containing many different parts in causal interaction, or experienced it as an intentional totality that is itself "talking to" and "wanting something" from us (Sunden, 1967).

Religion, in Sunden's analysis, is an attempt to see and to grasp this intentionality. For the pious man, there is—when he attributes meaning to the totality through religious myths—neither chance, fate, or blind natural laws, but only the will of God. The religious man then switches from a naturalistic to a theistic attribution. In reality there is another "true reality," and this latter "reality is made visible by the dual roles of religious tradition" (Sunden, 1967, p. 42).

In this set of entries we can see the need for psychologists of religion not only to deal with submission or trust in a personal god, but to understand processes behind the religious legitimation of surrender, especially when God is experienced as silent, or dead.

Fate denotes the idea that everything in human life, society, and in the world itself, follows an immutable pattern. Fatalism, as the term for our resigned submission to fate (given an attribution of personal relevance), must not be mixed with a philosophical positivism convinced that science could uncover the laws of causal relationships in the world. Fate is, paradoxically, not seen as supreme, exclusive, and all powerful, but might even be superior to the gods.

It is interesting to observe that before Kees V. Bolle moves into his philological and comparative analysis in his entry on *Fate*, he starts with a psychological observation. Denying that fear should be the basic drive of every religious experience, he cannot avoid saying that, with respect to fate and fatalism, however, the function of a psychological ambivalence in many human situations seems hard to deny. Especially in the case of fatalism, that is, the full surrender to fate, an attitude of defeat is in evidence in the belief that the future is as inevitable and fixed as the past.

The ambivalence he refers to here consists of the renunciation of one's reason (and responsibility) and a hypothesis of the relational coherence of events in some other order. These observations on the role of fate must be compared with the role of trust or surrender in relation to a living and personally experienced God whose presence has been experienced and to whom man talks, acts, and responds. Fate means surrendering to a mechanistic law, at least in crisis or when one does not experience religiously legitimized answers to their prayers "after rationalization" or a search for "cognitive consistency," Bolle then gives an elaborated overview of fate in different religions.

Astrology, magic, and divinatory systems, through which one hopes to gain access to a knowledge of the unseen, appear to be accepted or elaborated in times of ambivalence. That is especially noticeable in practical or nontheistic efforts to attribute an overarching meaning to reality (which is itself an interesting problem for psychologists of popular religion). This problem is partly discussed under the entry *Chance*, where it is seen as "the negation of necessity and the opposite of determinism." That English word has a spectrum of associations, including coincidence, randomness, probability, hazard, risk, luck, and so forth. But many other words are related to chance, such as contingency, coincidential oppositorum, or the German *Zufall*, which indicates a binary structure, the coming together of two causally independent series of events. Michiko Yosa says that something happens, a situation or person is encountered by chance. Moreover, as a rare, unusual occurrence, chance approaches the idea of miracle. After those considerations Yosa states (emphasizing the indirect but important role played by a sociology of knowledge) that "ideas of chance are part of a world-view, whether it is indeterministic or deterministic."

A belief in chance has a double role to play in the practice of divination, in the methods (using principles of randomness) and interpretations of coincidence. We can observe this in African systems of divination and in the Chinese I Ching, where casting an arrow yields randomly determined odd or even numbers. Other systems of popular divination include bibliomancy, which consists in randomly opening the Bible, the Quran, or Virgil's Aeneid, as a vehicle for messages from the "real" world. Interpretations of these signs are of central importance for divination, and rely on the principles of coincidence or correspondence, through beliefs about a relation between human affairs and the larger cosmic or Divine Will. This is illuminating for the history of psychology of religion, especially in the work of Swedenborg; and we must remember that casting lots is familiar in both the Old and New Testaments (Joshua 6:14, Proverbs 16:33, John 1:17, Acts 1:26), when divinatory messages were regarded as sacred and mysterious. To desacralize, or find a neutral concept for such coincidences, Carl Jung talked about "acausal synchronicity."

Summary and Conclusion

In Zeusse's entry on Ritual, and in many other places, one finds an open and permissive, or some might say, too eclectic and vague ways of explaining religious phenomena. In nearly all of Eliade's 16 volumes there is an effort to let multidisciplinary approaches characterize the explanations and definitions: The various levels of symbolic reference in ritual help us to understand the applicability of many disciplines and theories to ritual. These can be seen applying to one or another aspect or level of ritual action, although obviously this applicability also suggests that any one theory or discipline in itself cannot claim sole truth and must be supplemented and corrected by other approaches.

This broad approach to the role of theory is especially marked in relation to the psychological aspects of religious phenomena, both for good and ill. In my opinion, the approach is a little too permissive. From the point of view of comparative religion it seems irrelevant whether one's psychological understanding is taken from a Jungian, psychoanalytic, or social psychological perspective. These perspectives have, among other problems, different basic assumptions and are in part contradictory. In this sense, I think that psychologists of religion, because of their formal training in social science theory and method, can contribute to a deepening and critical "use" of the theories of comparative religion.

In earlier Encyclopedias of Religion there was an implicit, and sometimes overtly hierarchical structure when they tried to describe different religions. Historical, philological, and systematic or comparative studies, especially of documents and historical artifacts, were seen as more scientific and "true" than functional, sociological, or psychological approaches. That view seems to be disappearing or has become only a part of the history of studies of religion. Sociology and psychology of religion are now respected and seen as relevant in their own right.

When they talk explicitly in terms of psychoanalytic origins, nearly every article implicitly stresses the role of (sub)groups, the legitimation provided by tradition and a symbolic universe which sculptures experiences, or in terms of social psychological theories and Jung's theories of archetypes and symbols, which have had an immense influence.

There is, however, a slide or an unsophisticated changing of levels in the scientific tasks undertaken. Authors often talk about the phenomena as such (whether conversion, mysticism, possession, or ritual) and the cultural, societal, and personal functions or psychological conditions that are behind and within these experiences. To a psychologist, this is unsatisfactory but understandable.

Nevertheless, these enormous, scholarly, and highly readable books demonstrate the necessity of mutual exchange between religions, *Wissenschaft*, and psychologists. If historians or phenomenologists do not try to use and work with relevant psychological theories, their aim to "understand religious man" can be irrelevant and a bit esoteric. And the opposite is also the case. If psychologists do not try to understand scholars working on the total context in which religious man is embedded, their efforts will continue to remain marginal to their main task.

Psychologists need closer contact with scholars who, on the one hand, describe a multidisciplinary and nonconfessional approach to the study of religion, and on the other hand, separate such study from theological or other assessments that are entirely proper when applied within a single tradition. Religious phenomena can be described from observation, rather than as creeds to be followed. This implies a serious and—as far as possible—dispassionate study of material from the world's accessible religious traditions.

In a rapidly changing world, with multicultural communication, and a cross-fertilization of religious traditions that are completely different in ontology, cosmology, anthropology, eschatology and so on, this must be a necessity. Presumably a transcultural perspective leads to an even better understanding of religious experiences in comparison with aesthetic and moral experiences. It can also provide a better context in which to describe the essence of a scientific psychology of religion.

References

Batson, C.D. & Ventis, W.L. (1982). *The religious experience: A social-psychological perspective*. New York: Oxford University Press.

Eliade, M. (Ed.). (1987). *The Encyclopedia of Religion* (Vols. 1–16). New York: Macmillan.

Freud, S. (1991) *The Interpretation of Dreams*. Harrmonds Worth, Penguin.

Holm, N.G. (1988). *Scandinavian psychology of religion*. Åbo, Finland: Åbo Academy.

Katz, S.T. (Ed.). (1983). *Mysticism and religious traditions*. New York: Oxford University Press.

Smith, W.C. (1979). *Faith and belief*. Princeton, NJ: Princeton University Press.

Sunden, H. (1967). Bedingungen religiser Erfahrung. [Conditions for religious Lceharior *Archiv fur Religionspsychologie*, *9*, 41–49.

Van der Lans, J. (1987). Meaning giving behavior. A neglected but urgent research task for the Psychology of Religion. In Wikström, O. (Ed.) *Religionspsykologi nu. Proceedings from the first Scandinavian Symposium in Psychology of Religion* (pp. 3–10). Uppsala, Sweden Uppsala Teologiska Institutionen.

Wikstrom, O. (1987). Attribution, roles, and religion. *Journal for the Scientific Study of Religion*, *26*(3), 390–400.

Wikström, O. (1993). The psychology of religion in Scandinavia. *The International Journal for the Psychology of Religion* 1993, Vol. 3.

Yinger, J.M.A. (1977). A comparative study of the substructures of religion. *Journal for the Scientific Study of Religion*, *16*, 67–86.

4
Religion and Mental Health: A Case Study of the Finnish-Swedish Popular Writer Joel Pettersson

NILS G. HOLM

This study is based on a large amount of manuscript material left behind by Joel Pettersson, the popular writer from Finland. In the light of the psychology of religion, this material is extremely interesting, and the present study combines approaches from social psychology and depth psychology to interpret it. A religious training was relatively normal among writers at the turn of this century, but the psychosocial development of Joel Pettersson has particularly interesting links with his religiosity: in his teens he became religious, above all to escape problems of a sexual nature connected with his approaching manhood; and during the third decade of his life, he protested strongly against religious and paternal authority, before returning a little later to a madonna-like piety. His life ended (in 1937) in a mental asylum at the age of 44.

Introduction

The relationship between religion and mental health is a complicated one. There are a number of studies dealing with this problem, but in the present context it is sufficient to refer to Batson and Ventis's account in *The Religious Experience* (1982), which includes a review of research in this area. No simple connections can be made, although it may be concluded that, under certain conditions, religion contributes to mental illness, whilst in other cases it can alleviate and even prevent outbreaks of this kind. Those judgments clearly depend very much on the definition of health with which one is operating. This is another complex area, which I cannot discuss here, although we are dealing with mental illness when an individual himself, or those close to him are seriously disturbed by the behavior.

Religion can be regarded as a cognitive and behavioral system which, according to how it is used in the lives of individuals or social groups, contributes to the maturing process of an individual, or to the development of mental disturbances. The functions acquired by religion in the life of a given individual are highly dependent, as I see it, on how the transmission of religion from one generation to the next has taken place, which means that factors related to the psychology of socialization must be taken into account. In this context, the emotional and psychodynamic charges linked with religious ideas and behavioral patterns are of very great importance. To understand an individual's use of religion—cognitively, behaviorally, and emotionally—one should therefore study the kinds of religious material that a person has been provided with during adolescence, as well as the actual training they have received. It is extremely important here to examine the mechanisms which, during one's life, have linked religion to specific emotional reactions and psychodynamic structures of experience. These often determine what kinds of use will be made of religion in the course of their later lifetime.

To illustrate what I mean by these suggestions, I will give a brief account of my study of the artist Joel Pettersson (Holm, 1987a and b). He was born in 1892 in Lemland, a parish in Finland, and died when he was only 44, in a mental hospital in the year 1937; the cause of his death was identified as schizophrenia, general blood poisoning, and pneumonia. His schizophrenia has been questioned by Nils Wiklund in Lund (Sweden), who offers an alternative diagnosis, based on solid psychological and psychiatric grounds, that Joel Pettersson had functional disturbances in his vestibular apparatus, and vascular injuries to the brain. There was a hereditary predisposition for this in his family (Wiklund, 1978). My aim, however, is to make a case study of the literary material left by this popular author, to examine how religion was transmitted to him during adolescence, the use he made of religious motives during adolescence, and—above all—to relate this to his psychosocial development. It is naturally difficult to state whether, in his case, religion contributed to or prevented the outbreak of illness. As I see the matter, the genetic potential for illness was so strong that sooner or later it would have led to some form of disturbance, but that, with its mythological content, religion helped to postpone the onset of illness. In any case, we have here an excellent example of the function of religious motifs in a person with rich artistic gifts and the capacity for self-expression.

The Material

Joel Pettersson was born in the home of a smallholder, to relatively old parents. He revealed artistic talents at an early age, beginning to write short stories and paint pictures. Through the efforts of the local pastor, he came into contact with painters who used to frequent the parish during the summer time. At the age of 21 he began to study at art school in Turku, but after about 2 years, suddenly broke off his studies and returned home. He subsequently helped his aging parents on their farm and became closely involved with the activities of the local youth club. He gave talks, wrote and produced plays, painted scenery, and so on. At the same time, he also began to write on a larger scale. He was encouraged in this activity by a teacher, Werner Ek, who kept up a correspondence with Joel. Another significant writing phase occurred a few years later, during a period when a medical student in Helsinki, Birger Bondestam, provided the important link.

In 1928, both parents died, and Joel took his mother's death particularly hard. As he was now alone, he tried to work on the farm and to paint studiously. External adversities piled up, however, and he arrived at the brink of suicide. Neighbors nevertheless took care of him, although it was not long before he had to be committed to a mental asylum, spending only 9 months there before he died.

Joel wrote vast amounts during the course of his life. This material comprises over 4,000 handwritten pages of folio size. After his death, it was transferred to the Åland museum* in Finland and is today kept in the Åland provincial archives. During his lifetime, Joel only had minor articles published in newspapers, and most of what he wrote lay at home in large boxes. The language he used is a popular dialect of Swedish. By the middle of the 1930's, Joel had obtained a measure of fame for his pictures, but he had by then already been committed to the asylum and was probably unaware of this renown. He painted in a style that was reminiscent of van Gogh, who was virtually unknown in Finland at that time, and Joel left about 160 paintings at his death.

After his death, Joel was almost completely forgotten, and it was not until the middle 1970's that he achieved more lasting fame. This came with the publication by the provincial dean, Valdemar Nyman, of four books with extracts from the collected manuscripts. The rich style of the narratives guaranteed the success of these works within the context of Finnish-Swedish literature. Nyman also wrote a lengthy biography of Joel Pettersson, called *Pojken och den gråa byn* [The Boy and the Grey Village], published in 1977. On reading this book I realized that there was much of interest from the perspective of religious psychology in Joel's material. My study of Joel appeared at the end of 1987 under the title *Joels Gud* [Joel's God] (in the Proceedings of Åland's Cultural Foundation, No 2).

Joel wrote a vast amount about God, the Church, and the priesthood, and he possessed a great capacity for narrative. He liked to reproduce popular stories and legends, together with reworked biblical narratives and myths. Predominantly, however, he wrote short stories of an autobiographical nature, revealing in his correspondence that the stories were

---

* Åland (Finland)

about himself, even if they were often written in the third person. It is not difficult to analyze this material and to interpret it with direct reference to Joel. But one must remember that the narratives represent not an external or observable reality, but an internal, personally experienced (mental) reality. Most of the stories are of such clarity that the interpretive models of depth psychology can be readily applied to them.

We can divide Joel's life into five different phases. (a) The childhood years from 1892–1907, (b) confirmation and the years immediately afterwards (1908–1912), (c) at art school in Turku and in commitments with his youth club (1913–1919), (d) early middle age (1920–1934), and (e) the period of acute illness (1935–1937). We have a fairly clear picture of the role played by religion during these phases of his life, except in the final period, of which we know very little about his religious outlook.

Piety in Childhood and Adolescence

Joel was brought up in a conservative Lutheran tradition. He lived only a few hundred yards from the church and visited it frequently. At home he learned to say his evening prayers and grace at meals. The reading of homilies and hymn singing occurred in the home, while there was also preparation for the texts that were to be learned by heart. Transmission of his religious tradition in this way was fairly common at that time. From his accounts of it, however, we can see that it included certain highly negative elements, particularly with regard to the grace at meals. He describes how he came rushing in late, tucked into the food and forgot to say grace. He then received a severe reprimand from his father, who forced him to spit out the food and say, "In Jesus' name we come to eat. . . ." According to Joel, it was then that he learned to hate the name of Jesus. The child's mind suspected that the divinity of Jesus was in some way linked in that prayer with the hateful display of authority exercised by his father. Through overexposure and negative conditioning, Jesus acquired a clearly negative association. While Joel had a poor relationship with his father, his mother emerged as a predominantly positive figure.

When Joel was 15, he started confirmation school and was confirmed in the normal way in the Lutheran church, where it is not particularly common for young people to experience confirmation as a fundamental event in their lives. For Joel, however, this was the case, and he underwent a kind of conversion and became pious. He often went to church and then sat at home in the evenings "shedding tears over the Bible and the life of Jesus." In particular, Joel paid attention to the priest's hands and fingers, saying that he had fallen in love with them since they were so angelically beautiful and supernatural. Putting his own hand in them, he dreamed of losing himself in a forest and being eternally near the priest in a kind of heavenly joy.

Joel's exercise of piety during these years may be linked with the problems he experienced with sexuality. He wrote of how shocked he was at seeing his parents' sexual intercourse and how he felt rejected by his mother. He no longer knew whether he should identify himself with his father or with his mother. Attempts to impress the opposite sex failed miserably for him, and he was left with only a gaping sense of insufficiency. "I should never have been a man, just a small boy," he writes sadly. One solution to problems of identity and sexuality is provided by a sentimental piety that was appreciated by his mother. The pastor, in turn, saw the results of his teachings. But with a sort of angelic quality, Joel tried to become sexless and canonized. If during Joel's early childhood religion had been charged with negative paternal authority, it now became—during his teenage years—an emotional sanctuary in which to escape the threat of sexuality and the demands of the male role.

Protest in Youth

This early spirituality did not, however, continue for very long in Joel's life. It disintegrated on contact with others of his own age and doubt set in. After his arrival at the Turku art school his situation changed radically: The childhood world and its sanctimonious attitudes finally collapsed. This contributed to the anguish experienced by Joel and led to the abrupt termination of his studies. His youth club activities then, were characterized by a highly critical stance towards God, the church, and the priesthood. In a talk entitled *Religion and the Young* he was particularly scathing about the God of Christianity. All the negative experiences from his childhood, but most of all, the intolerable paternal authority, were projected onto God. "It is wrong to call God, father. Mother and father are better, because mother and father are so good, so blessed compared with what God is," exclaims Joel. And he is particularly solicitous about the mother: "For mother is great. She is like an angel, like a god," he insists. The early symbiosis with the mother remained part of him, while the god-figure was allowed to attract all the negative projections, and he now felt free to protest against it.

This development of religiosity in Joel's life is connected with another method he used for resolving his psychodynamic tensions. He sought contact with young people, unselfishly sacrificing himself for them, and dreaming of his union with a beautiful young extravert who possessed all the positive qualities he himself seemed to lack. This took the form of homosexual dreams and fantasies, which he also recorded, not least in the play *Elis och Johan* [Elis and Johan], which is remarkable in view of the fact that it was written as early as 1917, when attitudes towards homosexuality were very severe. To attain the ideal of manhood which Joel himself had never been able to reach, it was necessary for him to reject any form of authority and control. Only through an intimate union with an idealized man would Joel's immaturity be restored. In the pursuit of this goal, paternal authority and Christian tutelage—represented by God and priests—were merely obstacles. The elimination of religion then became for Joel a condition for personal freedom and individual maturity.

Madonna-like Holiness in Early Manhood

The next stage in Joel's life begins when he falls in love with a woman. Through his protest against God, and as a result of his contacts with young people, he matured to the point where he dared to enter into a heterosexual relationship. Unfortunately he became deeply disillusioned when the object of his affections emigrated to the United States and remained there. His 30's were then transformed into a period of great searching and wavering, which is reflected in his correspondence with Bondestam, who became a point of support for Joel, as a friend he admired from a distance. A kind of platonic love developed on Joel's side, with the result that his religiosity was once again modified. The previous sharp criticism of God became considerably milder, as certain maternal and feminine features again entered the picture. He mentions in his letters that he has undergone a conversion and we can find clear evidence of his self-effacement there. The piety he then cultivated has certain features in common with the behavior he had displayed in his teens. The maternal principle is affirmed as he identified himself with worship of the Madonna and Child. He says he envies Catholics, who have the Virgin Mary to turn to and real, living confessors who will listen to their outpourings. "We Protestants have only the cold, frozen ether to pour our suffering into," writes Joel.

Joel thus developed a kind of madonna-inspired piety, which was something quite remarkable in the genuinely Lutheran environment in which he lived. He nevertheless found it difficult to accept the idea of atonement. The descent of Jesus on earth, to suffer and to die, and His subsequent appearance before God, are concepts against which Joel reacted. But identifying himself, on the other hand, with Christ as the stranger on earth, the outsider full of love and sacrifice, was something Joel could manage easily. And the longing for some kind of transcendental, heavenly state was typical of Joel at that time.

After the death of his parents, Joel tried to obtain success and renown by intensive work on the farm, and through his art. With many severe setbacks, he fell into a state of confusion. We know nothing of his religious circumstances during those final years, but everything seemed to disintegrate for him and religion no longer provided any forms of identification for him.

Summary

We may see in the case of Joel Pettersson a person who received a religious tradition under fairly typical conditions for his time. He revealed great artistic talent, together with homosexual and schizophrenic tendencies. On the basis of his writings, one cannot go closely into the reasons for his homosexuality, and far less into questions about his schizophrenia. It is, nevertheless, clear that there was a previous history of mental illness in his family. We see, therefore, a loner in a peasant society, who studied religious questions seriously and allowed his own psychodynamics to be reflected in the symbolic world of Christianity.

In his childhood he was given a traditional form of religion. From the perspective of learning theory, we might say that his affect towards the central religious concepts had been negatively conditioned. But those negative experiences colored his religion then, especially through the oedipal bonds that were connected with the central motifs of Christianity. In his teens he was forced into an exaggerated spiritual piety in the retreat from a threatening sexuality, and from demanding male roles. He then appealed to desexed religious symbols, and dreamed of heavenly bliss. That solution was not, however, lasting. When brute reality called him back to his senses, his reaction was to eliminate the authoritarian principles of religion, and of the father, since it was primarily God and the religious system against which he felt the need to protest.

A certain maturity can be observed in him then, but external disappointment again forced him to reassess his religion. The need to protest was partly resolved through struggle and hardship, and while Joel could consider himself converted, the piety which then developed within him followed only the maternal principle as he then identified himself with supplication to the Madonna, Christ was experienced primarily as a friend and comrade, and then once again, a transcendental longing emerged within him.

To summarize, we can say that religion for Joel became the ground from which his psychodynamic and social development was projected. The mythological and symbolic elements of religion focused his mental development, the impasses, possibilities of retreat and outright protest, and gave opportunities for partial identification and maturity.

To understand the role of religion as a mental or psychological process, completely bound up as it is with the development of mental health or illness, one must consider the religious elements that are transmitted by a tradition and the ways that transmission process has been managed. The reworking of religious motifs during the course of a person's life is intimately linked to the question of how the transmission occurred. Those motifs alone are not responsible for mental illness, and, particularly in Joel's case, it could have been that religion delayed the onset of his mental illness.

References

Batson, C.D. & Ventis, W.L. (1982). *The religious experience: A social-psychological perspective*. New York: Oxford University Press.

Holm, N.G. (1987a). *Joels Gud [Joel's God]*. Meddelanden fran Ålands kultur-stiftelse (Proceedings of Åland's Cultural Foundation No 2). Mariehamn, Finland.

Holm, N.G. (1987b). Scandinavian psychology of religion. *Religionsvetenskapliga skrifter nr 15*. Åbo Akademi University, Department of Comparative Religion. Åbo, Finland.

Nyman, V. (1977). *Pojken och den gråa byn. Joel Pettersson 1892–1937*. [The Boy and the Grey Village]. Mariehamn Schildts.

Wiklund, Nils (1978). *The Icarus complex: Studies of an alleged relationship between fascination for fire, enuresis, high ambition, and ascensionism*. Lund University, Sweden.

5
Happiness and Religious Belief

JOCELYN DELBRIDGE, BRUCE HEADEY, AND
ALEXANDER J. WEARING

That religion in some form is important for many people is shown by information from the *Australian Values Study* (1984) summarized in Table 5.1.

The countries represented in these tables were chosen because, as Organisation for Economic Co-operation and Development countries, they share a predominantly Judeo-Christian religious tradition. Even in Europe, only one person in six does not believe in God, while in the United States only 1 nonbeliever in 50 may be found. Corresponding with these findings, Campbell, Converse, and Rogers (1976) report that 60% of their American sample regarded having a strong religious faith as very important, a level that accords with results from the *Australian Values Study* (1984) in which 32% of the Australian, 59% of the American, and 24% of the European samples said that God was very important in their lives. In these findings Australia typically falls between Europe and the United States, although it is more similar to Europe.

Are religious people more satisfied with their lives? Research findings suggest that the answer is "yes." Clemente and Sauer (1976), using church attendance as a measure of religiosity in a national sample of adult Americans, concluded that those who attended church frequently had a higher level of life satisfaction than those who did not, a result replicated by Davis and Smith (1986), who also used a national sample. Other investigations confirm this result (Hadaway, 1978; Andrews & Withey, 1976). Witter, Stock, Okum, and Haring's (1985) meta-analysis of 28 studies also concluded that religion is positively associated with subjective well-being.

Two complementary explanations have been offered to explain this relationship between religion and well-being (Argyle, 1987). One is that religious ideas provide meaning and purpose, integration and direction in life (Argyle & Beit-Hallahmi, 1975; Freedman, 1978; Soderstrom & Wright, 1977). The second explanation is that the church is a primary source of social support (e.g., Moberg & Taves, 1965), so that church

50

TABLE 5.1. An international comparison of religious beliefs.

Which, if any of the following, do you believe in?		Australia %	USA %	Europe %
God	yes	79	95	75
	no	14	2	16
Life after death	yes	49	71	43
	no	34	17	38
Hell	yes	34	67	23
	no	52	26	64
Heaven	yes	57	84	40
	no	31	11	47

Note: The Australian Values Study, 1984. (The data are given in percentages, and "Don't know" answers are omitted.)

attendance, for example, seems to be associated with better health outcomes (Comstock & Partridge, 1972).

Nevertheless, even though there is a positive relationship between religion and happiness, that relationship is not strong. Witter et al. (1985), following their meta-analysis, reported that although the effect sizes ranged as high as .58, the 95% confidence interval lay between .14 and .25. More recent studies (e.g., Markides, 1983; Peterson & Roy, 1985; St. George & McNamara, 1984) and national surveys in the United States (Davis & Smith, 1986) confirm this result, finding a correlation between religiousness and global happiness of .17.

It is clear that although religion may be related to subjective well-being, not all religious people are happy. One account of this relatively low relationship is that both religion and well-being are complex concepts, and that the observed relationships may depend on how those variables are measured. Chamberlain and Zika (1989), in a recent review, point out that although religiousness and happiness are related, the relation may not be a simple one, since the empirical findings suggest that the nature of the relationship between well-being and religion may alter, not simply as the measures of religion change, but depending upon the way well-being itself is assessed. They note that most studies in this area have used single-item measures of happiness, overall life satisfaction, or satisfaction with particular domains (e.g., Clemente & Sauer, 1976; Hadaway & Roof, 1978; Steinitz, 1980; St. George & McNamara, 1984).

Recent work on well-being has suggested that it is indeed multidimensional (Diener, 1984; Headey, & Wearing, 1992; Grob, Luethi, Kaiser, Flammer, Mackinnon, & Wearing, 1989). Although a general dimension of well-being can be identified and measured (Stone & Kozma, 1985), its components have been shown to relate differently to separate variables (e.g., Diener & Emmons, 1984; Harding, 1982; Headey, Glowacki, Holmstrom, & Wearing, 1985). The three most commonly agreed dimensions of well-being are, however, life satisfaction, positive affect, and negative affect (Andrews & Withey, 1976; Diener, 1984; Headey & Wearing, 1992; Headey, Holmstrom, & Wearing, 1984, 1985).

Religiousness may similarly be regarded as multidimensional, even though the net outcome of much empirical work suggests that, over a variety of items and using heterogeneous samples, religion emerges as a single common factor (Dittes, 1969). Nevertheless, theologians, as well as psychological theorists have continued to draw distinctions between religion as expressed in an explicit form, for example, in formal beliefs and institutional connections, and religion expressed more subjectively as a concern with the spiritual dimension of life. The first form is sometimes labeled *intrinsic* religious belief, the latter, *extrinsic* (Allport, 1950), with evidence that the two orientations have different empirical consequences.

A study of undergraduate psychology students (Soderstrom & Wright, 1977) suggested that the more integrated the religious beliefs (or the more commitment there is to both God and man), the greater the experienced meaning in life. So, intrinsically motivated individuals experience a greater degree of meaning in life than extrinsically motivated individuals. Bolt (1975), who also used American undergraduate students in a study of Allport's (1950) distinction between extrinsic and intrinsic motivation in religious activity, supported the findings of Soderstrom and Wright, by demonstrating that individuals with intrinsic motivation have the greater sense of purpose and meaning in life.

To summarize, this research seems to lead to the following conclusions:

1. religiousness has a positive, but low relationship with well-being, indicating that whereas for some people religiousness and well-being go together, for others they do not,
2. explanations for the strength of the relationship in general are that religion "works" because it provides meaning and purpose in life, or social support (through membership of religious congregations), or both,
3. explanations for the weakness of the relationship are that well-being and religion are multidimensional, and that, in particular,
4. a distinction needs to be drawn between extrinsic religion, which might be easy to measure by church attendance, for example, and intrinsic religion, which is not so easily measured.

The conclusion from these findings is that more detailed study of the relationships between religiousness and happiness (or satisfaction) is called for. In particular, research designs that are experimental rather than correlational are needed, with studies that systematically vary religiousness and satisfaction. Since we are interested in the different relationships between religiousness and happiness with other aspects of life, the design of choice would be one in which "religious" and "nonreligious," and "satisfied" or "dissatisfied" people were compared.

Given that there seems to be a weak relationship between religion and happiness, we are interested in systematic outcomes independent of variations in religiousness and happiness. But what distinguishes the person who is religious and satisfied from the person who is nonreligious yet also satisfied?

A further difficulty is the problem of capturing the complexity of religiousness, and particularly the differences between intrinsic and extrinsic religion. This problem seems to call for open-ended survey questions, since in-depth interviews may provide details of the texture of belief that enable us to see some of the ways in which belief may or may not mediate happiness.

In view of these considerations the following two-stage research design was adopted. In the first stage, a sample of the population of the Melbourne metropolitan area in Australia was selected and interviewed, using a closed question schedule. In the second stage, 20 participants were selected from this sample and interviewed in depth, using open-ended questions. The participants were selected to represent four groups consisting of those who attended church often and were highly satisfied with their lives, those who never attended church but who nonetheless were highly satisfied with their lives, those who attended church often but were dissatisfied with their lives, and finally those who never attended church and were very dissatisfied with their lives. The aim of the study, in its broadest terms, was to deepen our understanding of religious and nonreligious (or secular) attitudes to life and of the ways in which those attitudes may influence satisfaction with life-as-a-whole. In particular, the study aimed to determine what variables mediated the links between religion and well-being, with special reference to the integrative role of religion, and the extent to which it gives purpose and meaning to life.

Participants

The participants in the first stage of the study were selected according to a stratified random procedure, from within three suburbs of Melbourne representing high, medium, and low socioeconomic status areas. A total of 555 persons were interviewed. The information obtained allowed the construction of four criterion groups for the second stage, based on two independent variables (religious versus secular or nonreligious, and high versus low satisfaction with life). Participants were therefore chosen who (a) either attended church once a week or more, or never attended church; and (b) were either very satisfied or very dissatisfied with their lives as a whole.

We also intended to balance the four groups for age, sex, and socioeconomic status. But the number available in the low life-satisfaction categories was small (see Table 5.2), and no one with *very* low life-

TABLE 5.2. Selection of participants from the sample survey to be interviewed in this study.

Category	Number in original sample	Not available		Final sample
Satisfied Religious (SR)	67 (greater) (than 14)*	7	1 not known at given address	5 (plus 1 incorrect categorization)
Satisfied Secular (HS)	160 (greater) (than 14)*	5	—	5
Dissatisfied Religious (DR)	9 (less than 10)*	8	2 refusals 1 refusal and moving 1 unknown	4
Dissatisfied Secular (DS)	32 (less than 10)*	9	3 moved 1 refusal and moving	4 (plus 1 incorrect categorization)
Total	268	29	9	20

* Scores on life satisfaction.

satisfaction scores was also religious. Because of this shortage of respondents in the low life-satisfaction and religious category, one person was included who attended church "most weeks but not every week," which resulted in the low life-satisfaction groups having 4 members each, instead of the intended 5, and who were not matched for age, sex, and socioeconomic status.

Perhaps one of the more interesting findings coming from Table 5.2 is that when religious observance is considered, the assertion made at the beginning of this paper, that religion is important for most people, is called into question, since only about one person in seven could be called "religious."

Interviewing Procedure

The second stage participants were initially contacted by letter, then either visited or telephoned and a time arranged to interview them in their own home. On arrival for the interview, the purpose of this study was explained in terms of allowing people to answer in their own words so as to obtain a picture of each individual's ideas. The focus on religious belief was not elaborated. It was stressed that we sought the person's own feelings and attitudes, that no right or wrong answers were involved, and that the information was confidential. The interviews, usually lengthy and wide-ranging, were taped.

A Comparison of Open and Closed Questions

As indicated above, the relative advantages and disadvantages of open-ended and fixed response or closed questions have been the subject of some debate. Open questions have been seen as advantageous in that they can be used "to understand respondent's feelings and motivation in depth" (Dohrenwend, 1965), as a basis for developing an adequate set of closed response alternatives (Schuman & Presser, 1979), and to produce a more valid picture of choices, uninfluenced by any given alternatives (Schuman & Presser, 1979; Campbell, 1945).

On the other hand, Walsh and Cummins (1976) claimed that studies using open-ended questions suffered from contradictory findings, failure in replication, and inadequate conceptualization on the part of the researcher. But studies comparing the effectiveness of the two techniques have tended to suggest that open-ended questions do not function as an alternative to closed-ended questions. Rather, open-ended questions are used as a supplementary source of information despite their shortcomings (Headey, Holmstrom, & Wearing, 1982).

Design of the Interview Schedule

The interview schedule was not only designed to investigate the relationship between religious beliefs and life satisfaction, but to provide a comparison between the closed questions used in the survey, and in-depth interviews using open-ended questions. The interviews covered the aspects or domains of life shown to have greatest impact on overall life satisfaction through leisure, occupation, friendships and social involvements, marriage and family (see e.g., Headey, Glowacki, et al., 1985; Headey, Holmstrom, & Wearing, 1984; Headey & Wearing, 1981, 1992). The participants were asked three sets of questions about each domain: what they found satisfying, what they found dissatisfying, and what changes they would like to bring about in their own situation. Questions dealing with their personal background, premarital relationships, and future aspirations were also included.

All the participants were asked about religion, although the questions were modified appropriately for each person. This provided everyone with an opportunity to explain whatever religious or religiously related beliefs they held. Since the first questions were designed to differentiate between specific types of beliefs, the participants were encouraged to explain fully the nature of their beliefs and the consequences of these beliefs for life, and for their feelings about life. A question on philosophy of life (adapted from Lane, 1962) allowed each respondent to discuss any life code that may have been omitted. This section sought the main factors in satisfaction and dissatisfaction, and tapped utopian ideas with a question about changing their lives. The question, "How do you feel about life as a whole?" allowed further consideration of the whole interview. Participants were questioned at the end of the interview, to elicit any further issues that had been omitted and to check on changes in their circumstances which may have occurred since the initial survey.

Questions in each area of the schedule therefore focused first on satisfactions, secondly on dissatisfactions, and finally on desired changes. This enabled the participants to begin with a positive rather than a negative focus at the conclusion of each set of questions. Questioning began with leisure as the least threatening and most impersonal area, progressing towards more potentially threatening and personal areas such as marriage relationships, when rapport developed though trust and confidence in the interviewer.

Results

The results fall into two parts, the first part coming from the survey from which the four "experimental" groups were drawn, and the second part from this experiment itself.

In the survey of the Melbourne metropolitan area we found that religious people were a distinct subset within the community. Those who reported a strong sense of religious fulfillment were more satisfied with their overall lives than those who reported a moderate or low sense of religious fulfillment. Apparently their contentment did not derive simply from the psychological and emotional support obtained from a church community, since regular church attenders who felt a strong sense of religious fulfillment were only marginally more content with their lives than irregular church attenders with a strong religious fulfillment.

In a sense, religion appeared to "work" for these people by providing a strong sense of purpose and meaning in life, in that self-fulfillment correlated strongly with satisfaction with life ($r = .73$). The question arises, however, as to whether people who were not religious but who nevertheless had a strong sense of purpose and meaning in life were equally content with their lives. The results did not provide a clear answer, but indicated that those who reported a strong sense of religious fulfillment may have been slightly more satisfied with their lives than those whose sense of purpose and meaning in life was derived only from secular sources.

The survey also showed frequent church attenders to be more satisfied with most aspects of their lives than other people. They were also more concerned with personal relationships, since the correlation between life satisfaction and concern with relationships with friends, family, and parents was higher for the religious group. This result confirms Chamberlain and Zika's (1989) conclusion that religiousness involves other variables which are also linked to happiness, with purpose and meaning in life being particularly important. The highest correlate of life satisfaction for both survey samples ($r = .73$) was a group of variables which appeared to measure self-concept and the respect of others for one-self, which was called the self-fulfillment index.

In showing that self-fulfillment is important for life satisfaction, these results provide support for the view that to the extent that religion is integrative, it is likely to contribute to happiness. From Table 5.2 it can also be seen that religion and life satisfaction were closely related in the survey sample.

A Comparison of the Four Groups

Group 1: High on Life Satisfaction and Religiousness

The common factor for this group was their faith in God, although these people did not appear to be significantly different from those who were high on life satisfaction and *not* religious, except for a faith which transcended all human difficulty and shaped their perspective on satisfaction. When there was sadness, their faith placed a different perspective on it from that held by the "satisfied secular" group.

Church involvement was a part of their religious activity and faith for the satisfied religious group, but was not central to it. Loyalty to the church was also stronger for the four Catholics than for the one Anglican. Of those in the "high religious" group, the one who seemed to have little emotional attachment or commitment to his faith found his family and especially his children central to his life and happiness. That man's faith was something he had been taught as a child, and he wanted to believe in it, but did not want to know too much about it, in case he was changed in some way. "I want to believe in what my mother said to me to believe in." At the same time his relationship with God was important to him and he felt his prayers had been answered.

Another person was restrained in his responses. During the interview the longest "speeches" he made were about his son, and about an experience of guidance by God, although he could not explain the way in which he had been guided, since "it just flowed." He was content living a quiet existence, with visits from his son, and assisting widows and others in the area. He seemed to have a deep sense of purpose that was intrinsic to his faith. "I'm quite sure that we're here for a purpose, whatever that may be, and I am just quite happy in knowing that we follow the right path and carry on."

Another felt that prayer was more important than anything else in her life. She trusted God in everything, was never afraid, and had never doubted, even when her husband died. No one else mentioned religion so specifically in connection with other areas of life. Her motto in life was "He (Jesus) conquered—why shouldn't I?"

A further person placed great emphasis on both the family and her faith in God. Prayer was first in life and she "never stopped praying," and her prayers were answered as when God prevented her from having a second miscarriage because she prayed. "I always go to Him and pray."

The most satisfied woman in the "satisfied religious" group seems fulfilled in every area of her life. The source of this fulfillment, although she did not talk about it except when asked, was her relationship with God. "I suppose the overriding important thing in my life is my faith and that would transcend all human relationships. That to me is the most powerful and important thing in my life. Through tragedy, through any-thing, *anything*. There is always a transcending hope. It's not something that's sort of a compartment. It's an ingrained part of your life."

For this group of participants, faith was the motivating factor in their lives, giving them a deep sense of purpose, since God could always be relied on.

Group 2: High on Life Satisfaction, and Secular or not Religious

This group appeared to be united by a positive attitude towards life and a concern for other people, with the partial exception of one person. Even though religion was not central to their lives, they did not deny a super-natural power or its potential force.

The only exception was a woman who expressed herself positively, but with an undercurrent of sadness and loneliness. Her husband had died a slow, painful death and she was estranged from her daughter and son-in-law. She lived for the rare occasions when she saw her grandchildren, and for the day-to-day contact with two friends living close by. She said, "It gets lonely at times, but I don't mind. I don't mind at all. My nights are the loneliest, you know, when you're here by yourself. It's extremely lonely. As I say, life goes on. It doesn't stand still for anybody." She was therefore similar in outlook to those in the "dissatisfied secular" group, but showed the need for people like those in the "satisfied secular" group. She did not really believe in God, because her husband had died despite her prayers, although being "Church of England" and having had her children baptised was very important to her.

Another person in this group centered his happiness around his friends, so that "being able to relate to others my age" made life worthwhile. He believed that there was something there, but wanted to have God prove Himself and to perform a miracle before that man would trust in Him.

One was happy with her husband and family so that relating to her children and being a good mother were very important to her. The fact that her father had died when she was young had had an important influence on her life and she believed that her father's spirit gave her reassurance and relaxation when she was in need of it. This involved the belief that there was some kind of entity which was around and within everybody, but not what she would call "God."

Another person also centered his life around his family and their happiness. Although his choice of career and his work were also very important, it was less so than his family. While he had reservations about religion, he said that he prayed in everything he did, which equaled doing what he wanted and thought was right. His religion was "basically a set of rules to live by." For him, involvement with God did not appear to be as deep and meaningful as it was for most of the "satisfied religious" group. For the other member of this group, family seemed less important than it was for the rest, although it was his family, and particularly his grandchildren, who made life worthwhile and happy. He emphasized making the most of life, whatever it might bring, and said he believed in God and respected the church, but did not pray. Of religion he said, "I've always accepted it as part and parcel of my life—but it has never dominated my life."

The enabling factor in life for this group tended to be family and friends. They did not bring the same sense of purpose and deep satisfaction that faith in God brought to the religious people, but the positive outlook on their lives was stronger than that of the religious group, and seemed more explicit than the religious group's quieter reliance on God and His purpose.

Group 3: Low on Life Satisfaction and Secular

The outlook on life for these people varied. For one person life was a disappointment, and for two of them life was bleak and in some ways unbearable. It was not clear why one other person was dissatisfied with his life since his outlook was similar to those in the "satisfied secular" group.

One member of this group was on methadone and could not stop taking drugs because he couldn't cope with social life without them. At the same time his addiction left him physically weak and with poor concentration, and there was nothing in his life that he felt was really worthwhile. When asked what would happen if he stopped taking drugs he replied, "Well, then I could start doing anything I wanted." He knew nothing about God, but was interested in yoga and meditation, through which he was learning that no one should degrade or elevate themselves.

Another person was crippled by arthritis, with extremely limited movement. That illness had begun after her husband died, and it seemed as if her life had ended with his death. "There's nothing in life that makes it worthwhile. Life doesn't mean anything to me. I'm no use to myself or anybody else . . . my main purpose in life is to go off suddenly . . . I'd rather be out of it." She did not believe in God, and felt that even if there were a God He would have to be a cruel God because the world is cruel.

Another member of this group was cynical and disappointed with life. "When one is young you think everything is going to be marvellous but looking back it was very humdrum. Don't let it happen to you." She felt isolated, and took up activities such as learning Italian, to keep her mind occupied. Her dissatisfaction extended to all areas of her life, and while she believed in God she didn't want to think about her belief. "If you think about it, I think you couldn't believe in it." She used to pray "morning, noon and night" and it was important to her, although "my husband was very ill, and all the praying in the world didn't do any good for him—so nothing's happened to make me a firm believer."

The last person in this group had recently changed his career to painting, partly due to high blood pressure. Regrets about decisions he had made in England about leaving England were important to him. His family situation was not happy and he looked on his wife mainly as a convenience. While he appeared to be someone who knew where he was going, and was happy in most areas of his life, he did not feel satisfied, and life was "too tame" for him. His belief in God was uncertain, and he said he preferred to have "a bit of a bet each way." It may be that just as family was a central factor in the "satisfied secular" group's lives, it made this man dissatisfied.

Physical and emotional disabilities had a profoundly negative effect on the lives of two people in this group, and while the "satisfied religious" group was motivated by faith, these people provided a stark contrast of despair. The dissatisfaction of the other two "dissatisfied secular" people was more pervasive but there was no obvious factor to account for that feeling.

Group 4: Low on Life Satisfaction and Religious

The members of this group were in various ways more similar to some members of the other groups than they were to one another. Two did not seem to be any more religious than those in the nonreligious groups. The other two were more religious, but in rather different ways. "Most of the time I tend to hide it (being depressed by the world situation) as I have on a happy face . . . and try to keep it to myself. I'm a sort of a pessimist." She believed in God, saying "it's just nice to know He's there. I couldn't imagine my life without God." Her religious beliefs had been influenced greatly by her mother who "makes me feel guilty if I don't pray every night."

Another person was also influenced by her parents' religious ideas. She believed in God, but did not want to become involved with Him. "I think that if I needed it then I could go to it and it would help me . . . it doesn't really affect me that much." But she went to church every Sunday, although she hated going, because that was what her parents wanted. She was the one most dissatisfied with her whole life, which had not been the same since she broke up with her boyfriend. "I always thought that I would marry him and my job then was satisfying because I was satisfied in every other way. And when we broke up my whole world seemed to fall apart."

Another lived quietly, with his children and his faith as the important things in his life. He was lonely, and yet happy to "battle on." God gave comfort when his wife died—"He creates and He takes away." He had been taught his faith as a child and he retained it as an adult.

The last member of this group was hard of hearing, and slightly misunderstood many of the questions. She seemed lonely but was trying to be content, although her answers were very defensive. When asked about her religious belief, she was more interested in ascertaining whether the interviewer also believed than in discussing her own beliefs, so that her faith appeared to involve living a good, decent life.

This group lacked the very positive attitude towards life of the "satisfied secular" group, and the commitment to their beliefs seemed limited when compared with the "satisfied religious" group.

The Four Groups as a Whole

Although the responses varied within these groups, similarities between participants in the two high life-satisfaction groups were less obvious for the two religious groups. But simple labels as "religious" or "not religious" and as "satisfied" or "not satisfied" identified the groups well.

But there was a reluctance in all groups to deny the possibility of a supernatural force so that the kinds of religious meaning, activity, and belief that were described varied within both the "religious" and the "secular" groups. This made it impossible to draw a clear line between what was religious and what was not. For example, although the commitment of one of the participants to her faith was strong, the meaning of her faith appeared limited to living a good life.

Another distinguishing concept may be the degree of centrality to life that faith held, which would be related to the extent to which faith in God operated as an "enabling" factor. The more faith in God enables a person to live with a positive and satisfied view of life, the more central it would be to their lives. So, for example, one person found faith central to understanding life, and it enabled her to be satisfied when facing death; whereas for another faith was present but not central or enabling. Involvement with the supernatural also varied among the participants, one person communicated with her dead father, whereas another believed in God but was not prepared to try and communicate with the dead unless some positive "proof" was given to him.

The function of religion and faith in God also varied: For some, God was something that looked after you whether or not you took much notice of Him. For others, God was someone who should act, believing it was His duty to alleviate suffering.

The Relationship between Religious Beliefs, Activity and Faith, and Satisfaction with Life

This study showed a positive relationship between religious belief and life satisfaction with religious belief making a difference to life through personal involvement and commitment as the "enabling factor." Soderstrom and Wright (1977) suggested that commitment to both God and man increases life satisfaction, although our interviews showed that other people, particularly children and family, could be more important for those who are nonreligious. While personal relationships were also important for those with religious faith, a relationship with God was the central factor that overshadowed other religious relationships and indeed, any other feature of their life. At the same time, the meaning of faith and its ramifications were only discussed (with one exception) when they were specifically asked about.

The inherent correlation between religion and life satisfaction meant that for the religious, there was no one who felt worse about their life than simply having "mixed feelings" about it. For the religious group there was no despair among the participants with physical ailments, or arising out of emotional problems that profoundly affected their view of life, and there was not the cynicism that could be seen in some secular participants. The variations in life satisfaction were small, particularly for religious participants committed to their faith.

The religious people therefore appeared to have a different quality of life satisfaction. Whereas satisfaction for the nonreligious appeared to be derived mainly from their immediate world, usually the family, for the religious people an important part of their satisfaction depended on their relationship with God. The "dissatisfied secular" group might be seen as those for whom something had gone wrong, since they were disappointed with life, disabled in some way, or felt they had failed themselves. This is typified by one person who, at the time of the survey, was very dissatisfied with his life, but in the in-depth interview appeared to be very satisfied. It was found that when he was first interviewed he had recently broken up the relationship with a woman with whom he had been living. She had just become engaged to another man and after an argument had tried to kill her previous lover. At the second (in-depth) interview he had recovered from this trauma, and was again living with a woman.

In contrast, the more religious participants seemed less dependent on external circumstances. It was not that these were unimportant to them, but that their faith in God gave them an independence from those things. They were comforted when sorrow came, by their knowledge that God was in control, and by their confidence in His love. God was a permanent and constant factor in their lives. The sources of satisfaction for the "satisfied secular" group were transient. Family or friends could move away physically or emotionally, or die. Those with a religious perspective might find those events tragic, but believed God would still be with them. Relationships with others, particularly in marriage, and fulfillment within the self, were associated with being religious, but other aspects of life were not as important.

Being taught religious beliefs as a child served as the origins of the current beliefs of the religious people. The main present focus of attention for them was their faith and ongoing relationship with God and what He had done for them.

While both religious and nonreligious participants showed that they would turn to God in times of trouble, as Allport (1950) suggested, the nonreligious or "less" religious turned to God only when in trouble. For the religious, seeking comfort from God was only part of that ongoing relationship.

Other Determinants of Life Satisfaction

Previous research suggested that life satisfaction would be related strongly to psychological adjustment, satisfaction in family life, and occupation. The results of the present study indicate strong support for this, although occupation did not emerge as an important correlate of life satisfaction in this study. The importance of that factor in previous research may have been related to the economic dependence of the family on occupation, which meant that it would be important for life satisfaction because the well-being of the family was crucial for their satisfaction.

But health was an important factor in low levels of life satisfaction, since the two participants who appeared to be most dissatisfied with life were both disabled by their health problems.

Although self-fulfillment did not emerge as particularly important in the in-depth interviews, as we have seen, it was the highest correlate of life satisfaction, probably because self-fulfillment was the starting point from which the participants could talk about their lives and feelings.

A Comparison of Open and Closed Questions

The open-ended questions in this study provided the opportunity suggested by Dohrenwend (1965) to understand more fully the deeper feelings and motivations of the participants, who were given room to explore their feelings. It appeared likely that more intimate material would only be elicited by open questions, and it is doubtful, for example, if a participant would have expressed the hopelessness of drug addiction in response to a closed question. Had he tried, it is unlikely to have been captured in a meaningful way.

Comparison of each participant's responses to the closed question survey and to the open questions in the interview used for this study showed that the separate participants were not easy to recognize in the survey material, which did not bring out the warmth or despair of each individual, or reflect the things that were most important to their lives. It appears to be a distinct advantage to use open and closed questions in conjunction with each other.

It has already been indicated, however, that material from the open questions generally supported the findings from the survey study. For example, the measures of life satisfaction in the survey and interviews were highly correlated, and church attendance appeared to differentiate, in limited ways, between the religious and nonreligious participants. Religious people seem to be a distinct subset within the community in that their attitudes and perspectives on life differ from those of the nonreligious, although for both groups self-fulfillment (however attained) appeared to be an important factor in determining their life satisfaction.

A common reaction to the questions in the interview was that they were difficult to answer. Not only did the questions encompass a range of life experiences and thinking, there were also questions the participants said they had not considered before. In the interview, when asked for reasons behind the answers, it was not always clear, however, if the opinions reflected a settled set of opinions, or were invented to meet the demands of the situation. At times, participants appeared to leave out material which, on the basis of their previous answers, might have been included. For example, one who had been devastated by her husband's death did not spontaneously say that she would have liked him to be alive again, but she did express this when prompted. It may have been that on these occasions the participants felt that such things were obvious and did not need mentioning again.

A certain level of ambiguity and lack of certainty in their responses appeared to be revealed in the in-depth interviews, which were masked by the unambiguous response alternatives of the survey. For example, one respondent began by saying that studying Italian was the most satisfying and enjoyable of her leisure activities. She then said that it was "beginning to be a bit of a drag now," and it seemed that her cynical attitude to life prevented her from being enthusiastic about anything. This kind of ambiguity increased the difficulty of coding the responses, which called for a judgment of the relative value of partially contradictory statements.

Campbell (1945) and Schuman and Presser (1979) suggest that ambiguity is a disadvantage in open questioning. In contrast, if ambiguity reflects the true state of a person's opinions, it would appear to be an advantage. Furthermore, "objective" situations may not be free of ambiguity themselves. In the case of the participant mentioned above, Italian was the most satisfying leisure activity, but she had ambivalent feelings about it.

Perhaps neither method is more accurate, since the degree of accuracy may vary with the person interviewed, and less fluent participants could have benefited from being offered alternative answers. On the other hand, presenting a choice between several categories could mask an uncertainty and ambiguity that is felt, but can be avoided by choosing only one category. Perhaps it is not possible for any participant to give definite answers about many situations.

Conclusions

We began by noting a consistent finding that religiousness is related to subjective well-being or life satisfaction, but that the relationship is not a strong one. The two complementary explanations that have been offered to account for this relationship are that religion provides meaning and purpose in life, and social support, which results in increased well-being. These explanations are too powerful, however, in that, given their validity, one would expect much higher correlations between religiousness and well-being than were actually observed. Factors which might attenuate those correlations are: (a) both religiousness and well-being may be multidimensional (so we distinguished between extrinsic and intrinsic beliefs), and (b) that only a relatively small proportion of the population is religious, so that while the overall correlation may be low, for people who are religious, its integrative capacity may be very important. To investigate these matters, we drew first upon a survey which showed that church attendance was not particularly important for well-being, but that fulfillment (through meaning and purpose in life) was. The second and major part of the study involved constructing four groups, consisting of respondents taken from the survey who had either high or low levels of well-being, and were either religious or secular, as shown by their church attendance. Every member of each group was interviewed in depth. The interviews showed that those who were also religious were marked by a central and deep trust in God that "enabled" their lives, whereas those who were satisfied and secular were marked by a strong concern for others, and a positive attitude to life, but with less of the deep sense of purpose that marked the religious people. For the nonreligious, the dissatisfied were marked by disappointment, health problems, and disabilities. The dissatisfied religious group turned out not to be really religious, but to the extent that they were, their religiousness could be seen as extrinsic. One of the problems of the study was, however, to find enough dissatisfied religious people (see Table 5.2). For our religious respondents, their religiousness certainly gave their life meaning and purpose. For the secular group, meaning and purpose came through involvement with others, mainly family and friends. But whereas belief in God seemed relatively invulnerable, family, friends, and other people were not always able to sustain them against the vicissitudes of life.

As a methodological note, although the findings from the interviews did not contradict the survey results, they added a sense of the depth and power of strongly held beliefs. It seems, then, that a simple correlation between religiousness and satisfaction does indeed fail to capture fully that relationship, not because the scales are inadequate, or because of the multidimensionality of either religion or satisfaction (the measures of each construct being all highly correlated with one another), but because of the depth and centrality (or the intrinsic quality) of religion. Moreover, the low levels of observed correlation are probably due in part to the relatively small number (perhaps about 15%) of religious people in the population as a whole. Indeed, the findings cited at the beginning of the paper indicating the widespread nature of religious belief, almost certainly overstate its position. At least in Australia, only a minority of the population is religious in terms of their belief and practice. Surveys are therefore more likely to underestimate the effects of a religion on its believers.

Does the high road to happiness run through religion? Only in part, it seems, since it can do, but need not. Most happy people are not religious because their lives receive purpose and meaning from other sources. Where religion gives purpose and meaning to life, religious people are happy, although the price that must be paid is a set of beliefs that constrain as well as enable, and may have baleful, as well as beneficent effects. Secular happiness may have shallower roots, but it may at least let the rest of us live in peace.

Acknowledgments. Jocelyn Delbridge is now deceased, killed in a motor accident. The authors wish to thank Elayne Caputi, Samantha Albert, and Franca Collina for preparing the manuscript. We are also grateful to Laurence Brown for detailed comments on an earlier version of this paper. Further information may be obtained from either Bruce Headey, Department of Political Science, University of Melbourne, Parkville, Victoria, Australia, 3052, or from Alexander J. Wearing at the same address.

References

Abrams, M. (1973). Subjective social indicators. *Social Trends, 4*, 35–49.
Allport, G.W. (1950). *The individual and his religion.* London: Constable.

Andrews, F.M. & Withey, J.B. (1976). *Social indicators of well-being*. New York: Plenum Press.

Argyle, M. (1958). *Religious behaviour*. London: Routledge and Kegan Paul.

Argyle, M. (1987). *The psychology of happiness*. London: Methuen.

Argyle, M. & Beit-Hallahmi, B.P. (1975). *The social psychology of religion*. London: Routledge and Kegan Paul.

Australian Values Study Survey: Revised Report of International Comparisons (1984). Melbourne: Roy Morgan Research Centre.

Bolt, M. (1975). Purpose in life and religious orientation. *Journal of Psychology and Theology*, *3*, 116–188.

Glock, C.Y. & Stark, R.S. (1965). *Religion and society in tensions*. Chicago: Rand McNallly.

Bradburn, N.M. (1969). *The structure of psychological well-being*. Chicago: Aldine.

Campbell, A.A. (1945). Two problems in the use of the open question. *Journal of Abnormal and Social Psychology*, *40*, 340–343.

Campbell, A.A., Converse, P.E., & Rodgers, W.L. (1976). *The quality of American life*. New York: Russell Sage Foundation.

Chamberlain, K. & Zika, S. (1989). Religiosity, life memory, and well-being: Some relationships in a sample of women. *Journal for the Scientific Study of Religion*, *28*, 411–420.

Clemente, F. & Sauer, W.J. (1976). Life satisfaction in the United States. *Social Forces*, *54*, 621–631.

Comstock, G.W. & Partridge, K.B. (1972). Church attendance and health. *Journal of Chronic Diseases*, *25*, 665–672.

Crittendon, K.S. & Hill, R.J. (1971). Coding reliability and validity of interview data. *American Sociological Review*, *36*, 1073–1080.

Davis, J.A. & Smith, T.W. (1986). *General Social Survey, 1972–1986*. Cumulative Codebook, Chicago, National Opinion Research Centre.

Diener, E. (1984). Subjective well-being. *Psychological Bulletin*, *95*, 542–575.

Diener, E. & Emmons, R.A. (1984). The independence of positive and negative affect. *Journal of Personality and Social Psychology*, *47*, 1105–1117.

Dittes, J.E. (1969). Psychology of religion. In G. Lindzey & E. Aronson (Eds.), *The handbook of social psychology* (2nd ed.), (Vol. 5, pp. 602–659). Reading, MA: Addison-Wesley.

Dohrenwend, B.S. (1965). Some effects of open and closed questions on re-spondent's answers. *Human Organisation*, *24*, 175–184.

Freedman, J.L. (1978). *Happy people*. New York: Harcourt Brace Jovanovich.

Grob, A., Luethi, R., Kaiser, F.G., Flammer, A., Mackinnon, A., & Wearing, A.J. (1989). *Berner Frageboden zum Wohlbefinder Jugendlicher*. (Berne Youth well-being questionnaire). Forschungsbericht 6, University of Berne.

Hadaway, C.K. (1978). Life satisfaction and religion—a reanalysis. *Social Forces*, *57*, 636–643.

Hadaway, C.K. & Roof, W.C. (1978). Religious commitment and quality of life in American society. *Review of Religious Research*, *19*, 295–307.

Harding, S.D. (1982). Psychological well-being in Great Britain: An evaluation of the Bradburn Affect Balance Scale. *Personality and Individual Differences*, *3*, 167–175.

Headey, B.W., Glowacki, T., Holmstrom, E.L., & Wearing, A.J. (1985). Modelling change perceived quality of life. *Social Indicators Research*, *17*, 276–298.

Headey, B.W., Holmstrom, E.L., & Wearing, A.J. (1982). Australians' priorities, satisfactions, and well-being: Methodological issues. University of Melbourne, Monographics in Public Policy Studies No. 8.

Headey, B.W., Holmstrom, E.L., & Wearing, A.J. (1984). The impact of life events and changes in domain satisfactions on well-being. *Social Indicators Research*, *15*, 203–227.

Headey, B.W., Holmstrom, E.L., & Wearing, A.J. (1985). Models of well-being. *Social Indicators Research*, *17*, 211–234.

Headey, B.W. & Wearing, A.J. (1981). Australians' priorities, satisfactions, and well-being. University of Melbourne, Monograph in Public Policy Studies No. 4.

Headey, B.W. & Wearing, A.J. (1992) *Understanding happiness*. Melbourne: Longman Cheshine.

Lane, R.E. (1962). *Political ideology*. New York: The Free Press.

Markides, K.S. (1983). Aging, religiosity, and adjustment: Longitudinal analysis. *Journal of Gerontology*, *38*, 621–625.

McNamara, P.H. & St. George, A. (1978). Blessed are the downtrodden: An empirical test. *Sociological Analysis*, *39*, 303–320.

Moberg, D.O. & Taves, M.J. (1965). Church participation and adjustment in old age. In A.M. Rose & W.A. Peterson (Eds.), *Older people and their social world*. Philadelphia: F.A. Davis.

Peterson, L.R. & Roy, A. (1985). Religiosity, anxiety, and meaning and purpose: Religion's consequences for "psychological well-being". *Review of Religious Research*, *27*, 49–62.

St. George, A. & McNamara, P.H. (1984). Religion, race, and psychological well-being. *Journal for the Scientific Study of Religion*, *23*, 351–363.

Schuman, H. & Presser, S. (1977). Open and closed questions. *American Sociological Review*, *44*, 692–712.

Soderstrom, D. & Wright, E.W. (1977). Religious orientation and meaning in life. *Journal of Clinical Psychology*, *33*, 65–68.

Steinitz, L.Y. (1980). Religiosity, well-being, and weltanschauung among the elderly. *Journal for the Scientific Study of Religion*, *19*, 60–67.

Stones, M.J. & Kozma, A. (1985). Structural relationships among happiness scales: A second order factorial study. *Social Indicators Research*, *17*, 19–28.

Walsh, R. & Cummins, R.A. (1976). The open field test: A critical review. *Psychological Bulletin*, *83*, 482–504.

Witter, R.A., Stock, A., Okun, M.A., & Haring, M.J. (1985). Religion and subjective well-being in adulthood: A quantitative synthesis. *Review of Religious Research*, *26*, 332–342.

6
Religious Life-styles and Mental Health

ALLEN E. BERGIN

This study continues a series of inquiries in which we have studied the relations between values and mental health (Bergin, 1991). In this chapter, we will first examine religious aspects of life-style and their relation to mental functioning in a sample of religious college students. We then summarize 3-year follow-up data for the same students.

The psychology of religious involvement is a growing area of research and scholarly activity (cf. Gorsuch, 1988). Work done in this area has been *theoretical* (e.g., Bergin, 1980a, 1980b, 1985; Ellis, 1980, 1988; Fowler, 1981; Walls, 1980), *empirical* (e.g., Bergin, Masters, & Richards, 1987; Bergin, Stinchfield, Gaskin, Masters, & Sullivan, 1988; cf. Spilka, Hood, & Gorsuch, 1985), and *meta-analytic* (Bergin, 1983; Donahue, 1985). However, apart from a few notable exceptions, much of the current literature represents a onetime effort on the part of an investigator (cf. Spilka, Hood, & Gorsuch, 1985).

Our reviews of previous work in this area (Bergin, 1983) and our own experiences in studying these problems left us dissatisfied. Many studies have been done, but the overall picture of the phenomena and the principles operating therein are ambiguous and inconclusive. Debates over the role of religion in mental health have therefore been difficult to resolve (Bergin, 1980a, 1980b; Ellis, 1980; Walls, 1980).

There are two ways out of the empirical and conceptual difficulties facing researchers in this area. One is to become much more precise in measuring and differentiating the religious dimension so that the ambiguities in global, undifferentiated assessments of this complex of psychosocial variables can be avoided. Progress is being made in this direction (Batson & Ventis, 1982; Bergin et al., 1988; Donahue, 1985; Kahoe & Meadow, 1981). The other avenue is more difficult. It involves a deeper, more naturalistic, and more descriptive immersion in the phenomena than can be achieved by the typical large-sample correlational or multivariate study of scores on paper-and-pencil instruments. We chose this avenue. Although we gave up a degree of precision by doing so, we felt that this would be offset by the benefit of a more penetrating exploration of processes that are still poorly understood.

Questions Explored

Previous data, alluded to above, led us to believe that religiousness might have both costs and benefits for psychological functioning, depending on how it operates in an individual's life. Consequently, we explored how different elements of religious life-styles related to the quality of mental functioning.

⌈Because our participants followed a comparatively regulated life-style entailing considerable self-discipline, we were interested in whether there would be benefits or significant psychological costs in connection with such high levels of self-control.⌉We also explored the possible consequences that might emerge when an individual's strict morality was compromised, as well as possible antecedents of the choice to violate a moral standard. It was also our intention to explore and describe the participants' religious experiences. What were they like, and did they play a role in adjustment? Finally, we addressed the issues of personal growth and therapeutic change during the 4 years of this study (1984–1987 inclusive).

It is our view that if the role of religion in psychological adjustment is to be better understood, longitudinal or life cycle research needs to be conducted (Worthington, 1989). This study therefore follows a sample of religious students over time, using a descriptive, intensive (Chassan, 1979) research approach. Since we think that the status of this area dictates an exploratory approach we have not made definitive tests of specific hypotheses. Nevertheless, we have developed a descriptive classification by examining some of the themes that were suggested in the early stages of this exploratory work.

Participants

The original sample was composed of 60 undergraduate dormitory residents (27 men and 33 women) who regularly attended a student ward (congregation) of 163 members of The Church of Jesus Christ of Latter-day Saints (Mormon) on the Brigham Young University (BYU) campus. The median age of the subjects at the beginning of this study was between 18 and 19 years. Subjects were primarily freshmen and sophomores from white, middle-class families, who came largely from urban areas. Half were from the West Coast (California, Utah, Oregon, and Washington), and half came from 15 other states, plus Canada and West Germany. They had an average high school grade point average of 3.51 out of 4.00. (The BYU average for incoming freshmen was 3.34 in 1984.) Ten were enrolled in the university honors program.

Participants were solicited through individual letters, announcements placed on bulletin boards, and a verbal announcement given prior to a church meeting. Participation was voluntary, but sample selection was influenced by the fact that the principal investigator was also the bishop (lay pastor) of the ward. A relationship of trust was therefore already established that could yield the kinds of disclosure and commitment to participation necessary for such research.

Participants, in contrast to nonparticipants, were rated as better adjusted ($M = 4.5$ vs. 4.0 on a 5.0 scale), more spiritually committed, and closer to the bishop (4.0 vs. 2.9). They were also more likely to have been missionaries (22% vs. 9%), to seek the counsel of clergy (36% vs. 21%), to be converts (12% vs. 2%), and to attend church regularly (96% vs. 80%). Thus, they were somewhat more religious and had a closer relationship with the principal investigator than did nonparticipants, which was considered an advantage, however, for this intensive study of the more religious students.

The potential for biases in and abuses of the special relationship between the principal investigator and the participants was guarded against by the appointment of a special oversight committee co-chaired by a church leader and the Dean of students. A majority of interviews and all testing was done by non-Mormon research team members. The entire procedure was also thoroughly reviewed by the university's Human Subjects Review Committee. A further protection against biases or distortions in the study as a whole was that our research team membership averaged 50% non-Mormon. These team members made critical evaluations during every phase of the research.

Religious Life-style

The participants structured their lives in conformity with the typical Latter-day Saint (LDS) behavioral pattern. All of them held unpaid volunteer positions in the ward as teachers, leaders, social activities or sports directors, service project coordinators, musicians, and records or financial clerks. Time commitments to these responsibilities ranged from about 2 to 10 hours per week, in addition to attendance at 3 hours of Sunday meetings. Nearly all subjects addressed the congregation during the weekly Sacrament Meeting in a brief sermon at least once during the year. The ward is, in a sense, a large family: not always a completely happy family but, nevertheless, a relatively close social network.

In addition to donating time to ward responsibility and activity, the participants (with few exceptions) donated generously of their funds and also followed standard Mormon strictures, such as chastity; abstinence from alcohol, tobacco, tea, coffee, and nonprescribed drugs; daily private prayer, regular scripture reading, and participation in a regular Family Home Evening. They were at the same time lively and in many respects typical American college students. They acted out ordinary dormitory pranks and played loud music. They included "jocks," modern dancers, and scientific intellectuals. They had their share of roommate conflicts, broken engagements, and individual problems. Although the research team saw them as a cut above the average, we also viewed them as normal young adults who were in the processes of adjustment and transition regarding many of the primary dimensions of their lives.

For the second phase of our inquiry, which took place 3 years after the initial inquiry, we were able to contact and interview all 60 (100%) of the initial subjects, and received completed test data from 56 (93%) persons. Since the time of the first inquiry, many changes had taken place in the lives of these subjects. Many were no longer in school; others had become married and had children. A number of our sample had also engaged in one of the most intense religious experiences of their lives in that they have served on a full-time, unpaid, 2-year mission for The Church of Jesus Christ of Latter-day Saints (LDS or Mormon). Twenty-one of our 60 subjects had been on their missions between our initial testing and the follow-up assessment. Thus, they provide interesting and informative pre- and posttest data concerning the possible mental health effects of the mission experience.

Initial Inquiry

The subjects read and signed an extensive informed consent form that was co-signed by a witness. Two interview guides, specifically designed by us for this study, were used in 1- to 2-hour semistructured interviews that elicited details of life history, values, life-style, personal conflicts, and religious experiences. One year later, we were able to contact two thirds of the original subjects and conducted follow-up interviews with them. A 3-year follow-up is discussed later in this chapter. Subjects were administered a battery consisting of a biographical inventory, the Minnesota Multiphasic Personality Inventory (MMPI), Eysenck Personality Inventory (EPI), California Psychological Inventory (CPI), Tennessee Self Concept Scale (TSCS), the Allport Religious Orientation Scale (ROS) and other experimental value inventories that are not part of this report.

Four of the 7 research team members studied the interviews and life histories of a sample of the participants, and, through group discussion, derived a set of prominent themes concerning the students' values and life-styles. Careful individual reviews preceded the group sessions in which interpretive themes were proposed. The main themes stood out relatively well, and a fairly rapid consensus concerning them evolved. This was perhaps the most creative and important phase of the study. These themes, or dimensions, provided a way of classifying the subjects' experiences into categories that appeared to be significant and relevant to the purposes of the study.

The categories were *Religious Development*, which included two possible ratings: (a) *continuous*, in which religiousness developed consistently and smoothly over the life span, and (b) *discontinuous*, in which religious involvement varied significantly between high and low over time, and *Impact of Religion on Adjustment*, which included four possible ratings: (a) no obvious impact, (b) *reinforcement* of developmental trends, in that religious influences complemented and supported family values and family relationships during the subject's socialization, (c) *compensating*, in which religion had a positive impact, prompting improved functioning following or during distress, and (d) *deleterious*, in which religion had a negative impact, prompting deterioration in functioning. There were also *Religious Experiences*, which included two possible ratings: (a) *intense*, in which frequent or strong religious experiences were reported, and (b) *mild*, in which mild to moderate degrees of religious experiences were reported. (These definitions will all be elaborated in this chapter.)

The selection and definition of these dimensions were based on judgments by the researchers and are original to the study. They are part of the exploratory purpose of the project and require cross-validation in further research.

The interviewers categorized their own interviewees according to this schema. The interviews and histories of a sample of two thirds of the cases were then subjected to an independent rating by a group of 4 persons, 2 of whom had done interviews and ratings on their own cases and 2 of whom had done neither interviewing nor rating. If the group rating was discrepant from that of the interviewer, a consensus rating was made after discussion. The initial attempts at categorizing, prior to using the consensus rule, yielded 95% agreement on Religious Development ratings, 89% on Impact of Religion on Adjustment, and 89% on Religious Experience. Because all ratings were dichotomous, 50% agreement would occur by chance. The category Impact of Religion was dichotomous because ratings occurred in only two of the four categories, namely, "reinforcement" of developmental trends and "compensating." Procedures were invoked to control for biases in the ratings, including bringing in one reliability rater who had no previous acquaintance with the study and one who had done no interviews and no ratings but who had helped to define the categories.

The rating scheme provided profiles of the religious life-styles of the subjects that allowed for useful subgroupings of the sample. The test scores of these subgroups were then compared.

Subgroups

The analyses that follow are based on subgroupings of the 60 participants according to the foregoing categories. A subgroup of 44 out of 60 was identified by "continuous" religious development over their life spans, as opposed to 16 who experienced a "discontinuous" development. The 44 appeared to come from orthodox families who followed the LDS life-style and who integrated religion with most other aspects of their lives. Of the 44 continuous subjects, 42 were also rated as "reinforcing." The impact of institutionalized religion on their lives simply reinforced developmental religious trends established within the family. Of these people, 33 also reported "mild" religious experiences during their lives that seemed well-integrated with other aspects of their development. These 33 constituted what we have labeled a "continuous-reinforcing-mild" subgroup.

The other group of 16 subjects manifested a different style. All were actively involved and committed in church at the time of the study, but their religious development was rated as "discontinuous" because of significant fluctuations in religious involvement and commitment over their life spans. Of these people, 7 also reported that religion tended to have a "compensating" effect on problems they had experienced during their lives. Of these 7 subjects, 5 also reported having "intense" religious experiences that seemed to make decisive differences in their lives. These 5 constituted a "discontinuous-compensating-intense" subgroup.

Several other small subgroupings occurred, which appeared to be less significant than the foregoing, and an analysis of them is not germane to this chapter.

Results

Table 6.1 summarizes the mental measurements for the entire sample at the initial phase of the study ($n = 60$). Mean scores on the MMPI for this sample were within the normal range on all scales, in comparison with other samples in this age group (Colligan, Osborne, Swenson, & Offord, 1983), and were similar to profiles compiled by Judd (1986) from previous studies of LDS (at BYU), Catholic, Protestant, and Jewish groups. In the light of these data, our sample may be surprisingly representative of lower-division BYU undergraduates and, possibly, other normal college samples.

There is no evidence of unusual defensiveness or faking on the validity scales. The relatively high group mean on the Hypomania scale is common among college student populations and is likely to be more indicative of a generally high level of activity than of pathology.

Distributions on the other personality scales were also typical, and some means appeared to be slightly above average in the positive direction, as might be expected from this rather selective sample. Scores on the Religious Orientation Scale were higher than usual on the Intrinsic dimension and lower on the Extrinsic dimension.

Table 6.1 also shows that those with a continuous religious development generally appeared to be more mentally healthy than the discontinuous group. Out of 15 clinical scores (8 MMPI, 3 CPI, 3 TSCS, and 1 EPI), the continuous groups were slightly better on 14, a highly significant

TABLE 6.1. Means and standard deviations for the total sample and subgroups.

Scale	Research sample (n = 60)		Continuous (n = 44)		Discontinuous (n = 16)		t
	M	SD	M	SD	M	SD	
MMPI							
L	51	8.3	52	8.0	48	8.5	1.74
F	55	5.0	54	5.0	57	4.7	1.95
K	58	7.7	58	7.3	57	9.0	0.64
Hypochondriasis	53	8.8	52	8.3	53	10.3	0.07
Depression	48	7.7	47	6.2	51	10.4	1.59
Hysteria	56	7.4	56	7.7	57	6.8	0.37
Psychopathic deviate	58	9.8	55	6.9	66	11.9	3.56**
Masculinity and femininity	56	12.7	57	12.9	52	12.7	1.28
Paranoia	55	7.7	54	8.2	58	5.4	2.35*
Psychasthenia	58	8.5	57	6.9	62	11.0	1.79
Schizophrenia	59	8.8	57	6.9	65	11.3	2.39*
Hypomania	63	9.8	62	10.0	63	9.3	0.18
Social introversion	50	8.0	50	8.6	49	6.1	0.47
CPI							
Factor 1 (Compliance)	48	8.3	49	7.7	46	9.4	1.33
Factor 2 (Mastery)	53	7.8	53	8.4	55	5.4	1.37
Factor 3 (Adjustment Level)	54	8.1	54	8.0	52	8.3	0.94
TSCS							
Total positive	53	8.5	55	7.8	49	9.4	2.20*
General maladjustment	49	7.9	47	7.1	53	9.1	2.04*
Personality integration	57	8.5	58	8.8	54	7.0	1.75
EPI							
Extroversion (E)	13	3.7	13	4.0	14	2.8	0.56
Neuroticism (N)	8	4.1	8	3.8	10	4.7	1.51
ROS							
Extrinsic	23	5.4	24	5.1	22	6.2	0.92
Intrinsic	38	5.0	38	4.6	37	6.0	0.97

Note: Minnesota Multiphasic Personality Inventory (MMPI). California Psychological Inventory (CPI) and Tennessee Self Concept Scale (TSCS) are all based on a standardized mean of 50 and a standard deviation of 10. Eysenck Personality Inventory (EPI). Form A means and standard deviations respectively, for American college students are 13 and 4 for E and 11 and 5 for N. There are no national norms for the Religious Orientation Scale (ROS). A fairly representative sample, taken form Purdue University undergraduates, yielded a mean Extrinsic score of 29 and a mean Intrinsic score of 28 (Donahue, 1985).

Scores for men and women were lumped together because (a) they were equally represented in the two groups (55% female in the continuous group and 56% in the group) and (b) there were no significant differences between their mean scores on any scales except MMPI Masculinity and Femininity and EPI Neuroticism. Sex differences therefore, cannot account for the significant differences obtained: *$p < .05$ (continuous vs discontinuous) **$p < .01$ (continuous vs discontinuous).

statistical trend when considered in terms of a nonparametric "sign" test or binomial distribution. Five of these were also statistically significant on t tests: MMPI Psychopathic Deviate, Paranoia, and Schizophrenia, and the TSCS Total Positive and General Maladjustment scores.

Analyses similar to those presented in Table 6.1, but not included here, were conducted on other subgroupings, such as "discontinuous" and "compensating" $(n = 7)$ versus "continuous" and "reinforcing" $(n = 42)$ and "continuous-reinforcing-mild" $(n = 33)$ versus "discontinuous-compensating-intense" $(n = 5)$.

All these comparisons showed the same pattern of differences, and all of them favored those with a continuous religious development, mild religious experience, and the reinforcing impact of religion on their development and adjustment. Although the continuous-discontinuous variable alone appeared to account for most of the variation in these cases, the largest number of statistically significant differences occurred between the small, homogeneous "continuous-reinforcing-mild" and "discontinuous-compensating-intense" groups. Although these final classifications yielded small subgroups, they provided the kind of context for discovery we were looking for.

Second Inquiry

As mentioned earlier, we were able to contact and interview all 60 of our initial subjects, 3 years later, receiving completed test data from 56 (93%) of these persons. Of them, 23 (41%) were male whereas 33 (59%) were female. All 4 of the persons from whom we did not receive test data were male.

Procedure

The purpose of the second inquiry was to understand the continued effect of religiousness on mental health, since 3 years had passed since the initial phase of the study. Semi-structured interviews were conducted using guidelines from the original interviews that were adapted specifically for the follow-up study. Questions were asked pertaining to the person's life-style, including life history, marriage, religious activities and experiences, family relations, values, daily activities, experiences while serving as full-time missionaries, personal problems and personal goals. Because some of our subjects were not available in the immediate area, we had to conduct a few of the interviews over the telephone. Participants were contacted in all geographic regions of the United States as well as in several European countries. A small number of participants was unavailable by phone but responded to a written form of the interview that was mailed to them. Subjects were also administered a test battery which included the Minnesota Multiphasic Personality Inventory (MMPI), the Allport Religious Orientation Scale (ROS; Allport & Ross, 1967) and other experimental value and religious inventories that are not part of this report.

Subgroups

The analyses that follow are based upon the subgroupings of these participants that were established in the initial phase of the inquiry. The religious development categorizations of continuous and discontinuous were again utilized, with the subjects placed in these categories according to their classification in the earlier study.

For purposes of the analysis of the missionary experience, the sample was divided into three subgroups. The first of these ($n = 11$) consisted of those who had gone on their missions prior to our first testing in 1984. The second group ($n = 21$) was those who went on missions between the first and second testings, of whom 12 were male and 9 female. The final group ($n = 24$) consisted of those who have not served a mission, of whom 23 were female. Our analyses focused upon the latter 2 groups since we had pre-post data on the group who went on missions ($n = 21$) that could be compared with those who had not gone ($n = 24$).

Results

Table 6.2 shows the means of the entire sample on the MMPI and ROS for both this and the previous testing, with means for the separate subgroups. To assess the patterns of change in the religious development subgroups, time (pretest, posttest) by group (continuous, discontinuous) analyses of variance were conducted using the MMPI and ROS scales as dependent measures. Table 6.2 displays the means for these subgroups.

For the entire sample, we were interested in changes over time. Significant main effects over time in which the group as a whole increased their scores away from the mean were found on the L ($F[1, 43] = 7.76, p < .01$) and K ($F[1, 43] = 15.60, p < .001$) scales of the MMPI. On the other hand, the F ($F[1, 43] = 5.57, p < .05$), Masculinity/Femininity (Mf) ($F[1, 43] = 6.09, p < .05$), Psychasthenia (Pt) ($F[1, 43] = 6.01, p < .05$), Schizophrenia (Sc) ($F[1, 43] = 8.44, p < .01$), and Hypomania (Ma) ($F[1, 43] = 19.18, p < .001$) scales of the MMPI all showed overall decreases toward the mean. Interestingly, the main effect of time on the Intrinsic scale of the ROS showed an increase in intrinsicness ($F[1, 40] = 5.08, p < .05$).

TABLE 6.2. Means for the total sample and subgroups at inital testing (1) and follow-up (2).

Scale	Total sample (N = 56)		Continuous (n = 41)		Discontinuous (n = 15)	
	(1)	(2)	(1)	(2)	(1)	(2)
	MMPI					
L	52	55	53	56	48	51
F	55	53	54	54	57	53
K	58	62	59	63	56	61
Hypochondriasis	53	51	53	52	53	51
Depression	47	50	46	50	52	50
Hysteria	56	59	56	60	57	58
Psychopathic deviate	58	58	55	57	66	60
Masculinity and femininity	55	52	57	53	53	51
Paranoia	55	55	54	54	58	57
Psychasthenia	58	55	57	54	62	55
Schizophrenia	59	54	58	53	65	56
Hypomania	62	57	62	57	62	56
Social	50	49	40	49	49	48
	ROS					
Extrinsic	23	21	23	21	22	22
Intrinsic	38	40	38	40	37	40

Note: Minnesota Multiphasic Personality Inventory (MMPI). Religious Orientation Scale (ROS) has no national norms. A sample of Purdue University undergraduates yielded a mean Extrinsic score of 29 and a mean Intrinsic score of 28, whereas religious students score higher on I (30 to 40) and variably on E (21 to 48) (Bergin, Masters, and Richards, 1987).

Scores for men and women were lumped together because they were about equally represented and there were no significant differences between their mean scores except on MMPI Masculinity and Femininity. Sex differences, therefore, cannot account for the differences obtained.

Significant differences and p values are given in the text.

From Masters et al. (1991), copyright © 1991 by the American Counseling Association, reprinted by permission.

For the subgroups, we were interested in the interaction between the different groups and time. Significant interactions were found for the F ($F[1, 54] = 4.45$, $p < .05$), Depression (D) ($F[1, 54] = 7.22$, $p < .01$), and Psychopathic Deviate (Pd) ($F[1, 54] = 6.34$, $p < .05$) scales of the MMPI. On the F scale, the interaction was accounted for by a significant regression toward the mean between testings in the discontinuous group's score. The interaction on the D scale was accounted for by the fact that the discontinuous group had a higher initial score and because the continuous group score increased toward the mean over time. The initial difference in the groups accounted for the interaction on the Pd scale.

Significant main effects for the subgroup variables were found on only three of the MMPI scales at the second inquiry, which indicate that the continuous group scored higher at posttesting than the discontinuous group on the L scale ($F[1, 54] = 6.99, p < .05$). The discontinuous group however, scored higher on the Pd ($F[1, 54] = 11.91, p < .001$) and Sc ($F[1, 54] = 4.49, p < .05$) scales.

Missionary Subgroups

An inspection of the data from the missionary and non-missionary subgroups indicated that there were no differences on either of the ROS scores, and virtually no differences on the MMPI. There was a significant interaction (Time × Group) on the Pd scale ($F[1, 43] = 4.02, p < .05$). This was due to differences at the posttest which showed that the missionary group had changed toward a higher mean score than the nonmissionary group, who stayed about the same. This difference disappeared, however, when a multiple analysis of variance was applied to the same data. The missionaries did have higher Pt scores in both analyses, although the mean difference was not large (58 vs. 54). Our small, nonrandom samples and modest differences make probabilistic interpretations difficult here, but we offer some impressions of the Pd scale findings because they were interesting and interpretable. The follow-up means (non-missionaries, $M = 56$, female missionaries, $M = 63$) demonstrate that the group, primarily female, who did not go on a mission scored lower on the Pd scale at both time points. The male missionaries also scored lower and more like the female non-missionaries than the female missionaries. The female missionaries therefore look distinctive on this one scale. Since this was somewhat puzzling, we examined the women missionaries' pre- and post-Pd responses item by item. This revealed positive changes on several items, indicating growth in independence and self-confidence, such as: "My conduct is largely controlled by the customs of those about me" (changed from "True" to "False"), "I wish I were not so shy," (changed from "True" to "False"). The observed increase in these women's Pd scores did not therefore reflect an increase in disturbance.

Findings from *interviews* with returned missionaries (RMs) proved more informative than the test results. The RMs discussed their missions freely and reflected upon personal changes that had occurred over their 2 years of service. The reports were generally very positive, but we were able to elicit negative themes in their experiences as well. A summary list of all the comments was then assembled and analyzed by 3 members of

TABLE 6.3. Self reports of mission effects. N = 21

Positive change		Negative change	
Values and Life-Style Development			
Developed values, goals, focus and life perspective	(11)	Less sense of direction	(1)
More responsible and self-regulated	(3)	Less self-disciplined	(1)
More independent	(1)		
More balance in life	(1)		
16 reports by 12 persons		2 reports by 2 persons	
Religious Development			
Increased religious commitment, understanding, and feeling	(15)	Less investment in Church	(1)
Personality Development			
More mature, altruistic and inwardly at peace	(4)	More cynical and critical of self and others	(4)
More flexible, less perfectionistic	(2)	Became depressed	(1)
Less critical and doubting	(2)		
More self-esteem	(2)		
Accept authority more	(2)	.	
More self-aware	(1)		
13 reports by 12 persons		5 reports by 5 persons	
Social Development			
More cultural awareness, respect, and altruism	(9)	Decreased social adjustment	(5)
Improved social and emotional relationships	(8)	Difficulty relating to opposite sex	(3)
Better communication and closeness with family	(4)		
21 reports by 17 persons		8 reports by 6 persons	

Note: Overall, 12 Ss reported only positive changes and 1 subject reported only negative ones, while 8 Ss reported both positive and negative changes.

From Masters et al. (1991), copyright © 1991 by the American Counseling Association, reprinted by permission.

our research team. These comments divided nicely into the four themes identified in Table 6.3.

The most positive responses occurred in the two areas of *Values and Life-Style Development* and *Religious Development*. *Personality Development* and *Social Development* also showed many positive results, and several negative consequences as well. A few became anxious, depressed, or interpersonally distressed but, generally, these 21 returned missionaries appear to have grown in self-esteem, purpose in life, social consciousness, and spirituality.

About half served in various countries of Latin America with the remainder distributed through Asia, Europe, and the United States. The stresses of these missionaries were real, as most had to adjust to a new culture, learn to work 12–14 hours each day and for 6 days a week, adapt to full-time missionary companions, leaders, and rules, and try at the same time to be a positive influence upon the people they worked with. This pressured existence created crucibles for change, as these people were forced to face self and others in new ways. While ordinary developmental processes were continuing, the mission experiences clearly intensified or accelerated the dynamics of conflict and of growth. In this sense the missions proved to be prolonged, intense religious and psychosocial experiences that had a substantial effect upon their life course, life-style and adjustment.

Case Studies

In the initial phase of the study we subdivided the religiously "continuous" participants ($n = 44$) and the "discontinuous" ($n = 16$) according to two additional categories: (a) "reinforcing versus compensating" to indicate that religious church participation and experiences had either *reinforced* developmental religious trends established within the family or had *compensated* for problems they had experienced in their lives; (b) "mild versus intense," which meant that their internal religious feelings or experiences had generally been mild, and integrated with other feelings and experiences, or had been intense and distinctive. On this basis we identified a subgroup of persons having "continuous-reinforcing-mild" religious life-styles ($n = 33$) and a subgroup of "discontinuous-compensating-intense" persons ($n = 5$). Although the continuous-discontinuous distinction, by itself, accounted for nearly all of the statistically significant differences that were obtained between various combinations of subgroups in the first part of the study, we found these two, more-completely defined but small groups, to be of great interest for our follow-up exploration.

Consequently, we studied 4 persons, 2 from each subgroup, more intensively. Their histories highlight the differing styles. There is no special significance in the fact that the two continuous cases are female and the two discontinuous ones male, since the overall male and female proportions in the various subgroups were virtually equal. We begin with the two "continuous-reinforcing-mild" cases.

Case L.

L. was a 19-year-old single woman when initially studied. At the time of follow-up, she was 22, single, and about to complete her undergraduate degree. Initially, she presented a picture of almost ideal mental health along with a very active and committed religious involvement. Her relationships with family members, friends, professors, and so forth were consistently open, mutually rewarding, and healthy. Her tests, interviews, life achievements, and affective integration yielded an assessment that might be called "supernormal." She did not experience life's ordinary stresses as stressful because they stimulated growth and adaptation.

At follow-up, she reported having experienced more intense stresses than ever before, mainly in deep relationships with men. She had been sexually abstinent all of her life and was surprised by the strong passions aroused in her by a particular boyfriend. This resulted in confusion and strain relative to her loyalty to the ideal of chastity. She ultimately determined to reserve sexual relations for marriage.

Her religious convictions and experiences, plus an activation of her resilient character permitted her to adapt well to the trials of romantic ups and downs. Although she seemed slightly more tense and depressed than before, her life generally continued to be marked by excellent achievement, a wide range of friendships, and a better than average integration of affect. She had felt real distress but it had tended to deepen her maturity rather than provoke unadaptive emotional disturbances. Her personality and her religiosity continued to meld within a stable and optimistic framework. She learned to absorb flexibly the new and unexpected experiences that had shaken her core traits and values. She had drawn upon spiritual resources to manage difficulties and to reconstrue her experiences in a broader context. Her religious values anchored her responses in ways she felt could maintain a life-style that would provide optimal rewards over the long term.

Case S.

S. was initially 18, and like her counterpart, L., had grown up in a typical Mormon family reflecting Mormon values and life-style qualities. Her case, however, illustrated internal concerns within an outwardly normal life pattern. Although in many ways she was like L.—a high achiever, a leader, and very religiously disposed—there was a degree of emotional alienation in her family life that disposed her to wall-off distress in a somewhat rigid way. Although she said her church was the most stabilizing influence in her life, it may also have weakened her adaptability.

While it was clear that religious influences helped her develop a regulated and productive life-style that allowed her to manage disruptive feelings, its heavy load of high standards also reinforced her tendency to strive for perfection and may have limited her adaptive capacities. She was therefore less able to experience emotion in a complete way or to approach crises in a flexible manner. Although her initial test profiles and life-style were similar to those of L., this outward picture of health obscured a vulnerability to depression.

At the time of follow-up we found that S. had returned to her home state, married, and left school. She was the mother of a newborn child and was experiencing several symptoms of depression. These symptoms had developed over a period of time, at first in response to her husband's high expectations and the dynamics of the relationship. As one who already expected a great deal of herself, she found that she could not keep up with both his external demands and her own internal schedule. On the affective side she also developed problems. Having difficulty in expressing specific personal needs and feelings, she was unable to focus on her own fulfillment, especially in the light of her husband's stronger role in the relationship. The birth of the child, with its attendant panoply of needs, and her own deepening fatigue left her feeling depleted and inadequate. Her test scores confirmed the interview impression that she was depressed, and so she (and her husband) were referred for treatment.

In her case, religiosity had provided an adaptation for emotional concerns over many years, and it worked pretty well. As long as she was adjusting, her values and life-style qualities propelled her toward continuing successes, but they outdistanced her emotional growth. She had come to believe that productive performances, religious and otherwise, were major measures of self-value. This belief set her up for emotional conflict in the face of new trials that could not be managed by her external life. Her capacity to love and be loved was weakened when she substituted action for self-valuing emotion. Believing that she was on the right course and that denial was the way to cope with unpleasant vicissitudes and vulnerabilities, she moved forward into new dimensions of life that were too complex for her mode of adaptation.

Case E.

E. was 24 and had married in 1984. He grew up in a religiously inactive family that was Mormon in name only. Due to the chaos and violence of the family, he became alienated, insecure, and somewhat deviant in his conduct. His school performance was very poor. Over the years he found religion on his own and became an active participant, reporting a number of intense religious experiences that he said helped compensate for his insecurity and find new direction and fulfillment. His academic performance improved and he became a leader in school. He served a successful 2-year mission prior to marriage.

He is now 27, in a stable marriage and the father of 4 children. He became a leader during college and has held executive positions in large organizations since that time. Despite the instability shown during his early life and adolescence, this has never reappeared.

We were curious, at the conclusion of the first study, to see whether people like E. would maintain the positive changes they had manifested as the result of a new-found religious experience and participation. Would the intense spiritual identification wear off, and would instability return? Would the compensating effects of religiosity yield to decompensation?

E. continues to show greater stability and maturity than would have been predicted from his background. The church was decisive in bringing him within a nurturant community that provided him with a sense of identity, a role, and satisfying affiliations, including marriage to a strong young woman. On tests, interviews, and life events data, he continues to manifest a comparatively strong adjustment. His personality seemed to soak up selectively the benevolent features of the religious environment, and he has not been plagued by the perfectionism that afflicts S.

Case G.

G. was also a male, 24 years old in the initial study, but he was single and a convert. He had been troubled by various forms of substance abuse, depression, sexual promiscuity, insecurity, and a lack of meaning in his life. After an LSD trip and his father's death, he experienced a crisis and turned to God for answers. Coincidentally, Mormon missionaries visited him and his roommate, and they joined this "new" religion.

G. interpreted his religious conversion as divine intervention in answer to his prayers. Like Eldredge Cleaver of the Black Panthers and Charles Colson of Watergate fame, intense religious experience brought a transformation in life-style more dramatic than can ordinarily be attained through professional psychotherapy. G. was able to abstain from drugs and gave up his active sex life. His depression lifted, he found new meaning in his existence, and went on to serve a successful church mission. It was after returning from his mission that he was first studied by us.

During the 3-year follow-up period, G. maintained his new life-style and emotional stability. He married and is now the father of one child. There have been some difficult adjustments in the marriage relationship, and it is apparent that he and his wife suffer from more stresses than E. and his partner. Nevertheless, G. provides additional evidence of a continuing integration of personal growth, with a deep faith. His religion appears to anchor his life and aid in his coping. His spiritual identification persists and there is no evidence of a decline in the compensating influence of religiosity on his previous symptomatology.

In the cases of both E. and G., missionary service seemed to solidify the personal growth previously achieved. Their belief systems deepened and extended from theology and self-identity toward practice and social concerns. The mission experience thus seemed to strengthen the fabric of personality change that we called "compensating," and these "compensators" appear to derive strength from religiosity. They did not suffer from the negative experiences that some missionaries reported.

Discussion

Religiosity and Mental Health

The data collected from this group of religious subjects demonstrated no evidence, for the group as a whole, of a link between orthodox religiosity and pathology. This finding is interesting since these subjects hold to absolute values of the kind that Ellis (1988) associated with emotional disturbance. On psychological tests, the group's average scores are comparable to those of other normal groups of young adults, which is similar to the results found with other samples (Bergin et al., 1987).

The present sample also appears to be distinctly intrinsic in their religious orientation, determined by their high scores on the intrinsic scale and correspondingly low scores on the extrinsic scale of Allport's measure. This finding is similar to those found in other (but not all) conservatively religious samples (Bergin et al., 1987; Bolt, 1977; Donahue, 1985; Paloutzian, Jackson, & Crandall, 1978; Shoemaker & Bolt, 1977), with intrinsic religiosity characterized by internalized beliefs which are adhered to regardless of the external consequences. The extrinsic orientation, on the other hand, is typically seen as being motivated by a desire to gain status, security, self-justification, or sociability (Allport & Ross, 1967).

Our findings suggest that religiousness can be correlated with benevolent development and identity formation and that high levels of self-control are not necessarily associated with lower levels of adjustment. On the other hand, vulnerable individuals may interpret religious pressures to conform to high standards in a detrimental way. We therefore hypothesize that the healthy features of intrinsic religiousness will be better actualized when the institutional and familial environments allow for honest recognition and acceptance of moral imperfections, thereby emphasizing growth relative to moral principles rather than an outward perfectionism that reinforces rigidity and ensures lowered adaptability.

Our group also tended to become more intrinsically religious over the three years. This finding is worth replicating with other samples from differing faiths, in order to determine if this is a typical developmental pattern for highly religious persons.

In a related area, we found that during the first phase of the study some subjects occasionally deviated from their moral standards. Those who did so appeared to be a more disturbed subgroup on the psychological tests, and in interviews they reported more conflicted relationships with their parents than did the other participants.

When asked how they dealt with violations of their consciences (or church standards) and the consequent feelings of guilt, a minority answered that they used the church-prescribed practice of confession and repentance. For the others, their responses were diverse, and included waiting until the feelings of guilt subsided by attempting to convince themselves that what they had done was really not that bad, that is, not a transgression; doing something righteous to balance their account and to alleviate their feelings of guilt; promising themselves (and God) that they would avoid it the next time; punishing themselves by calling themselves self-deprecating names and feeling bad for 1 or 2 days; trying not to think about it; and avoiding spiritual contexts because they felt themselves unclean.

These practices represent a variety of defense mechanisms (including denial, suppression, rationalization, and reaction formation), their purpose being to defend the integrity of the self-concept. We hypothesized that these people have defined themselves as righteous, and that therefore, evidence to the contrary, transgression threatens the integrity of their self-image. To follow the practice of confession and repentance would be to acknowledge unrighteousness, which is contrary to their righteous self-identity. This problem appears to reflect a conflict produced in vulnerable people by a subculture's putting emphasis both on maintaining an external image as a righteous person and on honest self-disclosure. It pits an extrinsic norm against an honest, intrinsic style.

To provide a further empirical context for our results, we examined literature on the general effects of college experience on religiosity. The data on the effects of college on religious commitment offer no clear trends, although at least one study (Christensen & Cannon, 1978) found that students at a religious institution (Brigham Young University) tended to become more conservative over their college years; which also seemed to be the case for our subjects. Fowler (1981) hypothesized that Stage 4 (Individuative-Reflective) faith, which seems similar to intrinsic religiosity, is likely to emerge, if at all, during young adulthood as this is a time of individuation and personal commitment. Our subjects were already, on average, intrinsic but they increased in intrinsicness over time, consistent with Fowler's notion. Concurrently, their mental health was somewhat improved. Based on these results and ideas, it seems that the factors which influence religious development during this stage of growth are worthy of further consideration (cf. Worthington, 1989).

Continuous versus Discontinuous Religious Experiences

A recurring finding from the initial interview data was that nearly all the subjects in the "continuous-reinforcing" subgroup of 42 cases displayed a remarkable adherence to parental and church values and norms. This was demonstrated by the subjects' (a) report that parents and church had the most influence on their life-styles, (b) acceptance of parental and church teaching, (c) resistance to peer influences that oppose parental and church standards, (d) life-styles of personal impulse restraint and family and church participation, and (e) stated desire to please parents and church figures.

There are a number of explanations for these findings. First, these students were relatively young and may not have individuated themselves fully from their parents; second, they may have thoughtfully and intentionally assimilated and integrated the values of their elders into their life-styles; third, conformity to parental and church norms is highly valued and reinforced, whereas the cost of nonconformance is high, including the potential loss of parental acceptance and approval, loss of in-group peer approval, and disciplinary action by church or university; fourth, since their religious affiliation places them in a cultural subgroup and, in some settings an out-group, they have an unusually strong identification with their subgroup and with their parents. As one subject said, "My friends may come and go, but my family will always be there."

Overall, this disciplined and emotionally interdependent life-style was associated with better mental health on both test data and interview assessments. High degrees of self-control were not associated with a cost in level of adjustment. This pattern reflects a degree of family cohesion and loyalty to traditional ideals that is more characteristic of an earlier era. The processes of Mormon socialization appear to stimulate the development of a sense of personal identity that is strongly linked to group identity.

In this connection, we noted little evidence of identity crises when we first examined the "continuous" group. It is as though their identification with family and church values progressed smoothly into young adulthood. Although they seemed to be developing the kind of mature identity described by Erikson (1968), they were getting there by a different process from the one he described, which involves mutual affection between parent and child and joint participation in a variety of activities. There was mixed evidence on whether these individuals had "foreclosed" the Eriksonian identity diffusion period in favor of a less mature conformity to external ideals. For some this may have been the case, while for others there seemed to be a reasoned "election" of parental values that was deeper and more integrated than mere conformity would allow. This seemed particularly clear among the returned missionaries who had found out for themselves the value of those ideals. In the process, some had experienced mini-identity crises, but nothing like Erikson's descriptions. This sample of highly religious subjects obviously found in their religious experiences during their development certain personal foci that precluded a typical identity diffusion. On the other hand, the "discontinuous" subjects' histories appeared to be more consonant with Erikson's seminal descriptions.

Although it was found that those whose life history reflects a continuous developmental pattern appeared to be better adjusted than those showing the discontinuous pattern, it is not possible to make statements about whether religion caused this difference, since familial factors in the adjustment of the participants were so intertwined with religion that the religious element could not be isolated from other influential factors. It appears, however, that familial influence in the continuous group involved both high parental control (over behavioral standards) and high parental affection, whereas subjects in the discontinuous group frequently reported that the parenting they had received lacked control, affection, or both control and affection.

For those individuals whose religion was positively integrated into their family life and their own emerging life-styles, their continuous development seemed to provide a source of stability that, in its turn, was related to better adjustment. At the same time, the less adjusted subjects in the discontinuous group appeared to have their adjustment level boosted considerably by intense religious experiences that were like Maslow's (1968) peak experiences, especially those described as "acute identity experiences" (p. 103), but with the addition of a specific sense of contact with God that transformed motivation and life-style as a result. Such therapeutic personal changes have also been documented by Linton, Levine, Kuchenmeister, and White (1978) and can be compared with equally profound but nonreligious transformations. The former tend to yield new levels of self-regulation, contentment, and group identification, whereas the latter produce more self-expression, exploration, and individualism.

That continuous religious development is associated with better functioning was deemed a finding worthy of description and further investigation. From a theory-building point of view, the idea that a developmental dimension is the major variable is interesting because it is long-lasting and pervasive and includes powerful social influences. In the second phase of the research, we attempted to determine if the continuous/discontinuous effect was maintained over the 3 years that had passed since the first inquiry.

The hypothesis that the continuous subjects would demonstrate more psychological stability over time relative to the discontinuous group seems not to have been generally supported across the entire study. Overall, the groups tended to regress toward the mean on the MMPI scales, and became more similar to each other, with the discontinuous group showing more decisive changes in this direction on the F, Pd, Pt and Sc scales. The continuous group, across both testings, showed slightly better functioning on the Sc, Pd, and Pa scales. Nevertheless, there is a trend for the discontinuous group to improve their scores and, therefore, for the two groups to become more similar.

Finally, the continuous group appears to be slightly more socially conforming, conventional, and self-controlled than the discontinuous subjects (on L, K, and Hy). This style could itself lower their clinical scores, so that the functional levels of the two groups may, in reality, be even more alike than is indicated by their scale scores. Perhaps, then, maturation has a stronger effect on mental health than does any religious developmental style.

Although the L, K, and Hy scores increased in both groups, given the socioeconomic status of the sample their scores are in a range reflecting improvement in several positive features of mental functioning. These include ego-strength, independence, self-reliance, clear thinking, and a good balance between positive self-evaluation and self-criticism (Graham, 1987). Interestingly, these positive changes coincide with an increase in intrinsic religious orientation, which other authors have noted is associated with positive mental health (Bergin et al., 1987; Donahue, 1985) and also with positive physical health (McIntosh & Spilka, 1990).

The Missionary Subgroup

With the exception of the findings on the Pd scale, it appears as though the mission experience had no significant effects on the functioning of the participants, as measured by the MMPI. All missionaries (both male and female) tended, however, to increase their Pd scores relative to non-missionaries (96% female), with the major difference being between the female missionaries and their non-mission serving female counterparts. Male missionnaries are the norm in Mormon culture and female missionaries are only now beginning to become common. The women in our sample who have served on missions may thus tend to be a less conventional, more independent group. While the missionaries did show an increase not found in the non-missionaries, they were still within normal limits for the population in general, and for their particular age group.

Interview reports, on the other hand, suggested a variety of significant changes, both positive and negative. It is likely that the MMPI is not a sensitive instrument for detecting these levels of changes in a normal population. As a 2-year intense religious involvement, the missions appeared to provoke a wide array of personal crises and peak experiences that, in many cases, seemed to accelerate a growth process, while for others their personal difficulties were either left unresolved or accentuated.

Limitations and Suggestions for Future Research

This project is both blessed and cursed by the nonrandom nature of the sample, and we must be careful to note that MMPI interpretations based on group data from a normal population may not be precise or descriptive and should, therefore, be digested with caution. Future studies of a longitudinal nature with other religious samples are therefore needed, along with comparisons with nonreligious groups going through the same college and young-adult experiences. In particular, the question of religious development as it relates to the Religious Orientation Scales, the effects of missionary experiences, and the overall effects of varying religious styles on mental health all need to be addressed in future studies.

With respect to Albert Ellis, it is noteworthy that the positive relations we have discovered between religion and mental health are based on a subset that is mainly intrinsic in religious orientation, while our smattering of negative findings appears to come from the more extrinsic and rigid believers. To a degree, this supports Ellis's (and our own) notion that there are healthy and unhealthy ways of being religious; but Ellis goes too far, and overgeneralized about religiosity when he classified all devout, orthodox, or absolute belief in the unhealthy category. We have found that healthy religiousness is not necessarily "liberal," yet its definition and measurement are continuing tasks for research (cf. Malony, 1988).

Our perspective, based on this series of studies through the 1980s, is that it is possible to be devout or absolute in conviction without being dogmatic, intolerant or rigidly unadaptive. Extrinsic fear and intolerance do signal unhealthy belief, but intrinsic devotion is a strengthening feature of personality.

All the preceding points provide potentially valuable insights for counselors, concerning the vicissitudes of conservatively religious students' life-styles. Our findings suggest that such students, including those with turbulent histories involving intense religious experiences, can be comparatively normal, or at least, that their religious interests and aspirations can be used in adjustment counseling, provided that the emphasis is on growth rather than external appearances. The continuous-discontinuous distinction may also be useful in diagnosis and counseling.

Because psychologists tend to be less religious than the United States norm (Jensen & Bergin, 1988), our results have the important implication that counselors need to be tolerant of religious students, and not automatically interpret their religiosity negatively.

Also pertinent to counseling is the fact that our descriptions of differing modes of religiousness can be put into a developmental perspective. The intrinsic, the continuous, and the nondefensive modes appear to involve higher levels of functioning. We did not measure other presumably high-level dimensions, such as Quest (Batson & Ventis, 1982) or Religious Autonomy (Kahoe & Meadow, 1981), but these, like our dimensions, can be compared with other views of positive growth, like those of Maslow (1968), Erikson (1968), Kohlberg (1969), Fowler (1981), Perry (1970), and Loevinger (1976). Conceptually, correlations between religious development and these other developmental schemes can be articulated and applied in the counseling setting. Our guess is that such an articulation in practice and research would show that religious development is most successful when it recognizes the religious dimensions we have described and the dimensions defined by these other theorists.

Diverse life-styles, whether religious or nonreligious, need to be compared and correlated with indices of disturbance and health, in order to extend the small set of findings reported here.

Acknowledgments. This chapter is a condensed integration of two studies done on the same sample, the first in 1984 and 1985 (Bergin, Stinchfield, Gaskin, Masters, & Sullivan, 1988) and the second in 1987 (Masters, Bergin, Reynolds, & Sullivan, 1991). Portions of these studies are reproduced here by permission of the American Psychological Association and the American Association for Counseling and Development.

We are grateful to the College of Family, Home, and Social Sciences at Brigham Young University, which provided several Faculty Research Grants to fund this research. We are also grateful for the valiant subjects who have cooperated so willingly in our study of their lives.

Co-authors of this paper are Kevin S. Masters, Randy D. Stinchfield, Thomas A. Gaskin, Clyde E. Sullivan, Emily M. Reynolds, and David W. Greaves, Brigham Young University.

References

Allport, G.W. & Ross, J.M. (1967). Personal religious orientation and prejudice. *Journal of Personality and Social Psychology, 5*, 432–443.

Batson, C.D. & Ventis, W.L. (1982). *The religious experience: A social-psychological perspective*. New York: Oxford University Press.

Bergin, A.E. (1980a). Psychotherapy and religious values. *Journal of Consulting and Clinical Psychology, 48*, 95–105.

Bergin, A.E. (1980b). Religious and humanistic values: A reply to Ellis and Walls. *Journal of Consulting and Clinical Psychology, 48*, 642–645.

Bergin, A.E. (1983). Religiosity and mental health: A critical reevaluation and meta-analysis. *Professional Psychology: Research and Practice, 14*, 170–184.

Bergin, A.E. (1985). Proposed values for guiding and evaluating counseling and psychotherapy. *Counseling and Values, 29*, 99–116.

Bergin, A.E. (1991). Values and religious issues in psychotherapy and mental health. *American Psychologist, 46*, 394–403.

Bergin, A.E., Masters, K.S., & Richards, P.S. (1987). Religiousness and mental health reconsidered: A study of an intrinsically religious sample. *Journal of Counseling Psychology, 34*, 197–204.

Bergin, A.E., Stinchfield, R.D., Gaskin, T.A., Masters, K.S., & Sullivan, C.E. (1988). Religious life-styles and mental health: An exploratory study. *Journal of Counseling Psychology, 35*, 91–98.

Bolt, M. (1977). Religious orientation and death fears. *Review of Religious Research, 19*, 73–76.

Chassan, J.B. (1979). *Research design in clinical psychology and psychiatry* (2nd ed.). New York: Wiley, Halsted Press Division.

Christensen, H.T. & Cannon, K.L. (1978). The fundamentalist emphasis at Brigham Young University: 1935–1973. *Journal for the Scientific Study of Religion, 17*, 53–57.

Colligan, R.C., Osborne, D., Swenson, W.M., & Offord, K.P. (1983). *The MMPI: A contemporary study*. New York: Praeger.

Donahue, M.J. (1985). Intrinsic and extrinsic religiousness: Review and meta-analysis. *Journal of Personality and Social Psychology, 48*, 400–419.

Ellis, A. (1980). Psychotherapy and atheistic values: A response to A.E. Bergin's "Psychotherapy and religious values." *Journal of Consulting and Clinical Psychology, 48*, 635–639.

Ellis, A. (1988). Is religiosity pathological? *Free Inquiry*, 27–32.

Erikson, E.H. (1968). Identity youth and crisis. New York: W. W. Norton.

Fowler, J.W. (1981). *Stages of faith: The psychology of human development and the quest for meaning*. San Francisco: Harper and Row.

Gorsuch, R.L. (1988). Psychology of religion. *Annual Review of Psychology, 39*, 201–221.

Graham, J.R. (1987). *The MMPI, a practical guide* (2nd ed.). New York: Oxford University Press.

Jensen, J.P. & Bergin, A.E. (1988). Mental health values of professional therapists: A national interdisciplinary survey. *Professional Psychology: Research and Practice, 19*, 290–297.

Judd, D.K. (1986). Religious affiliation and mental health. *AMCAP Journal, 12*, 71–108.

Kahoe, R.D. & Meadow, M.J. (1981). A developmental perspective on religious orientation dimensions. *Journal of Religion and Health, 20*, 8–17.

Kohlberg, L. (1969). Stage and sequence: The cognitive-developmental approach to socialization. In D.A. Goslin (Ed.), *Handbook of socialization theory and research* (pp. 347–480). Chicago: Rand McNally.

Linton, P.H., Levine, L., Kuchenmeister, C.A., & White, H.B. (1978). Lifestyle change in adulthood. *Research Communications in Psychology, Psychiatry and Behavior, 3*, 1–13.

Loevinger, J. (1976). *Ego development*. San Francisco: Jossey-Bass.

Malony, H.N. (1988). The clinical assessment of optimal religious functioning. *Review of Religious Research, 30*, 3–17.

Maslow, A.H. (1968). *Toward a psychology of being* (2nd ed.). New York: Van Nostrand.

Masters, K.S., Bergin, A.E., Reynolds, E.M., & Sullivan, C.E. (1991). Religious life-styles and mental health: A follow-up study. *Counseling and Values, 35*, 211–224.

McIntosh, D.N. & Spilka, B. (1990). *Religion and physical health: The role of personal faith and control beliefs*. In M.-L. Lynn & D.O. Moberg (Eds.). Research on the social scientific study of religion (Vol. 2, pp. 167–194). Greenwich, CT: JAI Press.

Paloutzian, R.R., Jackson, S.L., & Crandall, J.E. (1978). Conversion experience, belief system, and personal and ethical attitudes. *Journal of Psychology and Theology, 6*, 226–275.

Perry, W.G., Jr. (1970). *Forms of intellectual and ethical development in the college years: A scheme*. New York: Holt, Rinehart & Winston.

Shoemaker, A. & Bolt, M. (1977). The Rokeach value survey and perceived Christian values. *Journal of Psychology and Theology*, *5*, 139–142.

Spilka, B., Hood, R.W., Jr., & Gorsuch, R.L. (1985). *The psychology of religion: An empirical approach*. Englewood Cliffs, NJ: Prentice-Hall.

Walls, G.B. (1980). Values and psychotherapy: A comment on "Psychotherapy and religious values." *Journal of Consulting and Clinical Psychology*, *48*, 640–641.

Worthington, E.L. (1989). Religious faith across the lifespan: implications for counseling and research. *The Counseling Psychologist*, 17.

7
Personality and Religious Development during Childhood and Adolescence

LESLIE J. FRANCIS

The work of Hans Eysenck and his associates has had a major influence on the conceptualization and measurement of personality, and on the development of an empirically testable theory with potential for predicting or accounting for the relationships between personality and a range of individual differences (Gibson, 1981; Lynn, 1981).

Although Eysenck's approach to personality theory and scaling has generated considerable controversy and dispute (Modgil & Modgil, 1986), it has been applied to key areas of personal and social life, including *Crime and Personality* (H.J. Eysenck, 1977) and the *Causes and Cures of Criminality* (H.J. Eysenck & Gudjonsson, 1989), *Sex and Personality* (H.J. Eysenck, 1976a), and *The Psychology of Sex* (H.J. Eysenck & Wilson, 1979), *The Causes and Effects of Smoking* (H.J. Eysenck, 1980), "sport and personality" (H.J. Eysenck, Nias, & Cox, 1982) and *The Psychology of Politics* (H.J. Eysenck, 1954).

The aim of this chapter is to examine the potential in Eysenck's theories for explaining relationships between religion and personality during the years of childhood and adolescence.

Eysenck's Theory

Eysenck's theory of personality, developed and refined over 4 decades (H.J. Eysenck, 1947, 1952, 1970, 1981; H.J. Eysenck & M.W. Eysenck, 1985), maintains that personality differences may be most adequately and economically expressed in terms of a small set of higher order factors, built on observed correlations between the primary or lower order traits. The development of this theory can be traced through a sequence of personality tests, the earliest measuring two dimensions, extraversion and neuroticism, in the Maudsley Personality Inventory (H.J. Eysenck, 1959) and in its short form (H.J. Eysenck, 1958). The next generation of measures added a lie scale to extraversion and neuroticism, forming the Eysenck Personality Inventory (H.J. Eysenck & S.B.G. Eysenck, 1964a), with a short form (S.B.G. Eysenck & H.J. Eysenck, 1964b). Subsequently the PEN Inventory (S.B.G. Eysenck & H.J. Eysenck, 1968) added psychoticism to the measures of extraversion and neuroticism; so that the current Eysenck Personality Questionnaire (EPQ) (H.J. Eysenck & S.B.G. Eysenck, 1975) with the long and short forms of the Revised Eysenck Personality Questionnaire (S.B.G. Eysenck, H.J. Eysenck, & Barrett, 1985) measure extraversion, neuroticism, and psychoticism, together with a lie scale. Alongside these adult inventories, parallel measures have been developed for children and adolescents: the Junior Eysenck Personality Inventory (JEPI) (S.B.G. Eysenck, 1965), and the Junior Eysenck Personality Questionnaire (JEPQ) (H.J. Eysenck & S.B.G. Eysenck, 1975), with a short form of it (Francis & Pearson, 1988a).

While Eysenck's personality tests were largely developed and refined on British data, the basic structure and stability of these personality factors have been examined across a range of cultures, with their properties explored among children and young people in America (Jamison, 1984; S.B.G. Eysenck & Jamison, 1986; Middlebrooks & Wakefield, 1987), Australia (Hansford & Neidhart, 1977), Austria (S.B.G. Eysenck & Renner, 1987), Canada (S.B.G. Eysenck & Saklofske, 1983), China (Gong, 1984), Denmark (Nyborg, S.B.G. Eysenck, & Kroll, 1982), Greece (S.B.G. Eysenck & Dimitriou, 1984), Hong Kong (S.B.G. Eysenck & Chan, 1982), Hungary (S.B.G. Eysenck, Kozeki, & Kalmanchey-Gellenne, 1980), India (Gupta, 1971), Ireland (S.B.G. Eysenck & Kay, 1986), Japan (Iwawaki, S.B.G. Eysenck, & H.J. Eysenck, 1977, 1980), New Zealand (Saklofske & S.B.G. Eysenck, 1978), Nigeria (Maqsud, 1980), Spain (S.B.G. Eysenck & Seisdedos, 1978; Perez, Ortet, Pla, & Simo, 1986), Uganda (Honess & Kline, 1974), and Yugoslavia (S.B.G. Eysenck & Sipka, 1981). All these studies demonstrate the stability and independence of neuroticism, extraversion, and psychoticism across cultures, during childhood and adolescence.

Religious Attitudes

Eysenck understands the major personality dimensions as continuous variables, and his personality tests give interval measures of them. To maximize the potential for relating these scores to religion, it also must be conceptualized as a continuous variable, such as those underlying attitudes to religion that can be linked with Eysenck's work on the relationships between personality and social attitudes (H.J. Eysenck, 1961, 1975, 1976b).

The long history of the measurement of attitudes towards religion during childhood and adolescence has depended on the techniques of attitude scaling that were developed for use among adults. Thurstone's

(1928) technique has been used by Glassey (1945), Garrity (1961), Johnson (1966), and Povall (1971); Likert (1932) scaling has been used by Daines (1949), Wright (1962), Turner (1970, 1980), Hornsby-Smith and Petit (1975), Murray (1978), Turner, Turner, and Reid (1980), and Egan (1988); Edwards's (1957) technique has been used by Hyde (1959, 1965), Miles (1971), Richmond (1972), and Mark (1979, 1982); and the semantic differential (Osgood, Suci, & Tannenbaum, 1957) has been used by Miles (1983) and Francis (1987a).

In an earlier review of the appropriateness of these various techniques of attitude scaling for children and young people, Francis (1976) found Likert's procedure to be the most satisfactory. Following Fishbein's model of attitudes (Fishbein & Ajzen, 1975; Ajzen & Fishbein, 1980; Ajzen, 1988), Francis (1978, 1989a) therefore developed a 24-item Likert scale of attitudes towards Christianity which functions reliably among children and young people aged 8 years and above. That scale measures attitudes to God, Jesus, the Bible, church, prayer, and religion in school (Francis & Kay, 1984). While originally developed on English data, the reliability, validity, and unidimensionality of this scale have been upheld in Scotland (Gibson & Francis, 1989), Ireland (Greer, 1982), Kenya (Fulljames & Francis, 1987a), and Nigeria (Francis & McCarron, 1989). This scale has been used to monitor changes in attitude with age (Greer, 1981) and over time (Francis, 1989b); to assess the impact of Catholic primary (Francis, 1984), middle (Boyle, 1984), and secondary schools (Rhymer, 1983); to compare the influence of Church of England, Roman Catholic, and county schools at primary (Francis, 1987b) and secondary levels (Carter, 1979); to explore the effect of religious education syllabuses (Kay, 1981a), social class (Francis, Pearson, & Lankshear, 1990), parental marital happiness (Kay, 1981b), conversion experiences (Kay, 1981c); and to examine the relationship between religion and empathy (Francis & Pearson, 1987), openness (Greer, 1985), attitudes towards science, creationism, and scientism (Fulljames & Francis, 1987b, 1988). Scores on this scale of attitude towards Christianity have also been compared with scores on adult and junior versions of Eysenck's personality tests (Francis, Pearson, Carter, & Kay, 1981a, 1981b; Kay, 1981d; Francis, Pearson, & Kay, 1982, 1983a, 1983b, 1983c, 1988; Francis, Pearson, & Stubbs, 1985; Francis & Pearson, 1985a, 1985b, 1988a, 1988b; Pearson, Francis, & Lightbown, 1986; Francis, Lankshear, & Pearson, 1989; Pearson & Francis, 1989). This chapter aims to synthesize the results of these studies.

Neuroticism

Eysenck's neuroticism scales characterize high scorers as anxious, depressed, tense, irrational, shy, moody, emotional, suffering from guilt feelings and low self-esteem (H.J. Eysenck & Gudjonsson, 1989).

Within the psychology of religion, two conflicting accounts have emerged from the theoretical literature on relationships between religion and emotional stability (Batson & Ventis, 1982; Paloutzian, 1983; Spilka, Hood & Gorsuch, 1985; Brown, 1987). One account, which suggests that religion either fosters or is an expression of instability (Freud, 1950; Ellis, 1962; Vine, 1978), leads to a hypothesized positive correlation between religiosity and neuroticism. The other account suggests that religion fosters stability (Jung, 1938; Allport, 1950; Mowrer, 1960) with a negative correlation between religiosity and neuroticism.

Empirical studies, using a wide variety of indices of emotional stability, self-concept, or anxiety, can be found to support each hypothesis. So Brown and Lowe (1951), Bender (1958), Stanley (1964), McClain (1978), Sturgeon and Hamley (1979), Ness and Wintrob (1980), and Paloutzian and Ellison (1982) report that religiosity is associated with greater personal stability, adjustment, and well-being. On the other hand, Cowen (1954), Roberts (1965), Keene (1967), W. Wilson and Miller (1968), and Graff and Ladd (1971) suggest that aspects of religiosity are associated with low self-esteem, reduced self-acceptance, anxiety, neuroticism, and emotional immaturity. A third group of studies, including Brown (1962), Hanawalt (1963), Heintzelman and Fehr (1976), and Fehr and Heintzelman (1977), have found no significant correlations in either direction, while Baker and Gorsuch (1982), Watson, Morris, Foster, and Hood (1986) and Jobinson, et al. (1989) find that whether those correlations are positive or negative depends on the index of religiosity.

A confusing theoretical picture is therefore compounded by conflicting empirical results. Eysenck might argue, however, that this lack of agreement among empirical studies is a consequence of relying on measures of lower order personality traits, rather than measuring a higher order dimension like neuroticism (H.J. Eysenck & M.W. Eysenck, 1985). To test that view, Francis, Pearson, Carter, and Kay (1981b) administered the Junior Eysenck Personality Inventory (S.B.G. Eysenck, 1965) and Francis's Scale of Attitudes towards Christianity (Francis, 1978, 1989a) to 1,088 fifteen- and sixteen-year-olds within state-maintained schools in Britain, sampling the whole range of ability and social class.

Preliminary analyses of these data revealed a significant positive correlation between scores on neuroticism and religiosity ($r = +0.10$, $p < .001$).[1] Although this correlation is small and accounts for very little variance, it lends support to the notion that religion is associated with neuroticism.

More sophisticated analyses of those data, however, revealed two other important relationships. To begin with, the females in the sample obtained significantly higher scores than the males, on their attitude towards

---

[1] The greater the number of subjects in any study the smaller the correlation coefficients need to be, to reach statistical significance.

religion. This finding is consistent with a large body of research concerned with sex differences in religiosity during childhood (Francis, 1979), adolescence (Ekehammar & Sidanius, 1982), and adulthood (Argyle & Beit-Hallahmi, 1975). At the same time, the females also recorded higher scores on neuroticism, which is consistent with most of the work on sex differences in neuroticism during childhood, adolescence, and adulthood (S.B.G. Eysenck, 1960; Gutman, 1966; S.B.G. Eysenck & H.J. Eysenck, 1969; H.J. Eysenck, 1979; Jorm, 1987). But when sex differences were partialed out, the apparently significant relationship between neuroticism and religiosity disappeared, indicating that it was an artifact of the sex differences. This finding emphasizes the importance of controlling for sex differences in any psychometric exploration of relationships between personality and religion, and may account for some of the discrepant findings in earlier studies that have not taken this precaution.

Francis, Pearson, and Kay (1983b) checked that effect over a wider age range, employing the Junior Eysenck Personality Questionnaire (H.J. Eysenck & S.B.G. Eysenck, 1975). This questionnaire was completed by 1,715 young people between the ages of 11 and 17 years, and it was found that, after taking sex differences into account, neuroticism and religion were uncorrelated.

The lack of a significant relationship between neuroticism and religion has also been confirmed among 11-year-olds by Francis, Lankshear, and Pearson (1989), and among 15- and 16-year-olds by Francis and Pearson (1988b). Those results are consistent with the findings of studies using other indices of religiosity among 11- and 12-year-olds (Nias, 1973a), 13- and 14-year-olds (Pearson & Sheffield, 1976), first year undergraduates (Caird, 1987), 23- to 40-year-old graduates (Chlewinski, 1981), and 17- to 97-year-olds (Costa, McCrae, & Norris, 1981).

Extraversion

Eysenck's extraversion scales characterize high scorers as sociable, lively, active, assertive, sensation-seeking, carefree, dominant, surgent, and venturesome (H.J. Eysenck & Gudjonsson, 1989).

Although Eysenck himself has given little attention to the relationships between religion and extraversion, such a relationship is clearly at the heart of his theory of the links between social attitudes, conditionability, social learning, and socialization (H.J. Eysenck, 1954). Since introverts condition more readily than extraverts (H.J. Eysenck, 1967a), it follows that introverts should be more thoroughly socialized than extraverts and more inclined to adopt tender-minded social attitudes (H.J. Eysenck, 1961). According to Eysenck, while tough-minded social attitudes are concerned with immediate satisfaction of aggressive and sexual impulses, tender-minded social attitudes are concerned with "ethical and religious ideas which act as barriers to such satisfaction."

While Siegman (1963), the first to develop the implications of Eysenck's theory of social attitudes for the relationships between introversion and religion, argued that introverts should be more religious, his attempts to test that hypothesis produced conflicting evidence. His first study found a significant correlation in the opposite direction to that hypothesized. A second study found that although relationships between extraversion and two measures of religiosity were in the expected direction, only one was significant. His third study found that the relationships between extraversion and religiosity varied according to both sex and denominational background. But not only did Siegman have small samples, he used several indices of religion that are not strictly comparable. Similarly, when religion was measured by a subscale of Wilson and Patterson's (1968) conservatism scale, Wilson and Brazendale (1973) found a negative relationship with extraversion, Powell and Stewart (1978) found a positive relationship, and Pearson and Sheffield (1976) found no significant relationship.

In the previously mentioned sample of 1,088 fifteen- and sixteen-year-olds, Francis, Pearson, Carter, and Kay (1981a) report that simple correlational analysis and multiple regression analyses all produced a quite straightforward result, with a significant negative correlation between extraversion and religiosity ($r = -.15$, $p < .001$) and no significant interaction between sex and extraversion. The hypothesis that introverts are more religious than extraverts was therefore supported.

While this first study employed the extraversion scale of the Junior Eysenck Personality Inventory (S.B.G. Eysenck, 1965), in a second study among 1,715 young people between the ages of 11 and 17 years, Francis, Pearson, and Kay (1983a) found a somewhat smaller, yet significant negative correlation between extraversion and religiosity ($r = -.06$) using the Junior Eysenck Personality Questionnaire (H.J. Eysenck & S.B.G. Eysenck, 1975).

Although the correlations between extraversion and religion are statistically significant, and in the predicted direction in both studies, the small proportion of variance that is accounted for suggests that the relationship between extraversion and religiosity may not be straightforward. Eysenck's theory predicts that introverts condition more easily, that socialization is a process of conditioning which reflects in their social attitudes, and that tender-minded attitudes involve ethical and religious teaching. A major problem with this argument concerns the link between extraversion and conditionability. As originally conceived in Eysenck's theory, extraversion was understood to embrace sociability and impulsivity (Carrigan, 1960; S.B.G. Eysenck & H.J. Eysenck, 1963; Sparrow & Ross, 1964; Farley, 1970). H.J. Eysenck and Levey (1972) and Frcka and Martin (1987) later showed that impulsivity alone was responsible for the correlation between extraversion and conditionability. At the same time, however, the place of impulsivity within the construct of extraversion was questioned, since it was shown that the impulsivity items tended to load on both extraversion and psychoticism (Claridge, 1981; Kline & Barrett, 1983).

Consequently, recent versions of Eysenck's adult extraversion scale have been purified of impulsivity items, to define extraversion in terms of sociability (Pearson, 1979; Rocklin & Revelle, 1981). This shift in composition would have a major implication for the relationship between extraversion and religiosity, and could explain why Francis, Pearson, and Kay (1983a) found a smaller correlation between religiosity and extraversion using the recent Junior Eysenck Personality Questionnaire, than when the earlier Junior Eysenck Personality Inventory was used (Francis, Pearson, Carter, & Kay, 1981a).

To test this effect, Francis and Pearson (1985a) administered the Junior Eysenck Personality Inventory (S.B.G. Eysenck, 1965), the Junior and Adult Eysenck Personality Questionnaires (H.J. Eysenck & S.B.G. Eysenck, 1975), and Francis's scale of attitude towards Christianity (Francis, 1978, 1989a), to 191 fourteen- to sixteen-year-olds. If impulsivity were a critical determinant of the relationship between extraversion and religiosity, the strongest correlation with religiosity should emerge for the Junior Eysenck Personality Inventory and the weakest for the Adult Eysenck Personality Questionnaire. The results were as predicted, with the strongest correlation on the Junior Eysenck Personality Inventory ($r = -.17, p < .01$), the lowest on the Adult Eysenck Personality Questionnaire ($r = -.08$, NS), and the Junior Eysenck Personality Questionnaire in the middle position.

Francis and Pearson (1988b) then took these comparisons a stage further, adding the extraversion scale from the short form of the Revised Eysenck Personality Questionnaire (S.B.G. Eysenck, H.J. Eysenck, & Barrett, 1985) to the other measures in another sample of 181 fifteen- and sixteen-year-olds. In that study the largest correlations were with the Junior Eysenck Personality Inventory ($r = -.19, p < .01$), and the Junior Eysenck Personality Questionnaire ($r = -.17, p < .05$). There were no significant relationships with the other measures.

These relationships are consistent with the findings of recent studies among adults. For example, Chlewinski (1981) found a negative relationship between extraversion and religiosity using a Polish translation of the Maudsley Personality Inventory, while Watson, Morris, Foster, and Hood (1986), Caird (1987), and V. Egan (1989) found no relationship between extraversion and religiosity using the Eysenck Personality Questionnaire.

These results suggest that among teenagers and adults, introverts tend to be more religious when the measure of extraversion includes impulsivity. Once extraversion is defined in terms of sociability alone, without including impulsivity, the relationship between introversion and religiosity disappears.

This relationship between introversion and religiosity, when extraversion involves impulsivity, can be explained in terms of social learning (Bagley, Verma, Mallick, & Young, 1979), which increases through childhood and adolescence, but which may not be well developed during the preteen years.

To test this relationship, Francis, Lankshear, and Pearson (1989) administered the short form of the Junior Eysenck Personality Questionnaire (Francis & Pearson, 1988a) and Francis's scale of attitude towards Christianity (Francis, 1978, 1989a) to 421 eleven-year-olds. Although Francis and Pearson (1988a) had found a negative relationship between this index of extraversion and religiosity among 15- and 16-year-olds, no such relationship emerged among 11-year-olds ($r = -.04$, NS). Other studies have also failed to find significant negative correlations between extraversion and religiosity among junior pupils, using the Junior Eysenck Personality Questionnaire (Powell & Stewart, 1978), and among low-ability pupils with a mean mental age of 10.2, using the Junior Eysenck Personality Inventory (Francis, Pearson, & Stubbs, 1985). The fact that a negative correlation between religiosity and introversion emerges among teenagers but not among younger children supports the view that this relationship involves social learning.

Personality Quadrants

While the relationship between religion and neuroticism and between religion and extraversion can be reviewed as separate issues, it is a key feature of Eysenck's theory that these personality dimensions should be viewed together as quadrants covering neurotic introverts, stable introverts, neurotic extraverts and stable extraverts.

So far, it is clear that neuroticism is not directly correlated with religiosity, that introverts tend to be more religious than extraverts when extraversion is operationalized as a combination of sociability and impulsivity, and that these relationships may be explained in terms of conditioning or socialization into tender-minded social or religious attitudes. Although early versions of Eysenck's theory did not implicate neuroticism in conditioning (Franks, 1957), as the theory was developed into studies of crime and personality, neuroticism was assumed to have a role there (Passingham, 1972; H.J. Eysenck, 1977). If neuroticism is regarded as a state of heightened emotionality, and emotionality is regarded as a drive (H.J. Eysenck, 1966) that can potentiate the effect of introversion in facilitating tender-minded attitudes, and of extraversion in resisting those attitudes, there could be a hierarchy in which neurotic introverts are more religious than stable introverts and neurotic extraverts less religious than stable extraverts.

On the other hand, if high neuroticism scores are an index of anxiety (Crookes & Pearson, 1970), it could be that neurotic introverts and neurotic extraverts would both conform to social norms, and adopt tender-minded attitudes defensively. This view involves a hierarchy in which neurotic introverts might be more religious than stable introverts, and neurotic extraverts more religious than stable extraverts (cf. Wilson, 1973). On this account it is impossible to determine an order for stable introverts and neurotic extraverts (H.J. Eysenck, 1967b). When Francis, Pearson, and Kay (1982) reexamined their original data from the 1,088 subjects who completed the Junior Eysenck Personality Inventory, they found that neuroticism appeared to interact with extraversion to predict scores on religiosity, although when sex differences were taken into account, this interaction disappeared.

Psychoticism

Eysenck's psychoticism scales identify a personality trait which underlies psychotic mental disorders. High scorers are characterized by H.J. Eysenck and S.B.G. Eysenck (1976) as cold, impersonal, hostile, lacking in sympathy, unfriendly, untrustful, odd, unemotional, unhelpful, lacking in insight, strange, and with paranoid ideas that people are against them. Low scorers are empathic, unselfish, altruistic, warm, peaceful, more pleasant, and possibly less socially decisive.

Furthermore, as impulsivity is more closely associated with psychoticism than with extraversion (Beyts, Frcka, Martin, & Levey, 1983), H.J. Eysenck and Wilson (1978) argued that psychoticism rather than extraversion is fundamental to tough-mindedness. Since religion belongs to the domain of tender-minded attitudes, a negative relationship between psychoticism and religiosity can therefore be expected, as a mirror image of the mature religious personality (Becker, 1971).

But the empirical evidence for that relationship is equivocal. While Eaves and H.J. Eysenck (1974) reported that psychoticism correlates positively with tough-mindedness, no relationship was found by McKelvie (1983). During childhood and adolescence, significant negative correlations between religion and psychoticism were found among 11- and 12-year-old boys and girls (Nias, 1973a) and among 8- to 10- and 11- to 15-year-olds (Powell & Stewart, 1978). On the other hand, Kay's (1981d) correlations for boys and girls within the 1st, 2nd, 3rd, and 4th years of secondary school separately, showed a significant negative correlation for boys in each of the four groups, but not for girls in any of those groups.

Kay thought the most satisfactory explanation concerned "cultural norms and stereotypes," and that a biological basis of psychoticism might be found in sex hormones (H.J. Eysenck & S.B.G. Eysenck, 1976). Kay argued that girls may score highly on psychoticism because their oestrogen-androgen balance predisposes them to do so, although a fuller expression of this bias may be inhibited by the cultural norms which channel a girl's sexual identity towards dependence. Furthermore, the junior psychoticism scale that Kay used may not operationalize psychoticism in an appropriate way for both sexes. Not only has Powell (1977) argued that its items are male-oriented but the majority of children, unlike adults, are distinguished by only a few scale points.

To examine these relationships, Francis and Pearson (1985b) administered the psychoticism scales from the Junior Eysenck Personality Questionnaire and the Adult Eysenck Personality Questionnaire (H.J. Eysenck & S.B.G. Eysenck, 1975), and the Francis scale of attitude towards Christianity (Francis, 1978, 1989a), to 132 fifteen-year-old boys and girls. Before sex differences were examined, a significant negative correlation was found between attitudes towards religion and psychoticism, as measured on both the junior ($r = -.16$, $p < .05$) and adult ($r = -.22$, $p < .01$) scales, with a strong negative correlation between sex and the junior scale ($r = -.34$, $p < .001$), but not between sex and the adult scale ($r = -.06$, NS). A multiple regression analysis showed a significant negative relationship between psychoticism and attitudes towards religion for the adult but not the junior scale. These findings suggest that there is a significant negative correlation between psychoticism and religion for both male and female adolescents, if the adult scale is the more valid measure of psychoticism.

Impulsivity

While impulsivity has an important place in Eysenck's personality theory, it is not, however, a simple construct, having been used in both a broad and narrow sense (S.B.G. Eysenck & H.J. Eysenck, 1977). In the broad sense, impulsiveness breaks down into four components, identified as narrow impulsiveness, risk-taking, non-planning, and liveliness (cf. Eaves, Martin, & Eysenck, 1977; Martin, Eaves, & Fulker, 1979; and Glow, Lange, Glow, & Barnett, 1983). To combine Eysenck's scales with Zuckerman's sensation-seeking (Zuckerman, S.B.G. Eysenck, & H.J. Eysenck, 1978) suggests two factors, impulsiveness and venturesomeness (S.B.G. Eysenck & H.J. Eysenck, 1978; S.B.G. Eysenck & Zuckerman, 1978). According to this two-dimensional model, which is included in the Eysenck Impulsiveness Inventories for adults (S.B.G. Eysenck & H.J. Eysenck, 1978; S.B.G. Eysenck & McGurk, 1980; Rawlings, 1984) and children (S.B.G. Eysenck & H.J. Eysenck, 1980; S.B.G. Eysenck, 1981; Saklofske & S.B.G. Eysenck, 1983; S.B.G. Eysenck, Easting, & Pearson, 1984; Jamison, 1984), impulsiveness involves doing and saying things without thinking, or acting on the spur of the moment and without being *aware* of the risk involved, while venturesomeness involves sensation-seeking and risk-taking, with an awareness of the risks but a willingness to chance them. Eysenck, Easting, & Pearson (1984) found that impulsiveness correlates primarily with psychoticism, and somewhat with extraversion, while venturesomeness correlates mainly with extraversion and somewhat with psychoticism. Those correlations suggest that impulsiveness rather than venturesomeness is fundamental to tough-mindedness, and might therefore be more involved in shaping religiosity. The relationship between venturesomeness and religiosity is, however, problematic. According to S.B.G. Eysenck, Easting, and Pearson (1984), risk-taking involves the extraverted elements of impulsiveness and can not be attributed to tough-mindedness, since high scorers on psychoticism are unlikely to be aware of the possible risks. Venturesomeness would therefore be unrelated to social attitudes. That sensation-seeking has been found to be inversely related to religiosity (Levin & Schalmo, 1974; Pearson & Sheffield, 1975; Zuckerman & Neeb, 1980) leads to the hypothesis that venturesomeness should have a weaker relationship with social attitudes than that for impulsiveness.

To explore more adequately the relationship between impulsivity and religiosity, Pearson, Francis, and Lightbown (1986) administered the Junior Eysenck Impulsiveness Inventory (S.B.G. Eysenck, Easting, & Pearson, 1984) and Francis's scale of attitude towards Christianity (Francis, 1978, 1989a) to 279 boys and 290 girls between the ages of 11 and 17 years. Bivariate correlation coefficients indicate that impulsivity and venturesomeness are positively related, but not equivalent ($r = +.23$, $p < .001$), and that religiosity is negatively correlated with impulsiveness ($r = -.12$, $p < .001$) and with venturesomeness ($r = -.15$, $p < .001$). Multiple regression analyses confirmed that those relationships remained, after controlling for sex and age differences, and are related to religiosity.

When Pearson, Francis, and Lightbown (1986) separated sensation-seeking and risk-taking, they found that risk-taking is negatively correlated with religiosity, while sensation-seeking is not. Moreover, risk-taking and impulsiveness both have a significant relationship with religiosity. Those findings clarify three issues. First, they indicate that Eysenck's and Zuckerman's constructs of sensation-seeking are different: Zuckerman's is negatively related to religiosity (Pearson & Sheffield, 1975), but Eysenck's is not. Second, they do not support S.B.G. Eysenck, Easting, and Pearson's (1984) notion that the risk-taking element in venturesomeness describes only the extraverted aspect of impulsivity. Third, they suggest that S.B.G. Eysenck & H.J. Eysenck (1977) were correct in regarding risk-taking as an independent component of impulsivity.

Lie Scale

Lie scales were originally introduced to personality inventories to detect the tendency of some respondents to "fake good" and so distort their personality scores (Dahlstrom & Welsh, 1960; O'Donovan, 1969). The concept of a lie scale is not, however, a simple one, and it has been interpreted as a measure of personality in its own right (McCrae & Costa, 1983; Furnham, 1986), because the internal consistency of a lie scale is independent of the need to dissimulate (S.B.G. Eysenck, H.J. Eysenck, & Shaw, 1974). It is therefore important to discuss the relationships between lie scores and religiosity.

Eysenck's lie scales have shown significant positive correlations with religiosity among children (Nias, 1973a; Francis, Pearson, & Stubbs, 1985; Francis, Lankshear, & Pearson, 1989), young people (Powell & Stewart, 1978; Francis, Pearson, & Kay, 1983c; Francis & Pearson, 1988b) and adults (Wilson & Brazendale, 1973; Nias, 1973b). While some other studies have not found such a positive relationship (Pearson & Sheffield, 1976; Watson, Morris, Foster, & Hood, 1986; Caird, 1987), none has shown a significant negative relationship. At face value these empirical findings, which suggest that religious people dissimulate as much as, or more than nonreligious people, are consistent with Crandall and Gozali's (1969) interpretation of that finding as a defensive denial. They argue that religiosity may lead to the denial of unacceptable thoughts or behavior and the consequent need to present oneself in a socially desirable light.

If, however, lie scales measure an underlying personality trait, an explanation of the positive relationship between lie scores and religiosity may itself be more complex. While Finlayson (1972), H.J. Eysenck and S.B.G. Eysenck (1976), Powell (1977), Massey (1980), and O'Hagan (1981) suggested that lie scales measure social acquiescence, or conformity to social rules and pressures, the fact that religious people are more socially conforming was explained by Nias (1973a) in terms of the internalization of parental values, with socially acquiescent children picking up the attitudes of the groups upon which they depend.

On the other hand, Dicken (1959), S.B.G. Eysenck, Nias, and H.J. Eysenck (1971), Crookes and Buckley (1976) and Kirton (1977) suggest that lie scales measure a lack of self-insight. Francis, Pearson, and Kay (1983c) accepted this view and argued that this effect involves immaturity, reflected both in a lack of self-insight (S.B.G. Eysenck, Nias, & H.J. Eysenck, 1971) and in religiosity (Pohier, 1965).

Furthermore, Michaelis and H.J. Eysenck (1971) argued that the correlation between neuroticism and lie scores indicates a tendency to "fake good," while S.B.G. Eysenck, Nias, and H.J. Eysenck (1971) argued that correlations between extraversion and lie scores are an index of social acquiescence. To explore these interpretations, Francis, Pearson, and Kay (1988) analysed the responses of 1,555 boys and 1,673 girls, between the ages of 11 and 16 years, to the Junior Eysenck Personality Questionnaire (H.J. Eysenck & S.B.G. Eysenck, 1975) and to Francis's measure of attitude towards Christianity.

The correlation between neuroticism and lie-scale scores in these data was $-.11$, which does not support "faking good" and detracts from the suggestion that religious children are bigger liars, while the correlation between extraversion and lie scores of $-.19$ in these data does not support the lie scale as a measure of social conformity or acquiescence. It does imply, however, that religious children are less mature (Francis, Pearson, & Kay, 1988), although that conclusion is unsatisfactory since others have suggested that high lie-scale scorers are more likely to tell the truth, being more honest (Loo, 1980), truthful (O'Hagan & Edmunds, 1982) and conscientious (McCrae & Costa, 1985). A further set of studies suggests that high lie scorers are more responsible, more socially mature and less inclined to delinquent behavior (Rushton & Chrisjohn, 1981; Furnham, 1984; Emler, Reicher, & Ross, 1987; Lane, 1987).

These discrepancies in interpretation could depend on specific items functioning in different ways (Wen, 1976) or on the fact that lie scores do not constitute a single facet of personality (Elliott, 1981). Contemporary perspectives on the multidimensional nature of lie scales and social desirability inventories include distinctions between "attribution responses" that claim socially desirable characteristics for the self, and "denial responses" that disclaim undesirable characteristics (Millham, 1974; Roth, Snyder, & Pace, 1986), or between "desirability" and "defensiveness" (Kusyszyn & Jackson, 1968), between "self-deception" about what is judged to be universally true but psychologically threatening, and "other-deception" about what is judged socially desirable but statistically infrequent (Sackeim & Gur, 1979, 1985) or between "self-deception" and "impression management" (Millham & Kellogg, 1980; Paulhus, 1984).

To establish whether Eysenck's lie scales contain more than one dimension, Pearson and Francis (1989) analyzed correlations between the responses of 191 fourteen- to sixteen-year-olds to the lie scales in the Junior Eysenck Personality Inventory (S.B.G. Eysenck, 1965), the Junior Eysenck Personality Questionnaire and the Adult Eysenck Personality Questionnaire (H.J. Eysenck & S.B.G. Eysenck, 1975) and Francis's scale of attitude towards Christianity. Significant positive correlations were found between each of the lie scores and religiosity (JEPI, $r = +.21$, $p < .01$; JEPQ, $r = +.30$, $p < .001$; EPQ, $r = +.17$, $p < .05$), and the variation in those correlations suggests that the psychometric properties of these scales should be closely examined.

Exploratory factor analyses and item analyses suggested that the 53 items in these three scales belong to two distinct components. Since both components correlate negatively with neuroticism and with psychoticism, Eysenck's theory suggests that both scales may measure aspects of "faking good" (H.J. Eysenck & S.B.G. Eysenck, 1976), although the two components have different relationships with extraversion and religiosity. The factor that correlates negatively with extraversion and positively with religiosity contains items concerned with a well-behaved, socially conforming individual, which is consistent with Eysenck's view that introverts condition more readily into both religious attitudes and socially conforming behavior. On this account, religious adolescents are more likely to endorse the behaviors listed in this component as truthful indicators of their personal practice. Although this interpretation does not establish that religious adolescents are more truthful, it challenges the view that they are less truthful.

The other component, which does not correlate with either extraversion or religiosity, has items less concerned with social conformity than with desirable but unlikely behavior and with undesirable but likely behavior. This component may, therefore, be functioning as a more independent and adequate index of "faking good." The fact that religious adolescents score neither more nor less highly on this component provides no evidence that religious adolescents are either bigger liars or more truthful.

Pearson and Francis (1989) concluded that this dual character of Eysenck's lie scale places the positive correlations between religiosity and lie scores in a fresh light. Religious children and adolescents are neither bigger liars nor more immature, but reflect the social conformity implicit in Christian teaching.

Conclusion

By carefully exploring religious development during childhood and adolescence within the context of Eysenck's theory of personality, this chapter demonstrates the links between some personality characteristics and attitudes towards Christianity. While an association is clear, it is too loose to explain religion as a function of personality, or to delimit the range of personality or individual differences to be found among adherents to a broadly Christian faith.

References

Ajzen, I. (1988). *Attitudes, personality and behaviour*. Milton Keynes: Open University Press, England.

Ajzen, I. & Fishbein, M. (1980). *Understanding attitudes and predicting social behaviour*. Englewood Cliffs, NJ: Prentice Hall.

Allport, G.W. (1950). *The individual and his religion*. New York: Macmillan.

Argyle, M. & Beit-Hallahmi, B. (1975). *The social psychology of religion*. London: Routledge and Kegan Paul.

Bagley, C., Verma, G.K., Mallick, K., & Young, L. (1979). *Personality, self-esteem and prejudice*. Farnborough: Saxon House.

Baker, M. & Gorsuch, R. (1982). Trait anxiety and intrinsic-extrinsic religiousness. *Journal for the Scientific Study of Religion, 21,* 119–122.

Batson, C.D. & Ventis, W.L. (1982). *The religious experience: A social-psychological perspective*. New York: Oxford University Press.

Becker, R.J. (1971). Religion and psychological health. In M.P. Strommen (Ed.), *Research on religious development: A comprehensive handbook* (pp. 391–421). New York: Hawthorn Books.

Bender, I.E. (1958). Changes in religious interest: A retest after 15 years. *Journal of Abnormal and Social Psychology, 57,* 41–46.

Beyts, J., Frcka, G., Martin, I., & Levey, A.B. (1983). The influence of psychoticism and extraversion on classical eyelid conditioning using a paraorbital shock UCS. *Personality and Individual Differences, 4,* 275–283.

Boyle, J.J. (1984). Catholic children's attitudes toward Christianity. Unpublished M.Sc. dissertation, University of Bradford, England.

Brown, D. & Lowe, W. (1951). Religious beliefs and personality characteristics of college students. *Journal of Social Psychology, 33,* 103–129.

Brown, L.B. (1962). A study of religious belief. *British Journal of Psychology, 53,* 259–272.

Brown, L.B. (1987). *The psychology of religious belief.* London: Academic Press.

Caird, D. (1987). Religiosity and personality: Are mystics introverted, neurotic, or psychotic? *British Journal of Social Psychology, 26,* 345–346.

Carrigan, P.M. (1960). Extraversion-introversion as a dimension of personality: A reappraisal. *Psychological Bulletin, 57,* 329–360.

Carter, M. (1979). The development of aspects of self in adolescence with reference to religious and moral education. Unpublished M.Phil. dissertation, University of Nottingham, England.

Chlewinski, Z. (1981). Personality and attitude towards religion in Poland. *Personality and Individual Differences, 2,* 243–245.

Claridge, G. (1981). Psychoticism. In R. Lynn (Ed.), *Dimensions of personality: Papers in honour of H.J. Eysenck* (Chapter 5). Oxford: Pergamon Press.

Costa, P.T., McCrae, R.R., & Norris, A.H. (1981). Personal adjustment to aging: Longitudinal prediction from neuroticism and extraversion. *Journal of Gerontology, 36,* 78–85.

Cowen, E.L. (1954). The negative concept as a personality measure. *Journal of Consulting Psychology, 18,* 138–142.

Crandall, V.C. & Gozali, J. (1969). Social desirability responses of children of four religious-cultural groups. *Child Development, 40,* 751–762.

Crookes, T.G. & Buckley, S.J. (1976). Lie score and insight. *Irish Journal of Psychology, 3,* 134–136.

Crookes, T.G. & Pearson, P.R. (1970). The relationship between EPI scores and 16PF second-order factors in a clinical group. *British Journal of Social and Clinical Psychology, 9,* 189–190.

Dahlstrom, W.G. & Welsh, G.S. (1960). *An MMPI Handbook.* Minnesota: University of Minnesota Press.

Daines, J.W. (1949). A psychological study of the attitude of adolescents to religion and religious instruction. Unpublished Ph.D. dissertation, University of London.

Dicken, C.F. (1959). Simulated patterns on the Edwards Personal Preference Schedule. *Journal of Applied Psychology, 43,* 372–378.

Eaves, L.J. & Eysenck, H.J. (1974). Genetics and the development of social attitudes. *Nature, 249,* 288–289.

Eaves, L.J., Martin, N.G., & Eysenck, S.B.G. (1977). An application of the analysis of covariance structure to the psychological study of impulsiveness. *British Journal of Mathematical and Statistical Psychology, 30,* 185–197.

Edwards, A.L. (1957). *Techniques of attitude scale construction*. New York: Appleton-Century-Crofts.

Egan, J. (1988). *Opting out: Catholic schools today*. Leominster: Fowler Wright.

Egan, V. (1989). Links between personality, ability and attitudes in a low-IQ sample. *Personality and Individual Differences*, *10*, 997–1001.

Ekehammar, B. & Sidanius, J. (1982). Sex differences in sociopolitical attitudes: A replication and extension. *British Journal of Social Psychology*, *21*, 249–257.

Elliott, A.G.P. (1981). Some implications of lie scale scores in real-life selection. *Journal of Occupational Psychology*, *54*, 9–16.

Ellis, A. (1962). *The case against religion*. New York: Institute for Rational Living.

Emler, N., Reicher, S., & Ross, A. (1987). The social context of delinquent conduct. *Journal of Child Psychology and Psychiatry*, *28*, 99–109.

Eysenck, H.J. (1947). *Dimensions of personality*. London: Routledge and Kegan Paul.

Eysenck, H.J. (1952). *The scientific study of personality*. London: Routledge and Kegan Paul.

Eysenck, H.J. (1954). *The psychology of politics*. London: Routledge and Kegan Paul.

Eysenck, H.J. (1958). A short questionnaire for the measurement of two dimensions of personality. *Journal of Applied Psychology*, *42*, 14–17.

Eysenck, H.J. (1959). *Manual for the Maudsley Personality Inventory*. London: University of London Press.

Eysenck, H.J. (1961). Personality and social attitudes. *Journal of Social Psychology*, *53*, 243–248.

Eysenck, H.J. (1966). Personality and experimental psychology. *Bulletin of the British Psychological Society*, *19*, 1–28.

Eysenck, H.J. (1967a). *The biological basis of personality*. Springfield, IL: Charles Thomas.

Eysenck, H.J. (1967b). Intelligence assessment: A theoretical and experiemental approach. *British Journal of Educational Psychology*, *37*, 81–98.

Eysenck, H.J. (1970). *The structure of human personality* (3rd ed.). London: Methuen.

Eysenck, H.J. (1975). The structure of social attitudes. *British Journal of Social and Clinical Psychology*, *14*, 323–331.

Eysenck, H.J. (1976a). *Sex and personality*. London: Open Books.

Eysenck, H.J. (1976b). Structure of social attitudes. *Psychological Reports*, *39*, 463–466.

Eysenck, H.J. (1977). *Crime and personality* (3rd ed.). St. Albans: Paladin.

Eysenck, H.J. (1979). Personality factors in a random sample of the population. *Psychological Reports*, *44*, 1023–1027.

Eysenck, H.J. (1980). *The causes and effects of smoking*. London: Maurice Temple Smith.

Eysenck, H.J. (1981). *A model for personality*. New York: Springer.

Eysenck, H.J. & Eysenck, M.W. (1985). *Personality and individual differences: A natural science approach*. New York: Plenum Press.

Eysenck, H.J. & Eysenck, S.B.G. (1964a). *Manual of the Eysenck Personality Inventory*. London: University of London Press.

Eysenck, H.J. & Eysenck, S.B.G. (1975). *Manual of the Eysenck Personality Questionnaire*. London: Hodder and Stoughton.

Eysenck, H.J. & Eysenck, S.B.G. (1976). *Psychoticism as a dimension of personality*. London: Hodder and Stoughton.

Eysenck, H.J. & Gudjonsson, G. (1989). *Causes and cures of criminality*. New York: Plenum Press.

Eysenck, H.J. & Levey, A. (1972). Conditioning, introversion-extraversion and the strength of the nervous system. In V.D. Neblitzyn & J.A. Gray (Eds.), *Biological bases of individual behaviour* (pp. 206–220). New York: Academic Press.

Eysenck, H.J., Nias, D.K.B., & Cox, D.N. (1982). Sport and personality. *Advances in Behaviour Research and Therapy*, *4*, 1–56.

Eysenck, H.J. & Wilson, G.D. (1978). *The Psychological Basis of Ideology*. Lancaster: Medical and Technical Publishers.

Eysenck, H.J. & Wilson, G.D. (1979). *The psychology of sex*. London: Dent.

Eysenck, S.B.G. (1960). Social class, sex, and response to a five-part personality inventory. *Educational and Psychological Measurement*, *20*, 47–54.

Eysenck, S.B.G. (1965). *Manual of the Junior Eysenck Personality Inventory*. London: University of London Press.

Eysenck, S.B.G. (1981). Impulsiveness and antisocial behaviour in children. *Current Psychological Research*, *1*, 31–37.

Eysenck, S.B.G. & Chan, J. (1982). A comparative study of personality in adults and children: Hong Kong vs. England. *Personality and Individual Differences*, *3*, 153–160.

Eysenck, S.B.G. & Dimitriou, E.C. (1984). Cross-cultural comparison of personality: Greek children and English children. *Social Behaviour and Personality*, *12*, 45–54.

Eysenck, S.B.G., Easting, G., & Pearson, P.R. (1984). Age norms for impulsiveness in children. *Personality and Individual Differences*, *5*, 315–321.

Eysenck, S.B.G. & Eysenck, H.J. (1963). On the dual nature of extraversion. *British Journal of Social and Clinical Psychology*, *2*, 46–55.

Eysenck, S.B.G. & Eysenck, H.J. (1964b). An improved short questionnaire for the measurement of extraversion and neuroticism. *Life Sciences*, *3*, 1103–1109.

Eysenck, S.B.G. & Eysenck, H.J. (1968). The measurement of psychoticism: A study of factor stability and reliability. *British Journal of Social and Clinical Psychology*, *7*, 286–294.

Eysenck, S.B.G. & Eysenck, H.J. (1969). Scores on three personality variables as a function of age, sex and social class. *British Journal of Social and Clinical Psychology*, *8*, 69–86.

Eysenck, S.B.G. & Eysenck, H.J. (1977). The place of impulsiveness in a dimensional system of personality description. *British Journal of Social and Clinical Psychology*, *16*, 57–68.

Eysenck, S.B.G. & Eysenck, H.J. (1978). Impulsiveness and venturesomeness: Their position in a dimensional system of personality. *Psychological Reports*, *43*, 1247–1255.

Eysenck, S.B.G. & Eysenck, H.J. (1980). Impulsiveness and venturesomeness in children. *Personality and Individual Differences*, *1*, 73–78.

Eysenck, S.B.G., Eysenck, H.J., & Barrett, P. (1985). A revised version of the psychoticism scale. *Personality and Individual Differences*, *6*, 21–29.

Eysenck, S.B.G., Eysenck, H.J., & Shaw, L. (1974). The modification of personality and lie scale scores by special "honesty" instructions. *British Journal of Social and Clinical Psychology*, *13*, 41–50.

Eysenck, S.B.G. & Jamison, R.N. (1986). A cross-cultural study of personality: American and English children. *Journal of Social Behaviour and Personality*, *1*, 199–207.

Eysenck, S.B.G. & Kay, W.K. (1986). A cross-cultural study of the personality of Northern Ireland and English children. *Irish Journal of Psychology*, *7*, 98–105.

Eysenck, S.B.G., Kozeki, B., & Kalmanchey-Gellenne, M. (1980). Cross-cultural comparison of personality: Hungarian and English children. *Personality and Individual Differences*, *1*, 347–353.

Eysenck, S.B.G. & McGurk, B.J. (1980). Impulsiveness and venturesomeness in a detention centre population. *Psychological Reports*, *47*, 1299–1306.

Eysenck, S.B.G., Nias, D.K.B., & Eysenck, H.J. (1971). Interpretation of children's lie scale scores. *British Journal of Educational Psychology*, *41*, 23–31.

Eysenck, S.B.G. & Renner, W. (1987). A cross-cultural comparison of personality: English and Austrian children. *European Journal of Personality*, *1*, 215–221.

Eysenck, S.B.G. & Saklofske, D.H. (1983). A comparison of responses of Canadian and English children on the Junior Eysenck Personality Questionnaire. *Canadian Journal of Behavioural Science*, *15*, 121–130.

Eysenck, S.B.G. & Seisdedos, N. (1978). Un estudio internaciones de la personalidad (An international study of personality). *Revista de Psicologia General y Aplicada*, 271–281.

Eysenck, S.B.G. & Sipka, P. (1981). Cross-cultural comparison of personality: Yugoslav children and English children. *Primijenjena Psihologija*, *2*, 175–180.

Eysenck, S.B.G. & Zuckerman, M. (1978). The relationship between sensation-seeking and Eysenck's dimensions of personality. *British Journal of Psychology*, *69*, 483–487.

Farley, F.H. (1970). Further investigation of the two personae of extraversion. *British Journal of Social and Clinical Psychology*, *9*, 377–379.

Fehr, L.A. & Heintzelman, M.E. (1977). Personality and attitude correlates of religiosity: Source of controversy. *Journal of Psychology*, *95*, 63–66.

Finlayson, D.S. (1972). Towards the intrpretation of children's lie scale scores. *British Journal of Educational Psychology*, *42*, 290–293.

Fishbein, M. & Ajzen, I. (1975). *Belief, attitude, intention and behaviour: An introduction to theory and research*. Reading, MA: Addison-Wesley.

Francis, L.J. (1976). An enquiry into the concept "readiness for religion," unpublished Ph.D. dissertation, University of Cambridge, England.

Francis, L.J. (1978). Attitude and longitude: A study in measurement. *Character Potential*, *8*, 119–130.

Francis, L.J. (1979). The child's attitude towards religion and religious education: A review of research. *Educational Research*, *21*, 103–108.

Francis, L.J. (1984). Roman Catholic schools and pupil attitudes in England. *Lumen Vitae*, *39*, 99–108.

Francis, L.J. (1987a). The decline in attitudes towards religion among 8–15 year olds. *Educational Studies*, *13*, 125–134.

Francis, L.J. (1987b). *Religion in the primary school*. London: Collins Liturgical Publications.

Francis, L.J. (1989a). Measuring attitude towards Christianity during childhood and adolescence. *Personality and Individual Differences*, *10*, 695–698.

Francis, L.J. (1989b). Monitoring changing attitudes towards Christianity among secondary school pupils between 1974 and 1986. *British Journal of Educational Psychology*, *59*, 86–91.

Francis, L.J. & Kay, W.K. (1984). Attitude towards religion: Definition, measurement and evaluation. *British Journal of Educational Studies*, *32*, 45–50.

Francis, L.J., Lankshear, D.W., & Pearson, P.R. (1989). The relationship between religiosity and the short form JEPQ (JEPQ-S) indices of E, N, L and P among eleven year olds. *Personality and Individual Differences*, *10*, 763–769.

Francis, L.J. & McCarron, M.M. (1989). The measurement of attitudes towards Christianity among Nigerian secondary school students. *Journal of Social Psychology*, *129*, 569–571.

Francis, L.J. & Pearson, P.R. (1985a). Extraversion and religiosity. *Journal of Social Psychology*, *125*, 269–270.

Francis, L.J. & Pearson, P.R. (1985b). Psychoticism and religiosity among 15-year-olds. *Personality and Individual Differences*, *6*, 397–398.

Francis, L.J. & Pearson, P.R. (1987). Empathic development during adolescence: Religiosity, the missing link? *Personality and Individual Differences*, *8*, 145–148.

Francis, L.J. & Pearson, P.R. (1988a). The development of a short form of the JEPQ (JEPQ-S): Its use in measuring personality and religion. *Personality and Individual Differences*, *9*, 911–916.

Francis, L.J. & Pearson, P.R. (1988b). Religiosity and the short-scale EPQ-R indices of E, N and L, compared with the JEPI, JEPQ and EPQ. *Personality and Individual Differences*, *9*, 653–657.

Francis, L.J., Pearson, P.R., Carter, M., & Kay, W.K. (1981a). Are introverts more religious? *British Journal of Social Psychology*, *20*, 101–104.

Francis, L.J., Pearson, P.R., Carter, M., & Kay, W.K. (1981b). The relationship between neuroticism and religiosity among English 15- and 16-year-olds. *Journal of Social Psychology*, *114*, 99–102.

Francis, L.J., Pearson, P.R., & Kay, W.K. (1982). Eysenck's personality quadrants and religiosity. *British Journal of Social Psychology*, *21*, 262–264.

Francis, L.J., Pearson, P.R., & Kay, W.K. (1983a). Are introverts still more religious? *Personality and Individual Differences*, *4*, 211–212.

Francis, L.J., Pearson, P.R., & Kay, W.K. (1983b). Neuroticism and religiosity among English school children. *Journal of Social Psychology*, *121*, 149–150.

Francis, L.J., Pearson, P.R., & Kay, W.K. (1983c). Are religious children bigger liars? *Psychological Reports*, *52*, 551–554.

Francis, L.J., Pearson, P.R., & Kay, W.K. (1988). Religiosity and lie scores: A question of interpretation. *Social Behaviour and Personality*, *16*, 91–95.

Francis, L.J., Pearson, P.R., & Lankshear, D.W. (1990). The relationship between social class and attitude towards Christianity among 10 and 11 year old children. *Personality and Individual Differences*, *11*, 1019–1027.

Francis, L.J., Pearson, P.R., & Stubbs, M.T. (1985). Personality and religion among low ability children in residential special schools. *British Journal of Mental Subnormality*, *31*, 41–45.

Franks, C.M. (1957). Personality factors and the rate of conditioning. *British Journal of Psychology*, *48*, 119–126.

Frcka, G. & Martin, I. (1987). Is there or is there not an influence of impulsiveness on classical eyelid conditioning? *Personality and Individual Differences*, *8*, 241–252.

Freud, S. (1950). *The future of an illusion*. New Haven: Yale University Press.

Fulljames, P. & Francis, L.J. (1987a). The measurement of attitudes towards Christianity among Kenyan secondary school students. *Journal of Social Psychology, 127*, 407–409.

Fulljames, P. & Francis, L.J. (1987b). Creationism and student attitudes towards science and Christianity. *Journal of Christian Education, 90*, 51–55.

Fulljames, P. & Francis, L.J. (1988). The influence of creationism and scientism on attitudes towards Christianity among Kenyan secondary school students. *Educational Studies, 14*, 77–96.

Furnham, A. (1984). Personality, social skills, anomie and delinquency: A self-report study of a group of normal non-delinquent adolescents. *Journal of Child Psychology and Psychiatry, 25*, 409–420.

Furnham, A. (1986). Response bias, social desirability and dissimulation. *Personality and Individual Differences, 7*, 385–400.

Garrity, F.D. (1961). A study of the attitude of some secondary modern school pupils towards religious education. *Religious Education, 56*, 141–143.

Gibson, H.B. (1981). *Hans Eysenck: The man and his work*. London: Owen.

Gibson, H.M. & Francis, L.J. (1989). Measuring attitudes towards Christianity among 11- to 16-year-old pupils in Catholic schools in Scotland. *Educational Research, 31*, 65–69.

Glassey, W. (1945). The attitude of grammar school pupils and their parents to education, religion and sport. *British Journal of Educational Psychology, 15*, 101–104.

Glow, R.A., Lange, R.V., Glow, P.H., & Barnett, J.A. (1983). Cognitive and self-reported impulsiveness: Comparison of Kagan's MFFT and Eysenck's EPQ impulsiveness measures. *Personality and Individual Differences, 4*, 179–187.

Gong, Y. (1984). Use of the Eysenck Personality Questionnaire in China. *Personality and Individual Differences, 5*, 431–438.

Graff, R.W. & Ladd, C.E. (1971). POI correlates of a religious commitment inventory. *Journal of Consulting Psychology, 27*, 502–504.

Greer, J.E. (1981). Religious attitudes and thinking in Belfast pupils. *Education Research, 23*, 177–189.

Greer, J.E. (1982). A comparison of two attitudes to religion scales. *Education Research, 24*, 226–227.

Greer, J.E. (1985). Viewing "the other side" in Northern Ireland: Openness and attitude to religion among Catholic and Protestant adolescents. *Journal for the Scientific Study of Religion, 24*, 275–292.

Gupta, B.S. (1971). Adaptation of a Hindi version of the Junior Eysenck Personality Inventory. *British Journal of Social and Clinical Psychology, 10*, 189–190.

Gutman, G.M. (1966). A note on the MPI: Age and sex differences in extraversion and neuroticism in a Canadian sample. *British Journal of Social and Clinical Psychology, 5*, 128–129.

Hanawalt, N.G. (1963). Feelings of security and self-esteem in relation to religious belief. *Journal of Social Psychology, 59*, 347–353.

Hansford, B.C. & Neidhart, H. (1977). An Australian evaluation of the Junior Eysenck Personality Inventory. *British Journal of Educational Psychology, 47*, 330–334.

Heintzelman, M.E. & Fehr, L.A. (1976). Relationship between religious orthodoxy and three personality variables. *Psychological Reports, 38*, 756–758.

Honess, T. & Kline, P. (1974). The use of the EPI and the JEPI with a student population in Uganda. *British Journal of Social and Clinical Psychology*, *13*, 96–98.

Hornsby-Smith, M. & Petit, M. (1975). Social, moral and religious attitudes of secondary school students. *Journal of Moral Education*, *4*, 261–271.

Hyde, K.E. (1959). A study of some factors influencing the communication of religious ideas and attitudes among secondary school children. Unpublished Ph.D. dissertation, University of Birmingham, England.

Hyde, K.E. (1965). *Religious learning in adolescence*. University of Birmingham Institute of Education, Monograph Number 7. London: Oliver and Boyd.

Iwawaki, S., Eysenck, S.B.G., & Eysenck, H.J. (1977). Differences in personality between Japanese and English. *Journal of Social Psychology*, *102*, 27–33.

Iwawaki, S., Eysenck, S.B.G., & Eysenck, H.J. (1980). The universality of typology: A comparison between English and Japanese schoolchildren. *Journal of Social Psychology*, *112*, 3–9.

Jamison, R.N. (1984). Differences in personality between American and English children. *Personality and Individual Differences*, *5*, 241–244.

Jobinson, R.C., Danko, G.P., Darvill, T.J., Bochner, S., Bowers, J.K., Huang, Y-H., Park, J.Y., Pecjak, V., Rahim, A.R.A., & Pennington, D. (1989). Cross-cultural assessment of altruism and its correlates. *Personality and Individual Differences*, *10*, 855–868.

Johnson, W.P.C. (1966). The religious attitudes of secondary modern county school pupils. Unpublished M.Ed. dissertation, University of Manchester.

Jorm, A.F. (1987). Sex differences in neuroticism: A quantitative synthesis of published research. *Australian and New Zealand Journal of Psychiatry*, *21*, 501–506.

Jung, C.G. (1938). *Psychology and Religion*. New Haven: Yale University Press.

Kay, W.K. (1981a). Syllabuses and attitudes to Christianity. *Irish Catechist*, *5*(2), 16–21.

Kay, W.K. (1981b). Marital happiness and children's attitude to religion. *British Journal of Religious Education*, *3*, 102–105.

Kay, W.K. (1981c). Conversion among 11–15 year olds. *Spectrum*, *13*(2), 26–33.

Kay, W.K. (1981d). Psychoticism and attitude to religion. *Personality and Individual Differences*, *2*, 249–252.

Keene, J.J. (1967). Religious behaviour and neuroticism, spontaneity and world-mindedness. *Sociometry*, *30*, 137–157.

Kirton, N.J. (1977). Characteristics of high lie scorers. *Psychological Reports*, *40*, 279–280.

Kline, P. & Barrett, P. (1983). The factors in personality questionnaires among normal subjects. *Advances in Behaviour Research and Therapy*, *5*, 141–202.

Kusyszyn, L. & Jackson, D.N. (1968). A multimethod factor analytic appraisal of endorsement and judgement methods in personality assessment. *Educational and Psychological Measurement*, *28*, 1047–1061.

Lane, D.A. (1987). Personality and anti-social behaviour: A long-term study. *Personality and Individual Differences*, *8*, 799–806.

Levin, B.H. & Schalmo, G.B. (1974). Self-rated liberalism is correlated with sensation-seeking. *Psychological Reports*, *23*, 298.

Likert, R. (1932). A technique for the measurement of attitudes. *Archives of Psychology*, *140*, 1–55.

Loo, R. (1980). Characteristics of the Eysenck Personality Questionnaire lie scale and of extreme lie scorers. *Psychology: A Quarterly Journal of Human Behaviour*, *17*, 5–10.

Lynn, R. (Ed.). (1981). *Dimensions of personality: Papers in honour of H.J. Eysenck*. Oxford: Pergamon Press.

Maqsud, M. (1980). Personality and academic attainment of primary school children. *Psychological Reports*, *46*, 1271–1275.

Mark, T.J. (1979). A study of cognitive and affective elements in the religious development of adolescents. Unpublished Ph.D. dissertation, University of Leeds.

Mark, T.J. (1982). A study of religious attitudes, religious behaviour, and religious cognition. *Educational Studies*, *8*, 209–216.

Martin, N.G., Eaves, L.J., & Fulker, D.W. (1979). The general relationship of impulsiveness and sensation-seeking to Eysenck's personality dimensions. *Acta Genet Med Gemellol*, *28*, 197–210.

Massey, A. (1980). The Eysenck Personality Inventory lie scale: Lack of insight or . . .? *Irish Journal of Psychology*, *3*, 172–174.

McClain, E.W. (1978). Personality differences between intrinsically religious and non-religious students: Factor analytic study. *Journal of Personality Assessment*, *42*, 159–166.

McCrae, R. & Costa, P.T. (1983). Social desirability scales: More substance than style. *Journal of Consulting and Clinical Psychology*, *51*, 882–888.

McCrae, R.R. & Costa, P.T. (1985). Comparison of EPI and psychoticism scales with measures of the five-factor model of personality. *Personality and Individual Differences*, *6*, 587–597.

McKelvie, S.J. (1983). Personality and belief in capital punishment: A replication and extension. *Personality and Individual Differences*, *4*, 217–218.

Michaelis, W. & Eysenck, H.J. (1971). The determinants of personality inventory factor patterns and intercorrelations by changes in real-life motivation. *Journal of Genetic Psychology*, *118*, 223–234.

Middlebrooks, K. & Wakefield, J.A. (1987). The Junior Eysenck Personality Questionnaire: An American sample. *Personality and Individual Differences*, *8*, 471–474.

Miles, G.B. (1971). The study of logical thinking and moral judgements in GCE bible knowledge candidates. Unpublished M.Ed. dissertation, University of Leeds.

Miles, G.B. (1983). A critical and experimental study of adolescents' attitudes to and understanding of transcendental experience. Unpublished Ph.D. dissertation, University of Leeds.

Millham, J. (1974). Two components of need for approval score and their relationship to cheating following success and failure. *Journal of Research in Personality*, *8*, 378–392.

Millham, J. & Kellogg, R.W. (1980). Need for social approval: Impression management or self-deception? *Journal of Research in Personality*, *14*, 445–457.

Modgil, S. & Modgil, C. (Eds.). (1986). *Hans Eysenck: Consensus and controversy*. Lewes: Falmer Press, England.

Mowrer, O.H. (1960). Some constructive features of the concept of sin. *Journal of Counselling Psychology*, *7*, 185–188.

Murray, C. (1978). The moral and religious beliefs of Catholic adolescents: Scale development and structure. *Journal for the Scientific Study of Religion, 17,* 439–447.

Ness, R.C. & Wintrob, R.M. (1980). The emotional impact of fundamentalist religious participation: An empirical study of intragroup variation. *American Journal of Orthopsychiatry, 50,* 302–315.

Nias, D.K.B. (1973a). Measurement and structure of children's attitudes. In G.D. Wilson (Ed.), *The psychology of conservatism* (Chapter 6). London: Academic Press.

Nias, D.K.B. (1973b). Attitudes to the Common Market: A case study in conservatism. In G.D. Wilson (Ed.), *The psychology of conservatism* (Chapter 16). London: Academic Press.

Nyborg, H., Eysenck, S.B.G., & Kroll, N. (1982). Cross-cultural comparison of personality in Danish and English children. *Scandinavian Journal of Psychology, 23,* 291–297.

O'Donovan, D. (1969). A historical review of the lie scale—with particular reference to Maudsley Personality Inventory. *Papers in Psychology, 3,* 13–19.

O'Hagan, F.J. (1981). Personality, reading ability and response to classroom lessons among a residential sample. *Research in Education, 25,* 41–46.

O'Hagan, F.J. & Edmunds, G. (1982). Teachers' observations on pupils' untruthfulness in relation to the "lie" scale. *Personality and Individual Differences, 3,* 335–338.

Osgood, C.E., Suci, G.J., & Tannenbaum, P.H. (1957). *The Measurement of Measuring.* Urbana: University of Illinois Press.

Paloutzian, R.F. (1983). *Invitation to the psychology of religion.* Glenview, IL: Scott, Foresman and Company.

Paloutzian, R.F. & Ellison, C.W. (1982). Loneliness, spiritual well-being, and the quality of life. In L.A. Peplau & D. Perlman (Eds.), *Loneliness: A sourcebook of current theory, research and therapy* (pp. 224–237). New York: Wiley-Interscience.

Passingham, R.E. (1972). Crime and personality: A review of Eysenck's theory. In V.D. Neblitsyn & J.A. Gray (Eds.), *Biological bases of individual behaviour* (pp. 342–371). London: Academic Press.

Paulhus, D.L. (1984). Two-component models of socially desirable responding. *Journal of Personality and Social Psychology, 46,* 598–609.

Pearson, P.R. (1979). How comparable are Eysenck's personality measures? *International Research and Communication System, 7,* 258.

Pearson, P.R. & Francis, L.J. (1989). The dual nature of the Eysenckian lie scales: Are religious adolescents more truthful? *Personality and Individual Differences, 10,* 1041–1048.

Pearson, P.R., Francis, L.J., & Lightbown, T.J. (1986). Impulsivity and religiosity. *Personality and Individual Differences, 7,* 89–94.

Pearson, P.R. & Sheffield, B. (1975). Social attitude correlates of sensation-seeking in psychiatric patients. *Perceptual and Motor Skills, 40,* 482.

Pearson, P.R. & Sheffield, B.F. (1976). Is personality related to social attitudes? An attempt at replication. *Social Behaviour and Personality, 4,* 109–111.

Perez, J., Ortet, G., Pla, S., & Simo, S. (1986). Test-retest reliability of the Spanish version of the Junior Eysenck Personality Questionnaire. *Personality and Individual differences, 7,* 117–118.

Pohier, J.M. (1965). Religious mentality and infantile mentality. In A. Godin (Ed.), *Child and adult before God* (pp. 19–42). Chicago: Loyola University Press.

Povall, C.H. (1971). Some factors affecting pupils' attitudes to religious education. Unpublished M. Ed. dissertation, University of Manchester.

Powell, G.E. (1977). Psychoticism and social deviancy in children. *Advances in Behaviour Research and Therapy*, *1*, 27–56.

Powell, G.E. & Stewart, R.A. (1978). The relationship of age, sex and personality to social attitudes in children aged 8–15 years. *British Journal of Social and Clinical Psychology*, *17*, 307–317.

Rawlings, D. (1984). The correlation of EPQ psychoticism with two behavioural measures of impulsivity. *Personality and Individual Differences*, *5*, 591–594.

Rhymer, J. (1983). Religious attitudes of Roman Catholic secondary school pupils in Strathclyde region. Unpublished Ph.D. dissertation, University of Edinburgh.

Richmond, R.C. (1972). Maturity of religious judgements and differences of religious attitudes between ages of 13 and 16 years. *Educational Review*, *24*, 225–236.

Roberts, F.J. (1965). Some psychological factors in religious conversion. *British Journal of Social and Clinical Psychology*, *4*, 185–187.

Rocklin, T. & Revelle, W. (1981). The measurement of extraversion: A comparison of the Eysenck Personality Inventory and the Eysenck Personality Questionnaire. *British Journal of Social Psychology*, *20*, 279–284.

Roth, D.L., Snyder, C.R., & Pace, L.M. (1986). Dimensions of favourable self-presentation. *Journal of Personality and Social Psychology*, *51*, 867–874.

Rushton, J.P. & Chrisjohn, R.D. (1981). Extraversion, neuroticism, psychoticism and self-reported delinquency: Evidence from eight separate samples. *Personality and Individual Differences*, *2*, 11–20.

Sackeim, H.A. & Gur, R.C. (1979). Self-deception, other deception, and self-reported psychopathology. *Journal of Consulting and Clinical Psychology*, *47*, 213–215.

Sackeim, H.A. & Gur, R.C. (1985). Voice recognition and the ontological status of self-deception. *Journal of Personality and Social Psychology*, *48*, 1365–1368.

Saklofske, D.H. & Eysenck, S.B.G. (1978). Cross-cultural comparison of personality: New Zealand children and English children. *Psychological Reports*, *42*, 1111–1116.

Saklofske, D.H. & Eysenck, S.B.G. (1983). Impulsiveness and venturesomeness in Canadian children. *Psychological Reports*, *52*, 147–152.

Siegman, A.W. (1963). A cross-cultural investigation of the relationship between introversion, social attitudes and social behaviour. *British Journal of Social and Clinical Psychology*, *2*, 196–208.

Sparrow, N.H. & Ross, J. (1964). The dual nature of extraversion: A replication. *Australian Journal of Psychology*, *16*, 214–218.

Spilka, B., Hood, R.W., Jr., & Gorsuch, R.L. (1985). *The psychology of religion: An empirical approach*. Englewood Cliffs, NJ: Prentice Hall.

Stanley, G. (1964). Personality and attitude correlates of religious conversion. *Journal for the Scientific Study of Religion*, *4*, 60–63.

Sturgeon, R.S. & Hamley, R.W. (1979). Religiosity and anxiety. *Journal of Social Psychology*, *108*, 137–138.

Thurstone, L.L. (1928). Attitudes can be measured. *American Journal of Sociology*, *33*, 529–554.

Turner, E.B. (1970). Religious understanding and religious attitudes in male urban adolescents. Unpublished Ph.D. dissertation, the Queen's University of Belfast.

Turner, E.B. (1980). General cognitive ability and religious attitudes in two school systems. *British Journal of Religious Education*, *2*, 136–141.

Turner, E.B., Turner, I.F., & Reid, A. (1980). Religious attitudes in two types of urban secondary schools: A decade of change? *Irish Journal of Education*, *14*, 43–52.

Vine, I. (1978). Facts and values in the psychology of religion. *Bulletin of the British Psychological Society*, *31*, 414–417.

Watson, P.J., Morris, R.J., Foster, J.E., & Hood, R.W. (1986). Religiosity and social desirability. *Journal for the Scientific Study of Religion*, *25*, 215–232.

Wen, S.S. (1976). Item validity of the lie scale of the Eysenck Personality Inventory. *Psychological Reports*, *39*, 880–882.

Wilson, G.D. (1973). A dynamic theory of conservatism. In G.D. Wilson (Ed.), *The psychology of conservatism* (Chapter 17). London: Academic Press.

Wilson, G.D. & Brazendale, A.H. (1973). Social attitude correlates of Eysenck's personality dimensions. *Social Behaviour and Personality*, *1*, 115–118.

Wilson, G.D. & Patterson, G. (1968). A new measure of conservatism. British Journal of Social and Clinical Psychology, *7*, 264–269.

Wilson, W. & Miller, H.L. (1968). Fear, anxiety and religiousness. *Journal for the Scientific Study of Religion*, *7*, 111.

Wright, D.S. (1962). A study of religious belief in sixth form boys. *Researches and Studies*, *24*, 19–27.

Zuckerman, M., Eysenck, S.B.G., & Eysenck, H.J. (1978). Sensation-seeking in England and America: Cross-cultural, age and sex comparisons. *Journal of Consulting and Clinical Psychology*, *46*, 139–149.

Zuckerman, M. & Neeb, M. (1980). Demographic influences in sensation-seeking and expressions of sensation-seeking in religion, smoking and driving habits. *Personality and Individual Differences*, *1*, 197–206.

8
Steps towards a Psychology of Prayer

EMMA SHACKLE AND LAURENCE B. BROWN

Because prayer is an essential feature of Christianity its practice is widespread. About half the adults in Britain, and slightly more in Europe, claim to need moments of prayer (Abrams, Gerard, & Timms, 1985, p. 60). Argyle and Beit-Hallahmi (1975, p. 12) noted that "about 44 per cent of the adult population" in Britain "claim to pray every day, mostly before going to bed," and to pray about "family and friends, especially for those who are ill, happier family life, peace, and help in crises," with more parents teaching their children to pray than who pray themselves. That more females than males pray daily (p. 73) gives a greater sex difference for prayer than for any other aspect of religious behavior.

While prayer may have become habitual for many people, little is known of the ways their *occasional* prayers are maintained, beyond the social recognition or acceptance, the pressing needs that cannot be resolved in other ways, and the conclusion that prayer works for them. Those who have decided to live under a religious rule are likely to have found other sanctions for their prayers, although the classical guides to prayer have psychological implications (cf. Miles, 1989), not least because of their concern with how to turn mind and body towards God. Finney and Malony (1985) (among others) note that psychological research has given "scant attention" to prayer, although the work that has been done was classified by them into developmental studies, the motive to pray, and the effects of verbal and of contemplative prayer, which they identify as its two major types.

The first modern statistical study of the effects of prayer was published in 1872. That study, by Francis Galton, investigated the longevity of the Royal Family and the clergy, because they were the ones most often prayed for publicly in Britain. He found, however, that they did not in fact live longer than others in the community. Despite that and other disconfirmations of the material efficacy of prayer, most people continue to take it for granted, and might even agree with William James, who looked at prayer "in the wide sense as any kind of communion" (1985, p. 376), noting "that by cultivating the continuous sense of our connexion with the power that made things as they are, we are tempered more towardly for their reception" (p. 373). When William James went on to find the essence of prayer in the fact that "the outward face of nature need not alter but expressions of meaning in it alter" (1985), he was close to the formal definition of a sacrament.

Petitionary prayer may be common but it is not its only form. Other prayers involve praise or thanksgiving and confession, and distinctions are drawn between the formality of public prayer and the intangibility of private prayer, the prayers of children and of adults, and between the prayer of those who are more or less mature, adept, or experienced with it.

The assumed intimacy of one's private prayers puts up barriers against psychological studies of those who pray unless, like C.S. Lewis, they publish their letters or memoirs, or, like Saint Augustine, Martin Luther, and other doctors of the Church, they make their views on prayer widely known in other ways. Even then, to interpret what anyone says about prayer could involve the psychologists' fallacy which, as William James (1985) pointed out, fails to keep existential judgments apart from "propositions of value" (p. 13) or from spiritual judgements that rest on some other kind of general theory. He also distinguished between "your ordinary religious believer" (p. 15) who has a second-hand religious life "made for him by others, communicated by tradition, determined to fixed forms by imitation, and retained by habit" (p. 15), from those whose "original experiences were the pattern-setters to all this mass of suggested feeling and imitated conduct." Individuals' interpretations of received doctrines, and the accounts they give of their experiences provide the best data from which to distinguish those for whom "religion exists not as a dull habit, but as an acute fever" (James, 1985). While the results of social surveys (e.g., Stark & Glock, 1968) can define the contexts within which such distinctions or patterns develop, more detailed inquiry is needed to establish the different ways in which prayer is construed.

Perhaps the first questionnaire study of prayer that aimed to give a detailed voice to "ordinary" church people was reported by Beck (1906). In the account of his findings, Beck noted that all those who replied, "regularly face the need of prayer," and pray both morning and evening. He thought this suggested that prayer was habitual, finding further support for that conclusion in the preference to kneel, and in the formal prayers of childhood. Nevertheless, he also found that prayers in maturity are for spiritual things, supported by feelings of dependence and communion, by a sense of "the presence of a higher power while in the act of praying" and by the desire "to find God's will." While it is not clear how the transition is achieved, Beck concluded that a mature expectation for subjective results in prayer ruled out the appropriateness for producing "a change in the weather" in the judgments of a majority of those who answered his "syllabus," although he found that those who pray were equally divided as to whether the sense of an unusual power "comes from without" or is a result of some already latent energy. His respondents did not think that accepting "one's dependence on a higher being weakens one-self." Beck also noted that, while "comparatively few have ever had remarkable answers to prayers," "conversion" was a commonly experienced outcome of prayer.

To establish how much stability there might have been in the attitudes and beliefs about prayer that Beck uncovered, we put most of his items into a questionnaire that also asked about how prayer is understood. This questionnaire was answered for us in 1987 by 26 Roman Catholic schoolgirls, with a mean age of 16.5, who were attending a Catholic girls' boarding school near London. (The answers of the only girl in that group who said she did "not pray now" have not been included in our analyses.) The questionnaire was also completed by 20 Roman Catholic women with a mean age of 53.2, whom we approached either through a network of ecumenical prayer groups in a cathedral city in the North of England, or at a British conference on Christian spirituality. Comparing the answers of these adult women with those of the schoolgirls should help to identify the attitudes of those who are more, or less mature, with maturity being identified by the explicit religious commitment of the adults in our study.

Results

Table 8.1 makes some bald comparisons between the practice and basic beliefs of the schoolgirls, who are still coming to terms with prayer, and of the mature women, whose lives are centred on its practice. Where they are available, Beck's (1906) figures are also shown. Strict comparisons between these three sets of data may be unfair, because of unknown biases in the sampling procedures, the small number of people we studied, and the absence of any detailed information in his paper about those who provided the data for Beck's (1906) study. There are, however, some similarities between the responses of his adults and our women, in that nearly all of them felt a need to pray regularly, believe that prayers can help those who pray, and said they have prayed most in their maturity.

There is a different focus shown among the schoolgirls from that shown among the adults, despite the fact that in each group of people, all said they pray either regularly or occasionally, and most said they were taught to pray, believe that prayer "can have an effect on them," use formal prayers (identifying, for example, "Our Fathers, Hail Mary's [sic], etc.," or "prayers learnt when younger"), and have preferred times for prayer. These replies suggest that prayer has a more or less routine character for those in both groups, rather like that which William James identified as "habitual." But the girls and women in our study diverge sharply in the ways they supported their answers.

TABLE 8.1. A comparison (in percentages) of schoolgirls' ($N = 25$) and adult women's ($N = 20$) answers to direct questions about prayer, together with Beck's (1906) results from an unspecified sample.

	Girls	Women	Beck
Feels a need to pray			
regularly	28	95	98
occasionally	72	5	—
Prays alone			
daily	32	100	"majority"
weekly	40	—	—
monthly	24	—	—
Says grace before meals			
daily	0	50	N/A
never	84	16	—
Adopts a particular position	8	60	"very few"
Has preferred times for prayer	60	60	25
Believe prayers can have an effect on those who pray	80	95	83
Was taught to pray	84	90	N/A
Regularly uses formal prayers	68	75	24
A mistake to pray to change the weather	40	50	>75
Prayer depends on their mood	72	20	N/A
Prayer depends on what has happened	72	40	N/A
Relieved to confess sins in prayer	36	70	19
Remarkable answers to prayers noted	20	65	"few"
Communion more important than dependence in prayer	10	45	22
Prayed most in their maturity	N/A	65	68
Prayer is easy to talk about	12	70	N/A
Prayers oriented to God	12	65	N/A
or to self	64	15	—
Prayer most needed in bad times	96	45	N/A

For many of the schoolgirls, but for fewer of the women, prayer is reactive, depending on their mood and on what has happened. They are therefore more likely to pray at bad times. While the schoolgirls tend to pray occasionally, nearly all the women pray regularly, in private as well as in church or with others, and in a preferred posture (46% prefer kneeling). While fewer of the schoolgirls than the women were aware of "remarkable answers" to prayer, the women's orientation there is toward God rather than self and the prayers of many (but not all) of them stress communion rather than dependence, as they "look for an answer in God's will and (being able to) learn something in the process" (as one of them said). While many of the women's detailed answers about their successes seem cautious and are in terms of healing and guidance, half the schoolgirls answered more formally with phrases like "God's will," "they are always answered but perhaps its not the expected way," "what you are asking for is perhaps not the best," or "will be answered in good time." When pressed, those in both groups would probably agree that when God says "no" the prayer is still answered, but there is a striking difference in the schoolgirls' emphasis on their own petitions and the women's stress on finding God's will. More of these adults said that prayer has beneficial effects on those who might have been prayed for, despite an aim of their prayer being to "establish a relationship with God."

Differences between the women and the schoolgirls were of course expected, since their prayers are differently contextualized, not only by the preferred places for prayer (especially those that are quiet), times of day (usually morning or evening), religious traditions, and by the experiences and reactions of those with whom they talk about it. While psychologists have neglected the effects of our actual (and expected) talk or discourse about prayer and what can be said about it, they have also neglected what is said about most other aspects of social and personal life. But when the women were asked who they talked to about prayer, it became clear that this is restricted to those they meet in their religious or domestic contexts. It is, however, noteworthy that a majority of both groups said that prayer has direct effects on them, although the women identified a wider range of positive and negative feelings (as in "love, rebellion, anger, repentance, sorrow, peace, and joy") than the schoolgirls, who stressed "comfort, security, hope." Most of the women also spoke of their need to concentrate when in prayer.

Our results suggest that the development of prayer is not independent of sanctions that may encourage people to accept, reconstruct, or reject recognized (if local) traditions of religious belief and practice.

Differences in the perspectives on prayer in these two groups can be seen more clearly in the particular constructions of prayer than are given in the broad data, because of a dialectic there between the information that is given or received, and what parts of that have been annexed in making their own practice of prayer personal rather than habitual. Welford's (1947) finding that prayer is commonly motivated by the need to reduce frustration or to help one adjust to unusual circumstances, and the use of prayer as a coping device (Parker & Brown, 1983) supports the assumption that for some people, including these schoolgirls, prayer has instrumental value. While Godin (1985) has argued that an expressive attitude is more appropriate since it reflects our "experience of the conflict of wishes" (p. 221) and not mere dependence, Oser and Reich (1987) argue that mature thinking consciously connects opposed processes and attempts to explain their relationship. The resolution of this tension is more apparent in the women's answers to our questionnaire than it is among the schoolgirls, whose answers suggest that their prayer reflects wishes or demands, without any attempts to identify it with their "reality."

The need to purify prayer in that integrative sense involves "allowing God to wish in us" (Godin, 1985, p. 217), and to acknowledge that the cries from our own misery "summon God (or the gods) to satisfy our needs with his gifts" (p. 218). That recognition forms the starting point for a religion that can be purified, by recognizing that the "harsh laws of the world and of men" (p. 219) need to be dealt with in terms of hope or love, and by refusing to repress unspoken wishes. Godin stresses that when people are confronted with the inevitability of events, and when they cannot change the order of things, they make changes by modifying their wish to agree with and even anticipate the divine plan (p. 219). He argues that this perspective should encourage an interest in the religious meaning of events, recognizing the inherent tension between a wish to unify, but also to modify a relationship.

The one schoolgirl who said she had given up praying said that "during confirmation I found I was beginning to feel nothing and became disillusioned . . . (but that) I still believe in God—just don't feel much. Still 'thank God' in church as we're made to go." She also noted that those who continue to pray "feel secure and hopeful that their prayers will be answered," and commented on the reflexive nature of prayer, saying that "prayer makes some believe in what they are praying for, so (there is an) element of hope and goodwill."

While few of the other schoolgirls expressed such doubt, their answers convey a sense of routine on one hand, perhaps because of their regular chapel services, and of the expediency, need, or crises in the circumstances of their spontaneous prayers, which are rewarded by a sense of "security, serenity, and calm," as one girl put it. She also said that "by learning simple prayers (you) can be encouraged to make up your own." So one said she prays, "when you need help, thanking God," and prayer can "put the person more at ease with herself and God" and that being "alone in a quiet room is a good place to pray." Successful prayers are immediate (like "finding lost possessions") and unsuccessful prayers are distanced, for example by praying for "less violence in the world."

Discussion

While our questionnaire was deliberately set out in a way that allowed those who responded to use their own words to convey their attitudes to prayer, quantifying the answers necessarily compresses them and conceals the directness of their expression. This is especially so with the answers of the adult women, which were, in all instances, more detailed. Perhaps that reflects a change from the innocence of youth to the experience and sense of intimacy inherent in prayers that do not *have* to "make them feel good" (to quote what one schoolgirl wrote). For the women, religion is not the only certainty in life, nor is it always there when you need it or want to use it "to bring peace and consolation in times of distress that is strengthened by prayer" or for "giving the will to work hard" (to quote other schoolgirls).

It is worth noting that some of the older girls said they found that they got "nothing from going to Church," yet they still prayed by themselves. This suggests that satisfying their feelings may be an important feature of prayer (or of religion itself) which not only supports a sense of its immediacy, but its propriety as well. Another girl said that prayer fits with religion, "like a key into a lock: it depends on who you are and what religion you belong to . . . (and) on your state of mind."

By contrast, the youngest of the women, who was 30, said that religion means "the expression of my faith together with others (past, present, and future)," and that prayer "transcends personal or communal ritual, focusing on God," giving "comfort, not being alone, strength, love, courage." It also involves "sorrow, desolation, consolation, love, anger, irritation." Another said that praying brings them to an "awareness of the divine mystery, its love and its demands, a sense of healing, acceptance, challenge, also bafflement, confusion. The fruits of acceptance should spill over into acceptance of others," She also noted that "small prayers, just a few words—can go on anytime, anywhere." Perhaps that involves a "talking" kind of prayer, with another, more extended, quieter prayer that is more like "listening."

An important feature of the adult women's prayer is therefore a tolerant elaboration in a rather introspective way, that is helped by "solitude, a regular pattern if possible . . . (and) a sense of the rightness of being in the right place at the right time even if nothing seems to be happening."

Prayer fits intrinsically into the lives of these women, "belonging" to it and to their religious stance. It does not appear to be "used" by them and most had said they would never pray for material gain, since "prayer is the food of the relationship with Christ (who guides me in daily life by the power of the Spirit, hopefully to the Glory of God the Father), the means of dialogue—the source of strength—the channel for response . . . (so that) it helps me see things in God's way and is the means of changing me." Aligned with that perspective is "beautiful scenery, the comfort of my own home, in front of the Blessed Sacrament," which were mentioned as "some of the good places" for that person to pray, as well as "being surrounded by others who pray (even if silently)." The same person went on to say that "there are so many things that seem truly remarkable to me—I'm not sure I can express them in writing for others, as they would seem remarkable to them." That this involves more than the privacy of prayer (and this woman said she spoke about her prayer life only with "my prayer group, my confessor, and on a different level, my pupils") emphasizes the central, constructive role of prayer, which is not primarily concerned with what is imposed or might have happened to you, but is well-balanced and interactive. This woman said that when she was asked to pray for a priest, she was terrified: "I'd never prayed for a priest before and I prayed for an hour before going with friends to pray over him."

Some of the accounts of these women read as if Otto's sense of the numinous stands behind them, although there are other readings of their texts, and of their paths in Christianity. It is of interest, however, that none of the women in this group wrote anything that suggested a conservative or fundamentalist perspective, nor did any of them use the questionnaire to imply a commitment to asceticism. The closest one gets to that is in the statement that prayer is "the lifeblood of religion and makes real and personal what is otherwise exterior and ritual." This stance itself implies that, as another woman said, "prayer is very private, but it is not difficult to talk about prayer in a general way."

The perspective that was offered in the questionnaire answers of these women presents the traditions of the church as a structure that is worked through by those who take up its meaning, and find group support in doing this. The schoolgirls find their support among peers, but with a different content from that given by the women. This can be seen most clearly in their contrasting reactions to successful and unsuccessful prayers. One of the women said that "successful prayer only means something foreseen by the prayer, unsuccessful (prayer) implies disappointment: but hidden results often occur and are recognized later . . . (and) strictly speaking I don't believe any prayer is unanswered." Most of the schoolgirls were less confident about the success of their prayers.

A Planned Replication That Failed

Granted that the questions we asked are close to commonsense, we had also planned to explore the experiences of women who are thought to be "expert" because of their life of contemplation or because they teach or write about prayer, as another comparison group. The questionnaire we developed for that study was based on one used by Moore (1956) to explore and then support his theologically principled analysis of a stage-based sequence in the development of an "interior spiritual life," with data from those in a contemplative life. In Moore's theory, maturity was recognized by "freedom from sin or by the level of his [sic] mental prayer" (Moore, 1956, p. 383), by experiences that distinguish "the mystic graces" from what "seemed to be derived from Satan" and by descriptions of "betrothal scene with Christ" (p. 385), by habitual mental prayer, a life of self-denial, and attitudes "towards sufferings and humiliations" (p. 384). These criteria lie at an opposite extreme to Beck's inductive approach, and were derived explicitly from a prescriptive reading of the works of St. Teresa of Avila rather than from popular accounts of prayer, or even from a contemporary psychological theory such as that advanced by Godin (1971), who assumed that a properly developed human maturity renounces "self-sufficiency and the desires of omnipotence" (p. 147) to make an entirely free commitment, "centering on faith in Christ" (Godin, p. 147). Elkind (1971) postulated a rather similar progression from "pre-religion" to a mature "personal religion' that is incorporated rather than imposed.

Moore's (1956) report noted that while some of his questions were "criticized by some respondents" (p. 304), he had wanted to find out what is the "usual life in the Catholic Church" (p. 392), the struggles it involves, and the evidence for the phenomena that were identified as natural events or "of divine origin" and so, miraculous (p. 393). He also noted that "a candid reader will be charmed by the simple spiritual beauty of the Catholic home of which we give a glimpse . . . (and of) what seems to be the inner life of the soul with God" (p. 393). (Such piety seems a little misplaced now.)

That the core of Moore's theory (and he was a psychologist) involved "a transformation for the better in one's spiritual life," stresses either its prescriptive rather than its normative character, or his emphasis on an effortful and individual striving, severe ascetic practices, and mystical phenomena, rather than "letting go," trusting in God, and a mildly ascetic emotional contemplation.

We approached a number of Catholic contemplative communities and some priests, nuns, and lay people who were recognized experts on prayer, asking them to find contemplatives who would be willing to fill in the questionnaire. Only 8 were returned of the 67 distributed (12%). They were all incomplete, although we had another six completed by lay-women. We received two letters from nuns telling us why they were unable to fill in the questionnaire. These, together with others' comments, indicated a general dissatisfaction with the "out-of-dateness" of its theological assumptions and emphases, except among 8 of the respondents, who described "special" or other graces. The evident unwillingness to accept Moore's rigorous views could be attributed to changes in Catholicism following Vatican II, although this interpretation disregards other factors that made the 1970's and 1980's so different from the immediate postwar period.

Conclusions

The incursion of psychologically based counseling and the current move of ecumenism into Catholic practice can, for example, be seen in Donoghue and Shapiro's (1984) identification of the period after 1962 as "anxious years." It aligned the (new) sacrament of reconciliation with celebrations such as Baptism and Marriage (p. 74), in which an examination of conscience covers social as well as personal sins while emphasizing spiritual guidance (p. 87). Jantzen (1987), using Julian of Norwich for her example, explored "personhood and its healing in rootedness in

God" (p. ix) from a theological perspective, and asked if "Christian theology has any implications for psychology" (p. 124). Those examples involve an important dialectic, since the psychological criteria of maturity (or mental health) must be clothed, and expressed, through a coherent set of concepts that is applicable to particular "kinds" of people and traditions. The problem is, however, to find links between the separate sets of surface and deep structures, in psychology and in religion, that might identify their similarities and ways in which they can be expressed that can convey meaning and not disorder. This is our problem, as much as it was a problem for William James.

A continuing question centers on "who is to blame" when people either defect from religion or do not develop towards what others judge to be a mature religious perspective about prayer, and in other attitudes to religion. This dilemma can be resolved only with better information than we have now about any criteria that might be applied, about the actual rather than the expected or assumed responses of separate groups to the meanings that prayer can carry. We need to know, for example, why self-referenced terms rather than theological doctrines were used in the answers that were given by the adults in our study: whether because that is how they think about prayer, or because our method of inquiry encouraged a psychological bias for their replies. It would clearly have been possible for them to have answered in biblical or theological terms that defined a closed world of the sacred, bounded by a forbidden mystery (to misquote Jaques Ellul). But none of the adult women did that, perhaps because their prayer is not marked off from the rest of their lives. Nor did they use fixed points of reference, beyond a commonsense understanding of what prayer "means." Prayer is therefore a resource for them, in their interaction with an everyday world that is understood "religiously." But we do not know what might help the schoolgirls to develop that perspective unless it is, as some have implied, a normal process from which many of them can be expected to defect.

More information is needed, however, about the roles that prayer has in the secular society to which they all belong in some sense, to find if the scientific facts about it complement (Oser & Reich, 1987) or compete against religion and its practices.

The adult women we studied are not strangers to interpretations of prayer that preserve more or less traditional religious perspectives, and readily use symbols, myths, and metaphors as tools to articulate their own experiences and religious practices (but especially prayer) that are explicitly sustained by group-based support within the broadly ecumenical traditions that they share.

References

Abrams, M., Gerard, D., & Timms, N. (Eds.). (1985). *Values and social change in Britain*. London: Macmillan.

Argyle, M. & Beit-Hallahmi, B.P. (1975). *The social psychology of religion.* London: Routledge and Kegan Paul.

Beck, F.O. (1906). Prayer: A study in its history and psychology. *American Journal of Religious Psychology and Education,* 2(1), 107–121.

Donaghue, Q. & Shapiro, L. (1985). *Bless me, Father, for I have sinned: Catholics speak out about confession.* Toronto: McClelland and Stewart.

Elkind, D. (1971). The development of religious understanding in children and adolescents. In M.P. Strommen (Ed.), *Research on religious development* (pp. 655–685). New York: Hawthorn Books.

Finney, J.R. & Maloney, H.N. (1985). Empirical studies of Christian prayer: A review of the literature. *Journal of Psychology and Theology,* 13(2), 104–115.

Galton, F. (1872). Statistical enquiries into the efficacy of prayer. *Fortnightly Review,* 18(12/68) New Series, 125–135.

Godin, A. (1971). Some developmental tasks in Christian education. In M.P. Strommen (Ed.), *Research on religious development. A comprehensive handbook* (pp. 109–154). New York: Hawthorn Books.

Godin, A. (1985). *The psychological dynamics of religious experience.* Birmingham, AL: Religious Education Press.

James, W. (1902). *The varieties of religious experience.* New York: Collier. Reprinted in Smith, J.E. (ed., 1985). *The Works of William James* (Vol. 15). Cambridge, MA: Harvard University Press.

Jantzen, G. (1987). *Julian of Norwich: Mystic and theologian.* London: SPCK.

Miles, M.R. (1989). *The image and practice of holiness: A critique of the classic manuals of devotion.* London: SCM.

Moore, T.V. (1956). *The life of man with God.* New York: Harcourt, Brace and Co.

Oho, R. (1958). *The Idea of the Holy.* New York: Oxford University Press. (Original work published in German in 1923).

Oser, F.K. & Reich, K.H. (1987). The challenge of competing explanations: The development of thinking in terms of complementarity of "theories." *Human Development,* 30, 178–186.

Parker, G.B. & Brown, L.B. (1983). Coping behaviours that mediate between life events and depression. *Archives of General Psychiatry,* 39, 1386–1391.

Stark, R. & Glock, C.Y. (1968). *American piety: The nature of religious commitment.* University of California Press.

Welford, A.T. (1947). Is religious behaviour dependent upon affect or frustration? *Journal of Abnormal and Social Psychology,* 42, 310–319.

9
The Social Representations of Death: A Study with Cancer Patients, Family Members, and Healthy Individuals

CLELIA MARIA NASCIMENTO SCHULZE

The topic of death has been much studied recently, especially by physicians (Kubler-Ross, 1970; Parkes, 1972; Saunders, 1985; Twycross, 1985) and others involved in counseling dying patients, and the bereaved.

D'Assumpcao (1984), analyzing reactions towards death in Brazilian hospitals, concluded that in general, patients, their relatives, and even the hospital staff are unprepared to deal with their own or with others' death. He also observed that family members, nurses, and doctors, as well as the patients themselves must go through the five stages described by Kubler-Ross (1970), of denial, anger, bargaining, interiorization, and acceptance, when preparing for death.

Our experience confirms what D'Assumpcao describes, and we dare say that appropriate psychological support when facing death is needed, not only for terminal patients and their relatives, but for the hospital staff, who may experience their own deaths vicariously when their patients die.

A psychosocial perspective on death has been considered by those involved in cancer prevention (Fobair & Cordoba, 1982; Martin, 1982), and in the support programs for terminal cancer patients (Hanks, 1986; Twycross & Lack, 1990). Because we believe that these approaches can make an important contribution to this subject, especially in relation to a patient's social representations or constructions of death, some relevant historical and sociological material on this subject will therefore be reviewed.

Background

In industrial societies, death is a negative event because of the importance that is given to production, and to consumers. So there is little place

130

there for those who are old, because death represents a defeat of the complex social and economic processes that focus on production, profit, and youthfulness. Philippe Ariès's (1974) account of the history of death in the Occident argues, however, that death is becoming a topic of interest again, because of a recognition that we must accept our own death and its circumstances. Knowing that we are going to die has made us fearful of sudden death, although across the centuries, as dependence on others increased, more and more support and preparation was needed to face one's own death. Into the 19th century, a "dying person" was active before their own death since everyone had to die in public. For that reason, those who were dying had the authority to give advice to family members and close friends.

While families and doctors are now expected to dissimulate to sick people about the gravity of their state, a common custom demands that patients will die ignorant of their approaching death. But Ariès does not accept that the dying person's role-inversion has anything to do with a fear of death, because that has always been present. Nevertheless, patients who are dying typically occupy the status of a "child," or of an underage or mentally retarded person, deprived of their right to prepare or organize their own death. Elizabeth Kubler-Ross (1986) noted, however, that even in the modern world, some traditional cultures offer those who are dying an active role in the time preceding their death.

Ariès also held that incurable diseases, particularly cancer, have taken over the ancient representations of death. When Glaser and Strauss (1968), in different hospitals in San Francisco, studied how family members and medical staff reacted towards the dying, their "symbolic interaction" analysis showed differences from that in the romantic period. They emphasized that the "styles of dying," as an "acceptable style of living while dying" or as an "acceptable style of facing death," were concepts through which to understand modern rules about death, in which family and staff members are more important than the patient. A hospital death must then occur in a way that will be acceptable to, or tolerated by the family, nurses, and doctors.

Since death seems to be incompatible with the regularity of modern daily life, an "acceptable style of dying" must avoid strong scenes that violate this harmony. Crying, tears, and desperation disturb a hospital's serenity, and an "embarrassingly graceless" dying is the opposite of an "acceptable dying," because it makes the *survivors* embarrassed. To avoid that, nothing is said to the patient about their real state, and they should also have the elegance and courage to be discreet about it. Patients must therefore behave in a way that allows the hospital community to forget the closeness of death, communicating with others as if death were not present. So Ariès argues that modern society deprives us of our death, giving it back only if we do not use it to disturb the living. Society also forbids the living to show strong emotion during a bereavement. Such behavior in hospitals has become a model for the whole society. Not only must the dying overcome their shock and collaborate with doctors and nurses, the bereaved survivors must hide their suffering. The time for dying has also changed. Even 50 years ago, people knew when they were going to die, and death came without hurry. No doctors interfered to postpone it, allowing time for forgiveness, testaments, and good-byes. In industrial societies now, the dying know little about the time of their death, because they should not know.

To be able to support dying patients and their family members, it is necessary to understand how they face and represent death. Although the arguments given by Ariès, and by Glaser and Strauss seem to hold in Brazilian hospitals, the sociological and anthropological literature points to different representations of death among other cultural groups. Souza Martins (1983) organized a series of articles written by Brazilian social scientists, called *Death and the dying in Brazilian society*, collecting data at Mato Grosso. He concluded that life and death were always considered simultaneously by those who were interviewed, since people are said to be born with the right date to die. Thus, the rituals after death are performed by the *caboclo*, with an order that aims to expel the dead person's soul from the home and from the family members, attaching it to the cemetery's space. These images and representation of death also vary across social classes.

Vidal (1983) found that the attitudes toward death among Kayapos Indians, for whom it is seen as negatively as is aging, depend on the belief that illness and death are caused by a break in eating habits, which elicits an attack by animal *mekarons* or spirits. Those examples show that it is unsafe to talk about social representations of death among Brazilians, since our country contains many cultural groups with distinct explanations of life and death. It is, however, likely that Ariès's conclusions about modern industrial societies and hospital contexts will apply to our urban reality. But cultural and regional differences must also be recognized if we are to offer good care and support for terminal patients.

The Present Study

Serge Moscovici (1981) defines social representations as "a set of concepts, statements, and explanations originating in daily life in the course of inter-individual communications. They are the equivalent, in our societies, of the myths and belief systems in traditional societies, and might even be said to be the contemporary version of common sense" (p. 181). In Moscovici's view, the role of social psychologists is to unfold this consensual universe and clarify the "shared" social cognitions that give order to an individual's world.

Our objective in developing the present work was to identify these commonsense explanations of death among a sample of patients attending

CEPON (the Center for Oncological Research), the family members of those cancer patients, and healthy people. We assumed that these groups would have different representations of death, since patients with cancer and their relatives would consider death a close possibility, while healthy individuals would avoid thinking about it, and so be more likely to deny the possibility of death than an ill person. We therefore assumed that these separate groups might show different levels of "awareness" about death.

The present sample of 15 males and 15 females had five people of each sex in each of three levels of awareness (cancer patients, relatives, and healthy individuals). Interviews with the patients and their family members were held in a vacant room at CEPON, which is in a hospital wing. The healthy subjects were interviewed at their work or at home. Patients were introduced to us after an appointment had been made, and we obtained permission to get extra information about them either from their doctor, the nurses, or from their files.

Once we were alone with the patients we said that our interview was very important, not only for our research but also for the hospital's purposes, to be able to offer a still better treatment to them. Because the information was important, we asked permission to have the interviews recorded.

Interview Schedule

The interviews were semi-directed, with a set of 10 questions as a guide although specific questions depended on previous answers.

The basic questions were:

1. How do you feel since you contracted the illness?
2. How do you feel and perceive your body? Are there any changes?
3. How did you feel before you contracted the illness?
4. How did your family react? What is your relationship with them now? How was it before?
5. Who has given you support?
6. When was the first time you experienced the first loss by death in your life? Please describe that.
7. What do you associate death with? What comes to mind when you talk about death?
8. How did your family teach you to face loss (or death)?
9. How do you explain death?
10. Does your way of explaining death have anything to do with your religious beliefs? What are those beliefs?

The answers to these questions were content-analyzed after each interview had been transcribed and typed on a blank sheet of paper with wide margins at each side. Subjects' answers were categorized by their distinctive themes, and a "figurative nucleus" was identified for the social representations of death.

Results

Most outstanding in the life stories of the female patients was the fact that for them all, life had been marked by successive unhappy events and diseases before they contracted cancer. Three of them revealed unfulfilled dreams, such as studying or making a career. The male patients, however, disclosed considerably less than the females, and their interviews were shorter than were those with the females.

All of the patients had a history of extremely hard work and the women said their work was associated with obligation rather than satisfaction. While the middle-class women talked about their unhappiness about body changes, the 3 women from the country showed no sign of distress about such changes or decay. Although the men disclosed less, in general they said they were depressed after receiving the diagnosis. All these patients complained about chemotherapy and its effects, and 2 women said they would prefer to die than go through that treatment again.

Among the patients' relatives there were no outstanding differences in the answers of males and females. All except one of them said that in their opinion, the diagnosis should have been hidden from the patients and only discussed with close relatives. Those who were Catholics offered similar representations of death.

Interviews with a male and a female doctor showed that both of them agreed that a diagnosis of cancer confronts the patient with the possibility of death, which they are in general not prepared for, although women were said to have more difficulty coping with their bodily changes, and that their self-image or self-esteem was also severely affected. These doctors thought that men have more difficulties than women in accepting death and coping with pain. They confessed that they had themselves questioned the meaning of life more deeply after working with cancer patients. The other healthy people who were interviewed showed no common elements or outstanding patterns.

Closer examination of all these interviews suggests that "awareness" was not a major factor acting upon the representations of death, although religious beliefs and social class were important. We noticed that spiritualists, converted Christians (no matter which denomination they belonged to), Catholics, and agnostics, had different explanations of death.

Five subjects were spiritualists, one of whom said that death does not exist for them. "Flesh dies but not the spirit. A spirit may even ignore the fact that its body is dead and very frequently a spirit has to be called to incorporate during a session equivalent to a church service to be convinced that its body has died." Death was also compared to birth, so that, "without a spirit," as one person said, "we cannot talk, we cannot think, we cannot desire." Another spiritualist said that the spirit evolves. "When a person dies, the matter disappears but the spirit remains vacant. A spirit will return and have several re-incarnations. Evolution comes from those reincarnations so that the more good a person does, the more the spirit is purified." These subjects said there is a right time for death, since a person's destiny is already written. Seven subjects were nominal Catholics, having been baptized, although they no longer went to church regularly. Two of them said that death is a tragedy that must be accepted, with suffering "a preparation for salvation." Another said that "the flesh has to suffer so that the soul gets purified," and one said that "Christ suffered and thus we too have to suffer." For these Catholics, when death occurs there is a separation of the spirit from the body. If a person has been good to others, their spirit will go to a place of rest, otherwise it goes to hell. One subject (from the relatives' group) believes that life is absolutely programmed, as in a computer.

Five subjects were Evangelicals, who argued that life involves suffering and that each person has a burden to carry. After death the spirit has to be presented to God to be judged, and that "Jesus will come to take His people with Him." Another 7 Christians, although belonging to different denominations, accept the Bible and a live relationship with God, and with Christ. For them, death does not imply losing something, but is simply "a passage from one dimension to another," "a passage to eternal life," or "a change of the state of life." "It does not mean a permanent separation from other believers," but is temporary, "taking a long journey and being sure that believers are hoping to meet again."

Doctor L. said that although physical suffering seems to be present for both believers and agnostics before death, he had observed that agnostics suffer more in spiritual terms than believers. He described two cases in which patients had died, "attached to their pride."

Six subjects declared that being atheists, they do not often think about death and do not believe in any of the religious explanations about death, life, and the universe. Two men confessed to being unable to explain death, saying that it could be compared to "switching off a light." But both of them said they became anxious when they thought about death.

A nurse said death is the final step in a life circle, and therefore natural. "Life animates beings, and death involves coming out of this vital circle."

Discussion and Conclusions

The theoretical considerations noted at the beginning of this paper find an echo in our data. Cancer is associated with death, as Ariès stressed. Although we did not ask the subjects about their associations between these two events, a fear of death, pain, and their close links with death were underlined in their discourse.

A majority of family members agreed that patients should not be told the truth about their illness. It is probable that the diagnosis of cancer deeply affects patients and their families, demanding life and identity changes and forcing people to consider their finiteness. Family members, and even some doctors therefore prefer to hide the diagnosis when they do not know how to perform the new roles this situation asks for, or how to avoid the embarrassment of not knowing how to support and comfort the patients, when they are themselves not on good terms with their own finiteness.

The data suggest that further studies should examine the social representations of life and death held by different religious groups, and that social class differences in self-esteem should be more closely examined, as well as the bodily representations that might be found among cancer patients.

References

Ariès, P. (1974). *Western attitudes toward death: From the middle ages to the present*. Baltimore: Johns Hopkins University Press.

Cullen, J.W. (1982). Role of the social and behavioural sciences in cancer prevention. In J. Cohen et al. (Eds.), *Psychosocial aspects of cancer* (pp. 33–37). New York: Raven Press.

D'Assumpcao, E.A. (1984). *Tanatologia e o Doente Terminal. Dialogo Médico.* 10(2), 22–32.

Fobair, P. & Cordoba, C.S. (1982). Scope and magnitude of the cancer problem in psychosocial research. In J.W. Cullen (Ed.), *Psychosocial aspects of cancer* (pp. 9–31). New York: Raven Press.

Fukui, L.G. (1983). *O culto aos mortos entre sitiantes tradicionais do sertao de itapecerica*. In Jose de Souza Martins (Ed.), *A morte e os mortos na sociedade Brasileira* (pp. 252–257). São Paulo: Hucitec.

Glaser, B.G. & Strauss, A.L. (1968). *Time for dying*. Chicago: Aldine.

Hanks, G.W. (1986). Management of pain in advanced cancer. In W. Siebert (Ed.), *Terminal care* (pp. 16–26). Siebert Puslications.

Kubler-Ross, E. (1970). *On death and dying*. London: Tavistock.

Kubler-Ross, E. (1986). *Death: The final stage of growth*. Englewood Cliffs, NJ: Prentice-Hall.

Martins, J.S. (1983). *A morte e os mortos na sociedade Brasileira* [Death and the dying in Brazilian society]. São Paulo: Hucitec.

Martin, L.R. (1982). Overview of the psychosocial aspects of cancer. In Cohen et al. (Eds.), *Psychological aspects of cancer* (pp. 1–8). New York: Raven Press.

Moscovici, S. (1981). On social representations. In J.P. Forgas (Ed.), *Social cognition* (pp. 181–209). London: Academic Press.

Parkes, C.M. (1972). *Bereavement: Studies of grief in adult life*. London: Tavistock and Pelican.

Saunders, C. (1984). The philosophy of terminal care. In Cicely Saunders (Ed.), *Essential elements in the management of terminal malignant disease* (pp. 232–241). London: Hogarth Press.

Twycross, R.G. (1985). *The dying patient*. London: Christian Medical Fellowship.

Twycross, R.G. & Lack, S.A. (1990). *Therapeutics in terminal cancer*. London: Churchill Livingstone.

Vidal, L. (1983). *A morte entre os indios Kayapo*. In J.S. Martins, *A morte e os mortos na sociedade Brasileira* (pp. 315–322). São Paulo: Hucitec.

10
Rigid Religiosity and Mental Health: An Empirical Study

HANS STIFOSS-HANSSEN

The present project relates to the empirical psychology of religion, where a main achievement has been the classification of religion into extrinsic and intrinsic orientations. Previous research has already made some effort to relate the concepts of religious orientation to psychopathology, and our aim has been to carry this effort one step further, and in doing so, to focus on the rigidity-flexibility aspect of religious orientations.

For this purpose, we developed a questionnaire which employs some items from previous instruments, and some new items. The experiment has been carried out with a control-group design, with psychopathology measured by a checklist procedure (SCL-90). Some unresolved problems remain as far as the interpretation of the results is concerned, but they nevertheless confirm our main hypothesis that there is a significantly higher rigidity in the religiosity of neurotic patients than in a control group. While this conclusion confirms previous findings, it calls for a further exploration of the relation between a rigid/extrinsic religiosity and psychopathology.

Introduction

Our aim was to establish a differentiation within religiosity that was (a) in accordance with current theory in the psychology of religion, (b) empirically measurable, and (c) could be used at a later stage as a predictor for the management of psychopathology.

We assumed that the most relevant and valuable contributions for this project came from the psychology of personality, and specifically from research on extrinsic and intrinsic religious orientations. These dimensions of religiosity were described by Allport (1950; Allport & Ross, 1967) and Allen and Spilka (1967), and further developed by Batson and Ventis (1982). Our ambition was to develop a method and an instrument that would demonstrate the occurrence of such dimensions in religiosity, and relate them to a measure of psychopathology. We have taken rigid-flexible religiosity as our key concept, assuming it to be a central factor in religious orientation.

The rigid-flexible concept is derived from Allen and Spilka's (1967) description of the extrinsic-intrinsic model, which states that extrinsic religiosity is characterised by rigidity. In relation to earlier instruments, our contribution was an expansion designed to include self-assertiveness in religiosity. Self-assertive or permissive religiosity being conceived as flexible (see there Factor 3, "nonpermissiveness"). The concept of rigidity-flexibility is also central in psychological theories in the line of Adorno et al. (1956), Rokeach (1960), and Rubenowitz (1963), whose research displays no direct measures of religiosity, although in the discussion he extensively implicates religion. Rubenowitz (1970) conceives religiosity to be associated with rigidity, but he also points out that it exists in a flexible form.

The existence of a rigid form of religiosity has been empirically demonstrated by Strommen, Brekke, Underwager, and Johnson (in *A study of generations*, 1972). This large study included the responses from more than 4,000 Northern American Lutherans to about 750 items, and the material was analyzed by various sophisticated statistical methods. Those analyses demonstrate that approximately 40% of the respondents showed what they call a "law-oriented," extrinsic, and rigid religiosity. But neither Rubonowitz (1963) nor Strommen et al. (1972) collected data concerning psychopathology.

The psychology of religion is also familiar with other efforts to separate religiosity into two or more different kinds or styles. As an example we can mention Erich Fromm (1950), whose distinction between authoritarian and humanistic religion has become well known, and the writings of James Fowler (1981) within the field of religious development, who describes a flexible, intrinsic religiosity as the optimal goal at the end of religious development (these points are elaborated by Batson & Ventis 1982, p. 149). I would emphasize, however, that all these analyses of human religiosity take their criteria not from theology, nor from the science of religion, but from psychology (and sociology).

Method

The Rigid-Flexible Religiosity Scale (RFR) was composed of several items from existing extrinsic/intrinsic scales, together with items based on the material mentioned above. Steps were taken to avoid biased responses, and the opinion of a group of professionals was sought. Subsequently, the instrument was tested in a small-scale study among 9 outpatients, 19 psychiatric nursing staff, and 7 chaplains. On the basis of that test, the instrument was revised, and the subscales rearranged.

TABLE 10.1. Demographic and religious characteristics.

Variable	Exp. group ($N = 56$)	Control group ($N = 70$)
Mean age (range)	43 (23–69)	40 (23–66)
Sex:		
Female	34	58
Male	22	12
Civil status:		
Married	30	50
Single	26	20
Professional status:		
High	24	14
Middle	17	52
Low	13	4
Religious attitude:		
Actively religious	21	48
Passive but positive	26	13
Negative	8	9
Church membership:		
Church of Norway	46	53
Other	5	9
None	5	8

Subjects

There were 56 volunteer hospitalized neurotic patients, approximately 72% of those available, who responded to the questionnaire.

Another 70 who were not receiving psychiatric treatment also responded as a comparison or "control" group. They were selected from psychiatric professionals and staff, of whom approximately 74% responded. The characteristics of these groups are shown in Table 10.1.

Assessment

Rigid religiosity and psychopathology were assessed by the RFR 50 scale (see above and Stifoss-Hanssen, 1987), and by the Symptom Distress Checklist SCL-90 (Derogatis, Lipman, & Covi, 1973).

Procedure

The questionnaires were distributed to each group, with a short introduction, and the respondents were asked to return the completed forms within at least 45 minutes. This allowed sufficient time, most taking about 30 minutes.

Hypotheses and Design

As a quasi-experimental, control-group design, the hypothesis was that the two groups would differ in their type of religiosity with the religiosity in the psychiatric patient group expected to be more rigid than in the control group, with similar sub-hypotheses covering the subscales that formed the questionnaire.

Statistics

The main goal was to evaluate differences between the two groups for the rigidity of their religiosity. To this end, analyses of variance were computed, followed by Student's t test where appropriate. Correlations were also computed to test the covariation between rigidity in religiosity and pathology (SCL-90).

Results and Discussion

The results, which are shown in Table 10.2, strongly support the hypothesis that rigidity in religiosity would be significantly higher among the patients than in the control group. Detailed analyses of the material show that this involves simplification and nonpermissiveness (in 2 of the 5 subcales, covering 20 of the 39 items).

Table 10.2 also shows the SCL-90 scores for the two groups, as a measure of difference in their psychopathology ($t = 8.75, p < .001$).

We also found significantly positive correlations between the total SCL-90 and RFR scores ($r = .19$), and between total SCL-90 and the RFR subscales for "Simplification" ($r = .21$ and $.55$) and "Nonpermissiveness" ($r = .27, .49$).

The items in those two factors are similar, and in a few cases, identical to those used by Hoge's (1972, p. 372) measure of intrinsic religiosity. Furthermore, three items (16, the exclusive truth claim of Christianity; 37, need for unchanging structure; and 43, need for religious absolutism) stem from Strommen's scales (Strommen et al., 1972, pp. 378–396).

We also computed a two-way Analysis of Variance (ANOVA) to examine the differences in psychopathology (SCL-90) between the low, medium, and high groups of self-reported religiosity which show a significant group effect ($F = 97.31, p < .001$), a nonsignificant belief effect,

TABLE 10.2. Means and (SD) of the Rigid-Flexible Religiosity (RFR) Scale.

Variable	No. of items	Exp. group $N = 56$	Control group $N = 70$	Significance t	p
Nonacceptance	7	1.56 (.88)	1.64 (.99)	−.52	NS
Simplification	8	1.69 (.62)	.95 (.48)	7.21	<.001
Nonpermissiveness	12	1.99 (.41)	1.52 (.41)	6.30	<.001
Literalism	6	2.48 (.65)	2.41 (.71)	.55	NS
Quest	6	2.07 (.68)	2.04 (.65)	.25	NS
All RFR variables	39	1.95 (.33)	1.72 (.37)	3.39	<.001
SCL	90	1.25 (.56)	.34 (.19)	8.75	<.001

and a significant interaction ($F = 4.73$, $p < .01$). A one-way ANOVA of SCL-90 by belief showed a significant belief effect ($F = 6.52$, $p < .002$). The high religiosity group was significantly lower on SCL-90 than the medium ($t = 3.60$, $p < .001$) and the low groups ($t = 2.05$, $p < .05$). That finding confirms Heskestad's (1984) results, among others, and invites further explanation and interpretation.

The RFR questionnaire, which included 11 items from Hunt's (1972, pp. 49–50) Literal, Auti-literal, and Mythological (LAM) scales (that is, all items except 13, 15–19, and 23) shows that Hunt's conception corresponds to those of the RFR (especially Hunt's items 12, 24, 3, and 2).

Conclusion

These results show that the religiosity of neurotic persons differs from that of psychologically healthy people in a way that can be described in rigid-flexible terms. Furthermore, it is reasonable to assume that this description is in line with the intrinsic-extrinsic tradition of analysis, which is well-established empirically within the psychology of religion. This conclusion agrees with the assumption that there is a connection between extrinsic religiosity and psychopathology (Batson & Ventis, 1982). Although no therapeutic interventions were planned within this study, we hope that this research might facilitate diagnosis, and eventually the development of therapeutic procedures.

Acknowledgments. The author wishes to thank Professor K. Gunnar Götestam, Department of Psychiatry and Behavioural Medicine, University of Trondheim for extensive supervision, and the Östmarka Hospital, University of Trondheim, and Modum Bad Nervesanatorium Psychiatric Clinic and Research Institute for financial support, access to research material, and professional support. This paper was written in cooperation with Modum Bads Nervesanatorium Psychiatric Inpatient Clinic and Research Institute, Vikersund, Norway.

References

Adorno, T.W., Frenket Brunswick, E., Leuinson, D.J., & Sanford, R.N. (1950). *The authoritarian personality.* New York: Harper.

Allen, R.O. & Spilka, B. (1967). Committed and consensual religion: A specification of religion-prejudice relationships. *Journal for the Scientific Study of Religion, 6,* 191–206.

Allport, G.W. (1950). *The individual and his religion.* New York: Macmillan.

Allport, G.W. & Ross, J.M. (1967). Personal religious orientation and prejudice. *Journal of Personality and Social Psychology, 5,* 432–443.

Batson, C.D. & Ventis, W.L. (1982). *The religious experience: A social-psychological perspective*. New York: Oxford University Press.

Derogatis, L.R., Lipman, R.S., & Covi, L. (1973). SCL-90, an outpatient psychiatric rating scale. *Psychopharmacology Bulletin*, *9*, 13–28.

Fowler, J.W. (1981). *Stages of faith: the psychology of human development and the quest for meaning*. San Francisco: Harper and Row.

Fromm, E. (1950). *Psychoanalysis and religion*. New Haven: Yale University Press.

Gorsuch, R.L. (1988). Psychology of religion. *Annual Review of Psychology*, *39*, 201–221.

Heskestad, D. (1984). Religiösitet og mental helse: En empirisk undersökelse. [Religiosity and mental health: An empirical study] *Nordisk Psykiatrisk Tidsskrift*, *3*, 353–661.

Hoge, D.R. (1972). A validated Intrinsic Religious Motivation Scale. *Journal for the Scientific Study of Religion*, *11*, 369–376.

Hunt, R.A. (1972). Mythological-symbolic religious commitment: The LAM Scales. *Journal for the Scientific Study of Religion*, *11*, 4252, p. II.

Rokeach, M. (1960). *The open and closed mind*. New York: Basic Books.

Rubenowitz, S. (1963). *Emotional rigidity-flexibility as a comprehensive dimension of mind*. Stockholm: Almquist and Wiksell.

Rubenowitz, S. (1970). *Personlighetspsykologi*. Stockholm: Aldus/Bonniers.

Stifoss-Hanssen, H. (1987). Religiös rigiditet og mental helse [Religious rigidity and mental health]. In O. Wikström (Ed.), *Religionspsykologi Nu* (pp. 67–80). Uppsala: Uppsala Universitet.

Strommen, M.P. (Ed). (1972). *A study of generations*. Minneapolis: Augsburg.

11
Religious Experience, Loneliness, and Subjective Well-being

Kathleen V. O'Connor

Transition from high school to university or college is a familiar and important experience for many young people. It involves "new beginnings" in several domains and requires dealing with novel physical and academic environments, building new social relationships, learning new ways of relating to parents and family, accepting new responsibilities and new roles in residential colleges or shared households, as well as developing personal, time, and financial management skills; learning the tenets of, and behavior for new professions; and finding new ways of relating to the demands and stresses of a tertiary academic system.

In Australia, few studies have been concerned with these experiences and their effects. Even more scarce are studies of the mediating factors that may influence students' capacity to adapt effectively to, and get the most from a new academic environment. While much of the research on Australian Universities and Colleges of Advanced Education deals with student success or failure (Caiden, 1964; Williams, 1982; Williams & Pepe, 1983), there is "general agreement that a high proportion of students either withdraw or fail because of adjustment or environmental factors rather than because of intellectual difficulties" (Williams, 1982, p. 1). Despite the lack of research, there has been some agreement that students coming into universities or colleges encounter difficulties in their adjustment, although it seems to have been assumed that these difficulties are the same for all students, and that they are dealt with in the same way by them all. It is suggested, however, that Australian universities are too impersonal and institutional, and that students in small universities and colleges probably experience this impersonality and its effects much less than do those at larger institutions (Williams, 1982). While clinical evidence derived from counseling and student services units supports this view, there is little systematic evidence about it.

Given the nature of the transition they must make, it is not surprising that loneliness and isolation are serious problems for students during their first year at university or college, and United States data suggest that

144

loneliness is probably one of the most important reasons for the high drop-out rates reported there (Newman, 1971; Cutrona, 1982). While loneliness can occur at any age, research also suggests "that late adolescence and early adulthood are times of especially high risk" (Cutrona, 1982, p. 292). Not only is this a time when ego and identity development are accelerated, as autonomy and assertiveness develop (presenting issues of separation), it highlights the transition to adulthood and the need to establish effective and satisfying adult social relationships (and a union with others). This is therefore a time when demands at both ends of the "Separation-Union" continuum are pressing (O'Dowd, 1986), which may also be true for those who, during their mid-life transitions, move into tertiary education for the first time.

Choosing to emphasize the experience of loneliness in this research is also significant because of the recent concern for "quality of life," usually measured through happiness and subjective well-being (cf. Bradburn, 1969; Campbell, 1976). Paloutzian and Ellison (1982) argue, for instance, that conditions or experiences of loneliness and spiritual-existential well-being "are facets of the more general concept of quality of life, and that loneliness is directly linked to the perceived quality of one's social life" (p. 224). While a study of loneliness and well-being among university and college students may highlight individual differences in the factors that contribute to successful social and academic adjustment during an important developmental transition (cf. Cutrona, 1982, p. 292), it could also yield data relevant to the experienced quality of students' lives. In the light of this, Paloutzian and Ellison (1982) argued that "the attempt to develop subjective measures is in part an attempt to assess people's interpretation of the things or events that affect them, as opposed to tabulating those things or events themselves" (p. 225). Their conceptual framework for loneliness has stemmed from the underlying assumption that one's history of intimate social interaction and current social experience both fundamentally affect the perceived quality of life. Life satisfaction seems in large part to be related to the quality of our social relationships. Lonely people are often depressed and unhappy (Paloutzian & Ellison, 1982).

Recent research on loneliness has also pointed to its possible relationship to a basic concern with intimate experiences in life through religiousness and religious experience. It has been argued that religious belief and practice, by promoting a sense of union and closeness with a personal God, or by enhancing a sense of security and belonging through shared experience and participation in religious social activities, can ameliorate loneliness and isolation and actively contribute to a sense of purpose, meaning, and direction in life. Paloutzian and Janigian (1986) have argued, however, that religiousness and religious experience, particularly at times or in settings that foster or necessitate aloneness, can provoke an intense and painful loneliness. Although the exact nature of the interaction between religious experience and loneliness remains unclear, it appears that "their interrelationship forms an intricate web that affects the quality of life" (Paloutzian & Janigian, 1986, p. 3).

This study affords an opportunity to investigate several aspects of the interrelationship between loneliness and religious experience among beginning university and college students, and the ways these aspects of experience interact and affect each other, and influence their sense of well-being. One goal of the study was to explore, in empirical, clinical, and theoretical terms, the importance of the factors that may enable some university and college students to make a satisfactory social and academic adjustment, and what prevents others from doing so (cf. Cutrona, 1982). The study therefore examined a wide range of factors related to loneliness among first year university and college students—including their feelings and experiences of belonging, alienation and isolation, the nature of their academic environment, and the personal characteristics that might make this initial adjustment more or less difficult. It also focused on different experiences of social relationships as they relate to feelings of loneliness and well-being. A final issue concerned the role of the religious environment and religious relationships in mediating adjustment and well-being.

Method

A questionnaire was constructed to cover demographic data, measures of happiness, early experience of university or college (Williams, 1982) and the satisfaction with that experience (Starr, Betz, & Menne, 1971; Walker, 1980), the quality of social relationships (Cutrona & Russell, 1987, based on Weiss, 1974), as well as loneliness (Russell, Peplau, & Cutrona, 1980), religious experience (Nagpal & Sell, 1985), and spiritual well-being (Paloutzian & Ellison, 1982).

The data to be reported are from 150 self-selected first year tertiary students with a mean age of 19.7, in Sydney, N.S.W., who in 1988 were among the 203 who accepted an invitation to participate in a study of the "Experiences of University or College Life." In the total group there were 129 students in education and biology at the University of Sydney

TABLE 11.1. Initial experiences, showing mean scores.

Scales	Univ.	College	F value
1. Institutional belonging	20.88	17.39	8.665*
2. Social involvement	22.65	20.26	3.968
3. Goal direction	15.90	13.39	6.409
4. Alienation	20.90	18.46	5.587
5. Academic achievement	24.66	22.91	2.182

F .05/5: 1,150. $Fc = 6.84$
Low scores represent more positive experience

TABLE 11.2. The satisfaction scales, showing mean scores.

Scales	Univ.	College	F value
1. Quality of education	31.82	36.89	20.953*
2. Social life	34.49	37.80	6.128
3. Compensation	31.56	33.44	2.848
4. Staff-student	31.02	35.98	18.116*
5. Participation in decision making	28.84	32.57	12.610*

F .05/5: 1,150. $Fc = 6.84$
High scores represent greater satisfaction

(65% of whom were females) and 74 students of teaching or nursing at Sydney's Catholic College of Education (84% being females). The majority in both of those groups (98%) were full-time students and single (95%). The 150 people for whom detailed information is reported here had completed all the separate measures.

Results

The two institutional groups were significantly different ($p < .05$) on the indices of happiness in general, and with university or College life. Fewer (3%) at the small, explicitly Catholic College said they were unhappy with college life (compared with 24% at the University), and that they were unhappy in general (5% compared with 21% at the University).

On the separate scales that measured initial experiences with their new institution, shown in Table 11.1, the two groups were significantly different only in "Institutional Belonging," with the Catholic College students feeling more identified and settled in their transition to life at their college.

On five aspects of satisfaction with campus experience, the groups were significantly different in their satisfaction with the "quality of education," "staff-student relationships," and "participation in decision making" because the Catholic College students expressed greater satisfaction in each case (shown in Table 11.2).

Those at the Catholic College also scored more positively on the two religious-experience scales (in Table 11.3), and on religious and spiritual well-being (shown in Table 11.4). There were, however, no differences

TABLE 11.3. Religious experience, showing mean scores.

Scales	Univ.	College	F value
1. Religious fulfillment	2.38	1.94	6.451*
2. Value of religious relationship	2.06	1.64	9.375*

F .05/2: 1,150. $Fc = 5.14$
Low scores represent more positive experience

TABLE 11.4. Spiritual well-being scale, showing mean scores.

Scales	Univ.	College	F value
1. Religious well-being	36.63	47.91	21.017*
2. Existential well-being	45.95	47.32	0.867
3. Total spiritual well-being	82.58	95.22	16.269*

F .05/3; 1,150. F = 5.89
High scores represent more positive well-being

between the two groups on the measures of loneliness, the quality of their attachments, or in their social relationships.

When the variables were factor analyzed across all subjects, a three factor solution was the most parsimonious (Table 11.5). It identified factors covering "Self-in-relationship" (accounting for 33% of the variance), "relationship to the academic environment" (14% of the variance) and "religious relationships" (10%). Obtained F values for each of the factors on the beanned contrasts were significantly different, with students at the Catholic College consistently scoring more favorably (Table 11.6).

TABLE 11.5. Factor loadings across 22 variables.

Scales % Variance	Factor 1 33.3%	Factor 2 13.9%	Factor 3 10.1%
A1 Institution	−.05	−.45	.46
A2 Course	−.09	−.42	.38
A3 Goal direction	−.32	.63	−.08
B4 Alienation	−.57	.68	−.07
B5 Academic achievement	−.27	.61	−.08
C1 Quality of education	.18	−.86	.25
C2 Social life	.34	−.64	.19
C3 Compensation	.26	−.75	.07
C4 Staff-student relations	.27	−.80	.17
C5 Decision making	.18	−.78	.15
D1 Guidance	.87	−.25	.13
D2 Assurance of worth	.80	−.25	−.02
D3 Social integration	.86	−.21	.09
D4 Attachment	.83	−.23	.16
D5 Nurturance	.66	−.25	.13
D6 Reliable alliance	.83	−.34	.10
E Loneliness	−.78	.46	−.16
F1 Religious fulfillment	−.09	.17	−.84
F2 Religious relationship	−.02	.11	−.87
G1 Religious well-being	.09	−.24	.95
G2 Existential well-being	.58	−.56	.25
G3 Total spiritual well-being	.34	−.44	.86

Factor intercorrelations 1 × 2 = −.28
1 × 3 = +.11
2 × 3 = −.21

TABLE 11.6. F values in a planned contrast analysis of factor scores.

Factors	F
1. Self in relationship	8.439*
2. Academic environment	27.060*
3. Religious relationships	39.481*

F .05/3; 1,150. $F = 5.89$

An attempt to obtain follow-up data at the end of the first semester in mid-year was only partially successful because of the low response rates, although the students at the University of Sydney who had replied showed little change, except for significantly decreased scores on loneliness, and an increased assurance of personal worth and social attachment ($p <$ .05).

Discussion

These results bear on macro-issues concerning students' relationships with their academic and institutional environment, and on more personal questions about social and religious relationships and feelings of well-being during a time of change and adjustment.

An analysis of the separate scales indicated that in the first weeks of their first semester, students in the small Catholic College were happier, more strongly identified with their college as an academic institution, had made an easier transition to life there, and experienced greater satisfaction with the education they were receiving, with staff-student relationships, and with their general participation in decision making, than did their counterparts at the University of Sydney. But it is not clear from these data how the Catholic College was able, so quickly, to facilitate a sense of institutional belonging and participation, heighten goal directedness towards academic achievement, and increase satisfaction with the quality of education and the social life to be found there, thereby contributing to positive feelings of well-being and happiness.

It could be that the environment of the smaller institution (with about 2,500 students) was able to motivate the students through the religious culture within which it is embedded, which facilitated an easier identification with it, compared with that among the 20,000 students at the University of Sydney. Furthermore, that the Catholic College was offering vocational training in teaching and nursing might also have helped that process, through better staff-student interaction and a more practical identification with their chosen profession. The philosophy of that College, the values shared by staff and students, and the religious involvement "in Christ's mission of teaching and healing" (*Catholic College Handbook*, 1988, p. 6), may all help to promote an explicit community ethos.

For the University of Sydney students, attachment, belongingness, and identification with the institution seemed to be particularly related to a growing sense of worth, and a lessening loneliness in its more impersonal academic setting. While the University actively promotes competence among administrative and teaching staff, the reduced opportunities for staff-student interaction makes personal contact and communication difficult.

While the University of Sydney shares professional and educational values with the Catholic College, the religious values underlying its philosophy, and the vocational emphasis that informs its training-orientation are quite different. It is clear that since "certain kinds of institutions attract certain kinds of staff and certain kinds of students" (Williams, 1982, p. 2), we can expect different institutions to be exposed to different social and environmental influences. But neither the social life scale nor the loneliness scale discriminated between students at the different institutions. Rather than loneliness itself being a problem for students, it is probably the unmet expectations about interpersonal relationships that are hardest to handle (cf. Paloutzian & Janigian, 1986). Loneliness is then a result of that lack, and the sense of well-being a consequence of rewarding social interactions. Positive social relationships that differ in type and degree of intimacy seem, therefore, to be inversely related to feelings of loneliness and alienation, and were in evidence earlier at the Catholic College than at the University.

Religious variables clearly distinguish the students at the two institutions, and relate more closely to religious and spiritual well-being than to loneliness or positive social attachments. While a person's religious beliefs or commitment generally involve "strong convictions about the nature of God, people's relationship to God, and the implications these beliefs have for people's interaction with each other" (Paloutzian & Janigian, 1986, p. 10), the Catholic College provides an environment where students can openly express and share such beliefs through self-disclosure, trust with peers, a sense of belonging, and a lessening of loneliness. The factor analysis in particular showed that religious relationships and religious fulfillment are linked directly with spiritual well-being, and not with loneliness.

Implications

In 1988, Australia had a system of higher education consisting of Universities and Colleges of Advanced Education, "with discernibly different objectives and student and staff interests" (Bartos, 1990, p. 12). By 1990, institutional amalgamations that were forced by the federal government had transformed that system from one "supported as a public good and funded on an assessment of its needs, to a system of autonomous universities which behave as private corporations in competition with each other" (Bartos, 1990). As these institutions increase in size, and come under pressure arising from the competition among them for their resources, environments will be able even less effectively to assist students' transitions into a university in a way that encourages their sense of belonging and identification. Counseling and support services for both students and staff will then become even more important in alleviating the problems that students will encounter in these new, more complex, and impersonal institutions.

Previous research has achieved several clarifications regarding religiousness and the religious variable, for example, that religion exists as both a matter of personal concern and commitment "and as an arena in which social-psychological processes operate" (Paloutzian & Janigian, 1986, p. 6). Religion is multidimensional, involving not only a mode of behavior but a system of beliefs and feelings. Vergote (1969) described it as, "a complex reality made up of beliefs, praxis and oriented feeling" (p. 10), which can be more or less central (i.e., intrinsic or extrinsic) in a person's life (Batson & Ventis, 1982), and conducive (or not) to a person's mental health (Bergin, 1983; Bergin, Masters, Richards, & Scott, 1987).

Given those clarifications as points of departure, this study brings into focus several aspects of the relationships between religion, personality, and mental health that warrant further investigation. Firstly, "religion" is preeminently an experience of relationship, consisting of an encounter between a person and the sacred or divine, in each person's response to this experience by their practice. Regardless of the forms this encounter and any practices might take, it is significant that they should involve the whole person as an intelligent and feeling being. Moreover, a person's religious responses involve the totality of their personal, natural, social, and cultural environment (or context) and as a "felt, practical relationship" (Thouless, 1971); so religion occupies an important place in the lives and experience of those who define themselves as "religious." Secondly, because of the particular nature and function of the "religious relationship" people not only refer to it but can use it existentially in times of personal change and growth, transition, or crisis to provide continuity and support, meaning and direction, and to find purpose, and examples that might facilitate their sense of well-being. The study reported here confirms the complexity and the importance of these experiences, meanings, and uses of religion (cf. Batson & Ventis, 1982).

References

Bartos, M. (1990). Further steps to a new educational order. *Australian Society*, 12–13.

Batson, C.D. & Ventis, W.L. (1982). *The religious experience*: A social-psychological perspective. New York: Oxford University Press.

Bergin, A.E. (1983). Religiosity and mental health: A critical reevaluation and meta-analysis. *Professional Psychology: Research and Practice*, *14*(2), 170–184.

Bergin, A.E., Masters, K.S., & Richards, P.S. (1987). Religiousness and mental health reconsidered: A study of an intrinsically religious sample. *Journal of Counseling Psychology*, *34*(2), 197–204.

Bradburn, N. (1969). *The structure of psychological well-being*. Chicago: Aldine.

Caiden, N. (1964). Student failure in Australian universities: A bibliographical review. *Vestes*, *7*, 35–56.

Campbell, A. (1976). Subjective measures of well-being. *American Psychologist*, *31*, 117–124.

Catholic College of Education. (1988). *Catholic College Handbook*. Sydney: Author.

Cutrona, C.E. (1982). Transition to college: Loneliness and the process of social adjustment. In L.A. Peplau & D. Perlman (Eds.), *Loneliness: A sourcebook of current theory, research and therapy* (pp. 291–309). New York: John Wiley & Sons.

Cutrona, C.E. & Russell, D.W. (1987). The provisions of social relationships and adaptation to stress. *Advances in Personal Relationships 1*, (pp. 37–67). JAI Press Inc.

Nagpal, P. & Sell, H. (1985). *Subjective well-being*. New Delhi: World Health Organization, SEARO Regional Health Paper No. 7.

Newman, F. (1971). *Report on higher education*. Department of Health, Education and Welfare. Washington, DC: U.S. Government Printing Office.

O'Dowd, W.T. (1986). Otto Rank and time-limited psychotherapy. *Psychotherapy*, *23*(1), 140–149.

Paloutzian, R.F. & Ellison, C.W. (1982). Loneliness, spiritual well-being, and the quality of life. In L.A. Peplau & D. Perlman (Eds.), *Loneliness: A sourcebook of current theory, research and therapy* (pp. 224–237). New York: John Wiley & Sons.

Paloutzian, R.F. & Janigian, A.S. (1986). Interrelationships between religiousness and loneliness. *The Psychotherapy Patient*, *2*, 3–14.

Paloutzian, R.F. & Janigian, A.S. (1987). Models and methods in loneliness research: Their status and direction. In M. Hojat & R. Crandall (Eds.), Loneliness: Theory, research and applications [Special issue]. *Journal of Social Behaviour and Personality*, *2*(2, Pt. 2), 31–36.

Russell, D., Peplau, L.A., & Cutrona, C.E. (1980). The revised UCLA loneliness scale: Con-current and discriminant validity evidence. *Journal of Personality and Social Psychology*, *39*(3), 472–480.

Starr, A.M., Betz, E.L., & Menne, J.W. (1971). *Manual: The college student satisfaction questionnaire*. Ames, IA: Central Iowa Associates.

Thouless, R.H. (1971). *An introduction to the psychology of religion* (3rd ed.). Cambridge: Cambridge University Press.

Vergote, A. (1969). *The religious man*. Dublin: Gill & Macmillan.

Walker, B. (1980). *Dimensions and Patterns of Satisfaction Amongst University Students*. Sydney: University of New South Wales, Student Counseling and Research Unit, Bulletin No. 17.

Weiss, R.S. (1974). The provisions of social relationships. In Z. Rubin (Ed.), *Doing unto others*. Englewood Cliffs, NJ: Prentice Hall.

Williams, C. (1982). *The early experiences of students on Australian University campuses*. Sydney: The University of Sydney.

Williams, C. & Pepe, T. (1983). *The early experiences of students on Australian College of Advanced Education campuses*. Sydney: The University of Sydney

12
Some Correlates of Well-being and Distress in Anglo-Jewish Women

KATE LOEWENTHAL, VALERIE AMOS, VIVIENNE GOLDBLATT, AND SEAN MULLARKEY

London Jewish women were sampled from "middle-" and "ultra"orthodox synagogue membership lists, and measures of well-being and distress, together with information on demographic and other factors, were obtained from 121 of them. For the whole sample, correlates of depression and well-being related to the wife-and-mother roles, and generally resembled the correlates that have been found in other groups of women, although the Jewish women with fewer dependent children were the more depressed. The two groups of women differed on a number of demographic characteristics, which might explain the slightly lower levels of distress and dissatisfaction in the ultraorthodox. For the middle-orthodox group, happiness relates to marriage, whereas for the ultraorthodox, happiness relates to integration into their community.

Introduction

It is now recognized that distress is not only unpleasant but dangerous for the sufferer (Brown & Harris, 1978, 1989). It is also known that in contemporary Western society, women are much more vulnerable than men to a very sinister form of distress-depression (e.g., Cochrane, 1984). Social factors are known to be very important in the etiology of distress, and it is known that the predictors and incidence of depression, for instance, differ in different groups of people, and may be affected by religious group membership (Prudo, Harris, & Brown, 1989).

Jewish groups have seldom been studied, however, although there are some data from the United States and Israel (Selavan, 1979). Fernando (1975) studied Anglo-Jewish depressed patients, but the catchment area was such that an atypical sample may have been obtained. In any case, Jewish communities are in a state of rapid transition associated with religious, educational, and occupational trends, and with migration and emigration, so the picture at the end of the 1980's is not likely to be the same as it was earlier.

This study focuses on Jewish women, and is preliminary to what will hopefully be a more thorough look at the causes of distress in the Anglo-Jewish population. We are particularly interested in the interplay between religion and the composition of the community—and the way that this in turn relates to distress—and, of course, to protection from distress. For instance, the "ultraorthodox" Jews live in small, closely-knit communities. Their religiously prescribed norm is for very large families, and the prolific woman receives a great deal of esteem, with the community organized to give a certain amount of practical support.

This nicely illustrates the interplay between religion, society, and distress factors. Having several young children to care for has been shown to make London women more vulnerable to depression, given a severe, threatening life event (Brown & Harris, 1978). But in the ultraorthodox Jewish community, values are such that the prolific woman is seen as heroic, bringing souls into the world and raising them in the religious path—rather than as a feckless increaser of the world's population and the irresponsible cause of her family's financial straits. This, and other factors to be discussed, may have a favorable effect on the self-esteem and well-being of ultraorthodox Jewish mothers of many children.

We are particularly interested in the two dominant styles of religious orthodoxy in the Anglo-Jewish community, designated as "middle-" and "ultra"orthodoxy. Those terms are umbrellas covering a heterogeneity of religious practices, recognizable to most members of Anglo-Jewry. In this study, the criterion of group membership was synagogue affiliation, and not individual levels of religious observance. So the criterion of middle-orthodoxy was affiliation to a United Synagogue, and of ultraorthodoxy, affiliation to a Union of Orthodox Hebrew Congregations synagogue.

Two thirds of Jewish households in London are affiliated with the United Synagogue. Future trends are unclear (Waterman & Kosmin, 1986) and the subject of some controversy, but it is likely that a large proportion will remain as at present, nominally orthodox and identifiably Jewish. While individual levels of religious observance vary greatly among United Synagogue members, the public image of this group is a "middle-of-the-road" Judaism.

While the proportion of households affiliated to the ultraorthodox group of synagogues (Union of Orthodox Hebrew Congregations) is approximately 5% (Waterman & Kosmin, 1986), this group is believed to be expanding rapidly by virtue of a very high birthrate, and by the addition of *Baalei Teshuvah* (returnees to Orthodox Judaism). This community professes itself to be an ethnic minority in local and national political dealings and is characterized by an assertively Jewish mode of dressing. It has many differences from the normative, middle-orthodox group, the main differences being in community structure, norms of religious observance, and social and family relationships. Probably most crucial for women are differences in the norms and attitudes to family size.

Community life among middle-orthodox may be very loose-knit, focused on the synagogue, and may be male-dominated. Synagogue membership chiefly involves a relatively small proportion of active members, from a total of hundreds or even thousands, and is perforce a matter of geographical convenience. Synagogue attendance, observance of kashrut, Sabbath, and festivals vary greatly within the middle-orthodox group. Social comparison between members of the group are therefore made in terms of how religiously observant (*frum*) individuals are.

The ultraorthodox group is characterized by a relatively uniform minimum level of religious observance. Frequent synagogue attendance (by men), kashrut, Sabbath, and festival observance are basic standards, as are full-time education of children in Jewish institutions, and adherence (by women) to religiously defined laws regarding modesty and menstruation. Men and women lead distinct and separate social lives, apart from in the home, where women may wield great matriarchal power. Home, rather than the synagogue, is the center of religious life. Social comparison is not normally made in terms of religious observance, but in terms of subgroup or sect membership, with several dozen distinct subgroups in the ultraorthodox community. Characteristically, each has it own (small) synagogue, and often schools and other institutions. Each group has its own leadership and philosophical or psychological outlook (called a *derech* or literally, "way" of serving G-d), with outward signs of group membership, such as norms of dress and religious customs, specific to the group. Synagogue membership is usually small enough for every member to know every other, and subgroup membership in the ultra-orthodox community is an important focus of social life and identity.

This study is of women only, partly because the norm for large families in the ultraorthodox community makes this an interesting group. Loewenthal (1988) found 5.1 children to date per household, although completed family size would be expected to be larger, estimated at about 7 children. Procreation is a religious duty (*mitzvah*), children are regarded as a blessing, and parents of large families are admired within the community. Note that in the middle-orthodox group, attitudes to family size resemble those of the host population, with birthrate slightly below replacement level (Waterman & Kosmin, 1986).

Kupferman (1978), an anthropologist, has estimated that the incidence of depression may be low in (ultraorthodox) Hasidic women, and suggested that this was due to the study of Hasidic philosophy, in which methods of avoiding depression, anxiety, and anger—and of obtaining a state of joy—are described. Kupferman's study did not involve clinical or psychometric assessments. We assessed several aspects of distress and well-being, using a rapid checklist measure. After discussion with a number of welfare workers in the communities under study, several factors were selected that might be expected to be associated with well-being and distress and which could be assessed with a questionnaire.

This study therefore aimed to discover, and compare some correlates of well-being, distress, and other factors in two groups of Anglo-Jewish women.

Method

Two defined groups of Anglo-Jewish women were recruited from synagogue listings. The first group was middle-orthodox, from the United synagogues, to which the majority of affiliated Anglo-Jewish households belong. The second group was ultraorthodox. Each participant filled in a brief, general form of the Multiple Affect Adjective Check List (MAACL) (Zuckerman & Lubin, 1965), which gives a rapid measure of well-being, depression, anxiety, and hostility, and answered questions about their age, marital status, children, own and husband's occupations, and levels of satisfaction with money, health, housing, and social support.

Subjects

For the middle-orthodox group, membership lists of three United synagogues were obtained after negotiations with their rabbis and other relevant officials. Since two of the synagogues were in the northwest London suburban area and the other was in the Redbridge area, the main centers of Jewish population in the Greater London area (Waterman & Kosmin, 1986) were studied. For two of these synagogues, 1 in 10 households was contacted by telephone, and the female head of household was asked if she would be willing to participate in the study. Of the 76 women who agreed to receive our questionnaires by post (plus a stamped, addressed envelope), 48 were returned. In the case of the third synagogue, officials were not willing for their members to be contacted by phone, and they agreed to send questionnaires by mail to a sample of 100 of their membership, with a covering letter from us, and another covering letter from them. Of those 100 questionnaires, 22 were returned. So 70 (of 176) middle-orthodox women returned our questionnaires, although in some cases not all the questions were answered.

For the ultraorthodox, there are published lists of all households affiliated with the Union of Orthodox Hebrew Congregations for the two main areas with high concentrations of ultraorthodox Jews in north and northwest London. One in 10 households were contacted by telephone until a total of 100 women had agreed to participate (50 from Northwest

London and 50 from North London). Fifty-one questionnaires were re-turned, with little missing information (51%).

In cases of failure to return our questionnaires, where subjects had been originally contacted by phone a follow-up call was made, which yielded a few more returns that have been included in the above totals.

While the representativeness of our sample is uncertain, we know of only one systematic difference between responders and nonresponders. All ultraorthodox returnees were still-married, though our lists showed approximately 10% as female heads of household in the ultraorthodox community, most of whom are widows, with a few divorcees and virtually no single women. All of those women declined to participate or failed to return their questionnaires. Generally, there was a degree of suspicion and unwillingness, which was anticipated because it has been reported by other researchers on these groups. So our recruitment methods were selected for their economy rather than their effectiveness. A final blow was a major disruption of postal services at the time of our study, and we have some definite evidence that questionnaires were lost in the post. We were able to put right only the cases we heard of, and a considerable loss is likely because of those difficulties. So the low response rate comes as no surprise, but we were pleased to be told by others currently doing research on Orthodox Jewish groups that the response rate we got was higher than is usual in research on this type of community.

Materials

All subjects received a covering letter explaining the purpose of the study, and given phone numbers to contact if further information or discussion was required. The questionnaire asked for details of age, occupation of head of household, marital status, unpaid and paid occupations of the woman and (where applicable) her husband, synagogue affiliation, details of children, and visual analogue scales to indicate levels of satisfaction with money, own health, family's health, housing, and level of support from family, friends, or community. The brief, general form of the Multiple Affect Adjective Check List (MAACL) (Zuckerman & Lubin, 1965) was used, and scored for depression, hostility, anxiety, well-being, and response bias.

Results

Table 12.1 summarizes the means and standard deviations for the variables studied, and significant differences between the two groups. Table 12.2 shows significant correlates and predictor variables for the depression, hostility, anxiety, and well-being measures for all the subjects. Since

TABLE 12.1. Means and standard deviations.

Variable	All		Middleorthodox		Ultraorthodox	
	Mean	SD	Mean	SD	Mean	SD
*Age (1 = 20s . . . 6 = 70s)	3.55	1.52	3.89	1.57	3.06	1.30
SES (1–6)	2.21	1.54	2.15	1.44	2.27	1.63
*Married (1/0)	0.82	0.39	0.67	0.47	1.00	0
*Divorced (1/0)	0.10	0.31	0.19	0.40	0	0
*Widowed (1/0)	0.07	0.26	0.12	0.33	0	0
*Live alone (0/1)	0.82	0.39	0.67	0.47	1.00	0
*Housewife role (1/0)	0.83	0.38	0.75	0.44	0.92	0.28
*Mother role (1/0)	.56	0.50	0.40	0.49	0.78	0.42
Work 1 (3–0)	0.78	1.05	0.78	1.11	0.78	0.99
Work 2 (1/0)	0.41	0.49	0.40	0.49	0.43	0.50
*Children (1/0)	0.83	0.38	0.73	0.45	0.96	0.20
*No. Ch. <16	1.26	2.21	0.38	0.75	2.42	2.87
*No. Ch. <5	0.41	0.86	0.14	0.53	0.75	1.06
Husband working (2–0)	1.49	0.78	1.42	0.82	1.55	0.74
Husband helps (1/0)	0.33	0.47	0.35	0.48	0.31	0.47
Vol. work (1/0)	0.20	0.40	0.14	0.35	0.25	0.44
*Retired (1/0)	0.26	0.44	0.37	0.49	0.10	0.31
Dissat. money (0–40)	16.81	9.52	17.03	9.70	16.87	9.61
*Dissat. health	13.12	10.68	15.78	11.88	9.68	7.53
Dissat. f. health	10.11	8.11	11.54	8.91	8.40	6.57
Dissat. housing	9.56	8.61	10.88	9.42	8.38	8.36
Dissat. support	11.00	8.83	12.14	9.89	10.13	8.26
Depression (0–24)	6.73	4.88	7.41	5.26	5.86	4.19
Hostility (0–14)	5.85	3.41	5.88	3.38	5.89	3.48
Anxiety (0–10)	3.05	2.36	3.08	2.56	3.07	2.05
Well-being (0–17)	8.51	5.14	8.09	4.75	9.02	5.68
Total (R. BIAS) (0–48)	14.56	7.53	14.41	6.80	14.86	8.53

Differences between middle and ultraorthodox were tested, using chi-square for dichotomous data and one-way ANOVAs otherwise. Significant differences between the two groups have been indicated by an asterisk * next to the variable name.

the two groups differed on several demographic and other variables, it was necessary to supplement the simple correlational analyses with further analyses to take out the effects of confounding variables. Forced-entry multiple regression analyses were therefore carried out, with the distress and well-being measures as dependent variables. The results of these multiple regression analyses must be viewed with caution, since the number of cases involved is rather small.

Intercorrelations between the different well-being and distress measures were generally high and negative, consistent with previous reports on the MAACL (Zuckerman & Lubin, 1963), although they are not reported here. Table 12.3 summarizes the main correlates of depression and well-being, and suggests that for middle-orthodox women, happiness relates to marriage, provided the husband is not retired. For the ultraorthodox, the

TABLE 12.2. Depression: significant correlations, and significant *t*-values on the regression analyses (all values significant at $p < .05$; values marked * significant at $p < .01$).

Variable	All		Middle-orthodox		Ultraorthodox	
	r	reg	*r*	reg	*r*	reg
Age	.21					
SES	.28		.36			
Married	−.34		−.37			
Divorced	.34		.41			
Widowed	.23					
Live alone	.42		.43			
Housewife role	−.21					
Mother role	−.18					
Work 1						
Work 2		2.39				
Children		−2.08				
No. Ch. <16	−.17					
No. Ch. <5						
Husband working					−.28	
Husband helps		2.78				
Vol. work	−.17					
Retired	.28	4.39		3.48		
Orthodox	−.18					
Dissat. money	.24		.33			
Dissat. health	.34	3.99	.35		.38	
Dissat. f. health					.44	
Dissat. housing	.25	−2.99	.32			
Dissat. support	.30		.30		.47	2.07

TABLE 12.3. Main correlates of depression and well-being.

	Depression	Well-being
Whole sample	Not working	Working
	Fewer children	
	Husband not helping at home	Husband helps at home
	Retired head of household	Not retired
	Dissatisfied with health	Satisfied with health
	Dissatified with housing	Satisfied with housing
	Not married	Married
Middle Orthodox	Retired head of household	Not retired
	Not married	
Ultraorthodox	Dissatisfaction with social support	
		Low socioeconomic status
		Husband does voluntary work

(Anxiety showed a similar pattern to depression, and hostility had very few correlates.)

pattern of variables suggests that happiness relates to integration into, and status within the community.

Of the possible predictive effect of combinations of variables, the only one selected for examination was a combination of large numbers of dependent children and inadequate income, which has been said to be very distressing. We looked at this effect in the ultraorthodox group, where the large number of children allows it to be tested. While neither family size nor money dissatisfaction by itself relates to distress among the ultraorthodox, family size (as the number of children under 16) *and* money dissatisfaction show quite strongly that the more children, the greater the dissatisfaction with money ($r = +.38, p < .01$). But the two variables combined failed to predict depression.

Discussion

In this discussion we will concentrate on the well-being and depression measures. As noted, they were strongly and negatively related, and tended to be associated (in opposite directions) with the same variables. Of the other distress measures, hostility showed little relationship with most variables studied, and the pattern of relationships shown by anxiety was similar in many respects to that shown by depression.

Correlates of Well-being and Distress in the Whole Sample

Virtually every variable studied relates to at least one of the distress measures in the correlational analysis. These variables had, of course, been selected on the basis of their expected association with well-being and distress. Many of those relationships are consistent with other findings of the effects of old age, retirement and unemployment, social class, and dissatisfaction with money, health, housing, and social support. Although several clusters of associations make particular sense in the context of the values of the communities under study, in one case they conflict with the direction of correlations found in other populations. This concerns the association between motherhood or childcare and well-being or low depression. Brown and Harris (1978) have shown that having several young children at home is a vulnerability factor for depression in urban British women, while childlessness has also been shown to be associated with high scores on distress for married women (Calhoun & Hennessey, 1988). Certainly in our ultraorthodox communities there are strong social pressures towards childbearing and, indeed, for very large families. This pressure is largely missing in the middle-orthodox, but in both communities (especially perhaps in the ultraorthodox) childless women occupy a marginal status, albeit a degree less marginal than those not married. We cannot tell whether an association between family size and lack of depression is due to the effect of not being childless, or shows the improved morale and status of the prolific women in the more orthodox groups. Consistent with Brown and Harris (1978), who showed that employment outside the home protected urban British women against depression, we found that working is associated with higher well-being and lower depression.

Another notable cluster of associations relates to marital status, since the married women tend to show high well-being and low depression. This effect is consistent with other findings (Cochrane, 1984) and it is predictable from the high value attached to the married state in Jewish life, which could be related to the extraordinary significance of the home in Jewish religious life, and the sanctity attached to it in the rabbinic tradition. In the ultraorthodox community, spinsterhood is almost non-existent, and sadly, widows and divorcees may feel that their status is marginal. Several widows approached in the ultraorthodox community were reluctant to participate because they "did not see how anyone could be interested in them." Depression may thus be "caused" by their not being married, especially because of its associated lack of status. An alternative causal interpretation is that the more cheerful women get and stay married, but we think this less likely, especially since the bulk of our not-now-married subjects were widows, to whom that explanation is not really applicable.

The married relationship seems to be important in other ways, too. Perceived helpfulness by husbands goes along with higher well-being and lower depression, and having a retired—and presumably often demoralized—husband to cope with, goes along with lower well-being and higher depression. This latter effect turns out to be particularly important for the middle-orthodox.

Dissatisfaction with health and housing—but not with money and social support—were also related to depression and well-being for the sample as a whole. Baker's (1990) research on Anglo-Jewish women in mid-life indicates that right across the religious spectrum, and regardless of whether they have careers or not, Anglo-Jewish wives attach primary importance to their roles as homemakers, wives, and mothers. Health and housing are therefore important to a woman's view of herself as a homemaker, which is an essential and primary corollary of her identity as a Jewish woman. If she has fears for her home, and fears for her physical health, which is essential to her ability to run the home, then her self-hood, or at least the most salient aspect of her identity, is threatened. This may explain why other dissatisfactions (with money or family health) are not crucial for well-being and depression, since they do not threaten identity in the same way.

The total picture that emerges shows the importance to the well-being of these women of their central role in family life. Contrary to evidence from other populations, larger numbers of dependent children may have a protective effect against depression. So too do other variables reflecting the extent to which women can carry out their traditional and normative "foundation of the home" role—which is highly regarded in Orthodox Jewish circles. The apparently cheering effect of working outside the home is not inconsistent with these findings, since in traditional Judaism, part of a woman's role in the family has been to assume economic responsibility, and she has been, and may still be the main breadwinner.

Comparisons of the Two Groups

Table 12.1 shows that the two groups were comparable in social class and in the number of women working outside the home, as well as in their husband's employment and his helpfulness at home. But the middle-orthodox were a little older than the ultraorthodox and had a somewhat higher proportion of those who had retired.

As expected, there are major differences between the groups with respect to the likelihood of being married, number of children, and in the profession of the housewife. (The data with respect to the number of children were disappointing, with many women being vague about that number, which suggests that those we have are an underestimate, at least for the ultraorthodox, many of whom are reluctant on religious grounds to state the number of their children. Furthermore, poor questionnaire design made it appear that we were only asking about school-age and pre-school children.) All the differences were, however, in the expected direction, and the ultraorthodox were more likely than the middle-orthodox to be married, have more children, and so on.

The middle-orthodox were somewhat less satisfied than the ultraorthodox, their depression was a little higher, and well-being a little lower, but not significantly so. The reported levels of anxiety and hostility were similar in both groups, and those differences were only significant in the case of satisfaction with money and health. On the correlational analyses, Table 12.2 shows that depression is less likely in the more orthodox, and that the other well-being and distress measures do not relate to orthodoxy. These differences in morale may be due to confounding stress factors that are hard to disentangle (in the present data) or to the use of religious cognitions, community support, and possibly other features by the ultra-orthodox group.

In general, comparisons between the two groups show that the middle-orthodox are older, more likely to have a head of household who is retired, and less likely to be still-married and to have dependent children. These factors have already been seen to be associated with low well-being in this sample, which means that the differences between these groups in levels of well-being, distress, and satisfaction may simply be confounded by the background factors on which they differ, and the effect of their religious attachment. Yet some of these background factors on which the two groups differ form part of the ultraorthodox way of life, with its emphasis on stable monogamy and large families.

The difficulty in interpreting differences when the variables are confounded does not apply when we look at the correlates of well-being or distress in the separate groups. In the middle-orthodox group, the most important effect was their married status, which is related to low depression and higher well-being. Although this did not appear important in the ultraorthodox group, that could be simply because all the ultraorthodox women who replied were now married. In the general population, marriage "protects" against depression, but less strongly for women than for men (Cochrane, 1984). Although we have no direct evidence, we suspect that marriage may be more "protective" for Jewish than for non-Jewish women. Alternatively, an unmarried status may make Jewish women more vulnerable to depression than are non-Jewish women.

In the middle-orthodox group the other important correlate of depression was the retired status of the head of household (usually the husband). This may be partly a consequence of financial difficulties. (The correlation between retirement and money dissatisfaction was significant.) Another likely explanation lies in the loss of status and morale of the married couple when the husband retires.

The three most important correlates of high well-being and low depression in the ultraorthodox are satisfaction with their level of social support, low socioeconomic status, and voluntary work by the husband. These may collectively indicate the importance of integration into, and status within the ultraorthodox community. Satisfaction with the level of support speaks for itself, and its absence indicates that the woman does not feel integrated into a community which is supposed to be characterised by high levels of concern and practical assistance. Low occupational status for the ultraorthodox may mean high status within the ultraorthodox community, since professionals of relatively high socioeconomic status, such as accountants, lawyers, and academics, are not as well integrated and may not be as highly regarded within the ultraorthodox community as are those whose education and careers have been totally within their religious community. For instance, many married men continue "learning" in specially designated institutions of religious learning (*kollelim*). They are well respected in the community as scholarly and pious, but would appear low on the socioeconomic scale, as would "butchers" or ritual slaughterers (*schochetim*), whose calling demands considerable erudition in Jewish law and a pious reputation. Voluntary work by the husband is very highly regarded in the ultraorthodox community, since an *askan* (who busies himself with communal welfare) is a dignified and respected figure.

When we look at the correlates and predictors of well-being and distress in the middle- and ultraorthodox groups we see some important differences. For both groups, there is evidence that the husband's status is important, though how this is determined differs, since among the middle-orthodox, status for the husband derives from working and earning, while for the ultraorthodox it is in terms of the norms and values of their community.

We have already described the general differences in communal organization between the two groups. Our analyses suggest that the different correlates of well-being and depression in each of them may be explained in those terms, and that ultraorthodox communities comprise small, cohesive groups, whose norms, attitudes, religious values, and support systems may function well to protect an integrated member against distress. But alas for the more marginal members!

Conclusions

Our results show that of great importance for Jewish women's sense of well-being is their sense of competence in carrying out a pivotal role in their family. The happier women are married, have more dependent children, work, have a husband who helps at home, and are satisfied with their health and housing. Although the middle- and ultraorthodox groups differ in a number of demographic characteristics, and appear to differ in their correlates of well-being and depression, these differences mask an underlying similarity in having a husband, and in the importance of his status for the wife's happiness.

Our data did not permit any serious causal analysis. We have almost no evidence on provoking agents, and none on the sequence of events, difficulties, or symptoms (Brown & Harris, 1978), though we have identified some probable vulnerability factors. Our study shows that what makes Jewish women happy may at least partly result from the Jewish community structure, and its attitudes and values.

Acknowledgments. Grateful thanks to the following for advice, help, and encouragement: Lady Amelie Jakobovits, Office of the Chief Rabbi; Tirril Harris, Medical Research Unit, Royal Holloway and Bedford New College; Judy Usiskin & others, Federation of Jewish Family Services; Dr. Tali Loewenthal, Myrna Potash & others, Lubavitch Foundation & Lubavitch Women's Organization; Rabbi Michoel Posen, Agudas Yisroel Community Services; Adrienne Baker & other members of the Family, Religion and Identity research group, Kings College & Royal Holloway and Bedford New College; Marleena Shmool & others, Board of Deputies Research Unit; Professor Sigmund Prais; Dr. Steve Miller, City University; Dr. Katherine Parkes, University of Oxford; Professor Laurie Brown, University of New South Wales; Professor Tony Winefield,

University of Adelaide Professor Geoffrey Alderman, Royal Holloway and Bedford New College; Dr. Robert West & Rosemary Westley, Psychology Department, RHBNC; the Rabbis and synagogue officials of the Finchley, Newbury Park and South Hampstead synagogues, and finally and most importantly, to the women who so kindly took the time to fill in and return our forms and questionnaires.

References

Baker, A. (1990). Role perceptions of Anglo-Jewish wives in mid-life. PhD, Kings College, London.

Brown, G. & Harris, T. (1978). *The social origins of depression*. London: Tavistock.

Brown, G. & Harris, T. (Eds.). (1989). *Life events and illness. A reference book for the caring professionals*. London: Unwin Hyman.

Calhoun, V. & Hennessey, T. (1988). The psychological adjustment of women experiencing infertility. *British Journal of Medical Psychology*, *61*, 137–140.

Cochrane, R. (1984). *The social creation of mental illness*. London: Longman.

Fernando, S.J.M. (1975). A cross-cultural study of some familial and social factors in depressive illness. *British Journal of Psychiatry*, *127*, 46–53.

Kupferman, J. (1978). *The mistaken body*. London: Paladin.

Loewenthal, K. (1988). Patterns of religious development and experience in Habad-hasidic women. *Journal of Psychology and Judaism*, *12*, 4–20.

Prudo, R., Harris, T., & Brown, G. (1989). Psychiatric disorder in a rural and an urban population: 3. Social integration and the morphology of affective disorder. *Psychological Medicine*, *14*, 327–345.

Selavan, I. (1979). Behaviour disorders of the Jews: A review of the literature. *Journal of Psychology and Judaism*, *4*, 117–125.

Surtees, P., Ingham, J., Kreitman, N., Miller, P., & Sashidrahan, S. (1983). Psychiatric disorder in women from an Edinburgh community: Associations with demographic factors. *British Journal of Psychiatry*, *142*, 238–246.

Waterman, S. & Kosmin, B. (1986). *British Jewry in the eighties: A statistical and geographical study*. London: Board of Deputies of British Jews.

Zuckerman, M. & Lubin, B. (1965). *Manual for the Multiple Affect Adjective Check List*. San Diego, CA: Edits.

13
Women Religious Professionals and Stress

CAROLE A. RAYBURN, LEE J. RICHMOND, AND LYNN ROGERS

Clergywomen, fairly new to the religious scene, are still feeling their way to define a role for themselves in the previously all-male religious hierarchies. Although women have been involved in clerical roles within some settings for over 50 years, the fact that as a class they have been subjected to much discrimination, and even given a derogatory image in other ecclesiastical surroundings, has left an unpleasant and unhealthy situation for those who would be religious professionals. This in turn has led to much stress, whether denied or expressed and recognized, among women clergy. Yet the very negative picture of women painted by early church theologians such as Augustine, Chrysostom, and Luther (Daly, 1973; O'Faolain & Martines, 1973) and by the papal sacred congregation for the doctrine of the faith in recent times (1976) may have discouraged women from looking realistically at the stress to which they are subjected. Such recognition might cause them to run the risk of appearing even more imperfect—though entirely human—to the male enclave that still holds some hope of eliminating women from religious professionalism and positions of leadership. Nonetheless, their stress serves to handicap these women in accomplishing all they might, in their roles as religious professionals. They must be able to recognize more adequately, deal with, and even accept some stress in their newly carved positions in order to function optimally.

Background

It would seem that nuns are among the first women who, as a group, were allowed to serve as religious professionals, yet it is ironic that they exist in these roles in an ecclesiastical setting that has been ultraconservative in its view of women. But nuns do not have permission from the Papacy to engage in many of the roles fulfilled by Protestant and Jewish clergywomen. Nor are nuns seen by the male hierarchy in quite the threatening way that some clergywomen are viewed. Much might be learned by comparing nuns to clergywomen for their roles and levels of stress.

While Roman Catholic nuns have been part of the religious scene for some time, clergywomen are new to the religious establishment. Nuns, who have usually worked in schools and hospitals, are traditionally viewed within the Roman Catholic Church as more like laity than clergy. Until recently nuns were not seen by Catholic priests or brothers, as their male counterparts, and by parishioners, as equal to or competitors of males in title, role, or other functions within the church. In contrast, Protestant and Jewish clergywomen have typically been regarded as challengers to the males in their settings, going against the traditions of established religious mores or beliefs.

What do these differences in roles and role models mean in terms of stress, strain, and coping mechanisms for nuns and clergywomen? Do nuns experience less stress and strain than clergywomen because they are seen as less of a threat? Do clergywomen sense a backlash from conservative members of their religious groups, or become stressed because their work structures are geared to male religious experiences or expressions of spirituality? This study attempted to answer some of these questions, by examining stress in women religious professionals.

Method

Altogether, 51 nuns, 45 Reform women rabbis (one less than the total number of women rabbis in the United States and Canada with synagogue or Hillel pulpits at the time of the study), 32 female Episcopal priests, 45 United Methodist clergywomen, 45 Presbyterian clergywomen and 36 female seminarians drawn from United Methodist and Episcopalian seminaries were studied. They were matched on age, years on the job and, in the case of the clergywomen, on pulpit assignment. They were drawn as volunteers in a stratified sampling to represent the denominations which have women religious professionals.

Procedure

All subjects completed Osipow and Spokane's (1981) Occupational Environment Scales, Personal Strain Questionnaire, and Personal Resources Questionnaire. These are paper-and-pencil questionnaires in which respondents indicate the stress, strain, and coping resources present in their lives. They also completed a 16-item Religion and Stress Questionnaire (Rayburn & Richmond, 1982) especially designed to study stress in religious professionals, which allows not only "yes" and "no" responses but essay-type explanations as well. In each group studied, 10% were interviewed in a structured fashion, for further clarification of their stresses.

Statistical Comparisons

The significance of differences between the various groups was evaluated by t tests.

Results

Nuns, the most traditional group in terms of their roles, as well as the oldest group historically, had the lowest overall scores on stress and strain and the highest scores on personal resources for coping with stress and strain. Reform rabbis, as the least traditional group, had the highest overall score on stress and strain and the lowest overall score on personal coping resources. In overall stress scores, the next lowest to the nuns were the female seminarians, followed by the Episcopalian priests, then the Presbyterian ministers, with United Methodist ministers occupying the next-to-the-highest position. In the next-to-lowest overall strain scores came the Episcopalians, then the United Methodists and the Presbyterians, while next-to-highest were the seminarians. In terms of personal coping resources, from the lowest to highest were the rabbis, Presbyterians, seminarians, Episcopalians, United Methodists, and then the nuns.

The extreme scoring groups were compared on the Osipow and Spokane scales (1981). Their Occupational Environment Scale measures six subcategories, covering role overload, responsibility, role ambiguity, role boundary, role insufficiency, and physical environment. On the first three of these scales, and on the total measure of occupational environment, the nuns scored significantly lower than the rabbis ($p < .001$). A significant difference was also found for the role boundary measure ($<.05$), suggesting that the rabbis experience their occupational environment as more stressful than did the nuns.

The Personal Strain Questionnaire, which indicates vocational, psychological, interpersonal, and physical strain, showed that rabbis experience significantly more strain than nuns in the vocational, psychological, and interpersonal areas. Furthermore, the nuns showed significantly more coping resources than rabbis ($<.001$), as measured by the Personal Resources Questionnaire, especially in physical, rational, and cognitive coping ($<.001$), and in recreation.

Compared to the other groups, rabbis suffered the most stress and strain, and they scored higher than the Episcopalians on role boundary and total occupational environment (both $< .01$), on vocational strain ($<.001$), role overload ($<.05$) and psychological strain ($<.05$).

When the Episcopal and Presbyterian clergywomen were compared, the Presbyterians were higher on vocational strain (<.001) and role boundary (<.05), and lower on stress from the physical environment (<.05). Presbyterian clergywomen were lower than rabbis on role overload (<.01), stress from the physical environment (<.05), and interpersonal strain (<.05), while the United Methodists had more stress from the physical environment than the Presbyterians (<.05), and better physical coping resources than the Presbyterians (<.05). Episcopalians and United Methodists had only one significant difference on role boundary, with the United Methodists being more stressed (<.01).

In the Religion and Stress Questionnaire, rabbis scored significantly higher than the United Methodists in the judgment that female seminarians have a greater need to excel than their male counterparts (<.05). The rabbis also scored lower than Episcopalians (<.001), United Methodists (<.05), and Presbyterians (<.001) in their judgments that women in religious settings do not have equal opportunities in job recruitment and hiring. While all these clergywomen think women get blamed for wanting nontraditional work, the rabbis realized this less than the United Methodists or Presbyterians (<.001). While the clergywomen prefer to use their birth names and gender-fair language, rabbis lead in birth name preference, especially when compared to the Protestant clergywomen as a group.

Nuns were less sensitive overall to issues concerning stress over women's participation in religious leadership than the Protestants and rabbis. In general, the nuns were only more sensitive to these issues when compared to the female seminarians. When compared to the rabbis, nuns were more likely to see female leaders in predominantly male enterprises being blamed for defying the establishment (<.001), and they were more likely than the rabbis to see women experiencing stress from institutional and personal pressures in work. The nuns were less positive than rabbis about reducing gender-bound language in church or synagogue texts and hymnals (<.001), in planning to use inclusive language for men and women in their religious setting (<.001), and less positive about women using their birth names (<.001). The seminarians were the next most insensitive to the stresses on women religious professionals.

Among the Protestant clergywomen, the United Methodists were less sensitive than the Presbyterians to women not having equal opportunities for recruitment interviews and actual hiring on church or synagogue staffs (<.01). On that issue, the Episcopalians were more sensitive than the United Methodists (<.01), while the Methodists were more likely to see their setting accepting women using their birth names than the Episcopalians (<.05). In addition, more Methodists than Presbyterians preferred using their birth names (<.05). Episcopalians were less sensitive to the blame attached to women leaders than Methodists (<.01) or Presbyterians (<.05).

Discussion

Nuns occupy a traditional place within a religious establishment that maintains the status quo. Although many of the nuns expressed activist and even feminist leanings, the church encourages the status quo and the nuns project an image of subservience in a traditional female role. Although some may be striving toward more priestly functions or roles, such changes would be tantamount to revising the hierarchical structure at a time when the Pope has reaffirmed his patriarchy. While seminarians often live in communities, nuns live in community with other women, for long periods of time. While nuns would not have to coexist on coed seminary campuses or to experience the stresses and strains such living might entail, they have a better chance to maintain an "old-girl-network." From this background, it is not surprising that nuns demonstrate the lowest stress from their occupational environment, the lowest strain overall, and the highest overall personal coping resources. But compared to other women religious professionals, nuns were less sensitive to the issues about women that produce stress and strain in a still non-feminist world. It is possible that, given a growing interest in the groups which promote a priesthood inclusive of women, such as the Women's Ordination Conference and the National Coalition of American Nuns, nuns wander between the traditional and contemporary worlds' concerns for the role of women in religious leadership and may have to deny or suppress much of what is happening in today's world, to survive within the framework of their religious establishments. Not only were they least likely to be offended by changes in language, they were the least positive in planning to use inclusive language in their own work or to favor gender-fair language in church texts and hymnals.

Women seminarians as clergy-in-training have not yet gotten into the full-time work force of religious professionals. Perhaps they too have a need to deny and suppress their frustrations and anger in having to function in a patriarchal system, not totally accepting the equality of women in religious roles. Goldsmith and Ekhardt (1981) reported that women seminarians were stressed by the unrealistic expectations that others place upon them. Furthermore, Hardesty (1979) suggested that the attitudes and language used in seminary become more sexist as the numbers of women there grows, so that both women and men are stressed.

Among the Protestant women, Episcopalians and Presbyterians occupied a middle position on occupational environment stress, while the United Methodists and Presbyterians were in the middle on overall strain. Being out in the religious "marketplace," having been through seminary, they may have given up some of their idealism and optimistic hopes about men and women functioning together as equals in religious leadership. They have probably accepted the stress and strain of being in an environment where they must daily prove themselves to a congregation that may refuse to let women celebrate the Eucharist, or to senior pastors who may see them as competitors or inferiors. They may be resigned to waiting for the time when clergywomen will be appreciated by all. Considering the quite recent acceptance of female Episcopalian priests, it is noteworthy that they showed less stress, and less strain than both the United Methodists and Presbyterians.

The female Reform rabbis had the image of being the least traditional of women religious professionals. Yet they are constantly aware that, to remain on a synagogue staff, they must please their congregations, and maintain an image of the dedicated, hard-working, and scholarly religious leader—one who may neglect adequate relaxation, rest, and vacation time. As a group, these rabbis were sensitive to the overall stresses caused by prejudiced attitudes toward women clergy, and seem more open about their thoughts and feelings, and willing to deal with their stresses. But they do not have the social support, role models, and recreational or relaxational opportunities to lower such stress and strain.

Conclusion

To have women as professionals in the religious work force is still relatively new. Such a change has brought stress and strain, and a need for adequate coping. Women are still struggling with their roles as priests, rabbis, ministers, and even as nuns and seminarians, caught in the middle of this changing tide. Some of the stress derives from the newness, the excitement, and creativity of more inclusive roles for religious believers. Other stress, however, depends on wear and tear and is destructive, leading to physical, vocational, psychological, and interpersonal strain. Psychotherapists, counselors, and church or synagogue officials and administrators need to be fully attuned to the problems faced by these women religious professionals. A greater awareness and understanding of them should afford insight into how to help them lower their stress, and increase their coping resources.

Acknowledgment. This study was supported in part by a grant from the Educational Foundation Program of the American Association of University Women.

References

Daly, M. (1973). *Beyond God the father*. Boston: Beacon Press.
Goldsmith, W.M. & Ekhardt, B.N. (1981). *Personality differences between seminarians and secular education students*. Paper presented at the annual meeting of the American Psychological Association. Los Angeles, CA.

Hardesty, N. (1979 February 14). Women and the seminaries. *Christian Century*, 96, 122–123.

O'Faolain, J. & Martines, L. (Eds.). (1973). *Not in God's image.* New York: Harper and Row.

Osipow, S.H. & Spokane, A.R. (1981). *The Occupational Environment Scales, Personal Strain Questionnaire and Personal Resources Questionnaire*, Form E-2. Columbus, OH: Marathon Consulting and Press.

Rayburn, C.A. & Richmond, L.J. (1982). *Religion and Stress Questionnaire.* Washington, DC: Copyright Office.

Sacred Congregation for the Doctrine of the Faith (1976). *Declaration on the Question of the Admission of Women to the Ministerial Priesthood.* Washington, DC: United States Catholic Conference.

14
Welfare Policies, Religious Commitment, and Happiness

Thorleif Pettersson

The relationship between an expanding welfare state and its citizens' participation in voluntary organizations, including the churches, can be interpreted in different ways. Some assume a negative relationship, so that the expanding welfare state generates civil privatism or narcissism, and individuals become increasingly removed from the public sphere and from voluntary organizations. Others depict the welfare state as encouraging participation in voluntary organizations. Since voluntary associations are considered necessary channels for the implementation of state policies, the welfare state is expected to promote strong and active voluntary organizations; others have linked the welfare state's expansion to the rise of new social movements. These movements, especially feminism, and the ecological and peace movements, are assumed to emerge in response to an unprecedented state penetration into many spheres of private life (for a review with special regard for religious organizations, see Wuthnow & Nass, 1988).

Religious organizations are, of course, not the only voluntary organizations. Therefore a discussion of the relationship between the expanding welfare state and voluntary organizations must not be limited to religious organizations. Although arguments could be advanced for choosing religious organizations as a proper context for testing this issue (Wuthnow & Nass, 1988), it should be acknowledged that different kinds of voluntary organizations show different relations to the expanding welfare state. In Sweden, for example, a country usually considered to be a welfare society, "ideological" organizations (with affiliations that reflect particular attitudes, norms, and convictions) have declined, while "identity" associations that depend on either/or types of human characteristics such as sex, and "interaction" associations that foster strivings for self-realization within a collective setting, expanded during the heyday of the Swedish welfare state. During the course of the postwar Swedish welfare society "movements whose rationale is based on composite ideology are on a downhill course, whereas those founded on identity and the desire to socialize and for recreation, have gained momentum" (Engberg, 1986). Relationships between the welfare state and a growing civil privatism, narcissism, and an experience of alienation are therefore complex.

Likewise, relationships between religious commitment and the believers' subjective appreciations of their lives are equally complex. Numerous studies of religion and mental health or disorder, and of religion and experiences of alienation, have yielded divergent results. Despite the theoretical confusion, this paper once again addresses the general question of the ways in which religious commitment relates to life situation, evaluation, and appreciation. That high-quality cross-national interview data are not often used by social scientists of religion is the excuse for presenting another discussion of this topic. As for theory, the social-psychological view advanced here assumes that welfare policies are secularizing and that the implementation of such policies may, in a certain sense, be detrimental to religious commitment as a source of subjective well-being and happiness. That the implementation of welfare policies is a necessary condition for many other aspects of psychological well-being is of course not to be disputed!

Welfare Policies and Religious Values

In a number of writings, Ronald Inglehart (e.g., 1977, 1981, 1982, 1984, 1985) contends that the basic value priorities of Western people are changing as Western societies move into a postindustrial era. The direction of their value shift can be summarized as a move from "Materialism" towards "Post-Materialism." Among younger generations, an increasing proportion adheres to "Post-Materialist" values instead of Materialism. That view is based on two key hypotheses: (a) *the scarcity hypothesis* (related to Maslow's need theory), which assumes that people value most highly the things that are scarce and (b) *the socialization hypothesis*, which assumes that adults' longitudinally stable values reflect conditions that prevailed during their formative preadult years. Taken together, these hypotheses imply that, as a result of rapid economic and social development, rising levels of public education, the absence of direct war experiences, and the expansion of mass media after World War II, postwar generations have developed a Post-Materialist value system. In contrast to prewar generations whose safety and sustenance needs were less properly satisfied during their formative years, the younger Post-Materialists should give a higher priority to the fulfilment of social and self-actualization needs (aesthetic, intellectual, belonging, and esteem). The accompanying change in basic value priorities then leads to a decline in the legitimacy of institutional religion and traditional Judeo-Christian values and norms, hierarchial authority, and social institutions. Cosmopolitanism replaces localism: Moral permissiveness replaces moral strictness. Man (sic) is viewed as just one species among others in a holistic ecological system, and not as a creature of specific worth, superior to the rest of nature.

With preserved and possibly enhanced levels of welfare policies and socioeconomic development, the percentage of Post-Materialists should gradually increase. As the older prewar and predominantly Materialist cohorts die, the younger postwar generations, with their trend towards Post-Materialism, will constitute an increasing proportion of the population. Inglehart thus advances the following explanation (Inglehart, 1984):

All of these changes are related to a common concern: the need for a sense of security that religion and fixed, absolute cultural norms have traditionally provided. In the decades since World War II, the emergence of unprecedentedly high levels of economic prosperity, and the relatively high levels of social security provided by the welfare state, have contributed to a decline in the prevailing sense of vulnerability. For the general public, one's fate is no longer so heavily influenced by unpredictable and unknown forces as it once was. . . . [T]his fact has been conducive to the spread of secular and Post-Materialist orientations that place less emphasis on traditional religious and cultural norms—especially as these norms conflict with individual self-expression.

This theory suggests that the implementation of welfare policies yields a change in value systems and that this value shift can be generally understood as a process of secularization. In the present context, secularization is understood as a continuous decrease in the proportion of the general population adhering to the Christian faith. With welfare policies in place, successive age cohorts become less and less committed to traditional Christian values and norms, and more Post-Materialist and secularized.

It should be noted that although Inglehart's explanation seems to be based on a kind of deprivation-compensation theory, most of those approaches to religion have failed to find empirical support (Spilka, Hood, & Gorsuch, 1985, p. 234).

Using the labels "traditional-conservative" and "radical-secular," Harding, Phillips, and Fogarty (1986) broadened the scope of the argument and suggested a link with theories of conservatism, in the "tendency to exhibit resistance to change, and to seek out and prefer traditional and conventional values, goals and behaviour." Harding et al. also questioned Inglehart's original explanation of the value system change. "No doubt, the relative affluence and physical security of recent decades has been instrumental in the apparent shift in values, but it is likely that additional explanations can be found in the many other changes, both cultural and economic, that have taken place within post-war Western Europe" (Harding et al., 1986, p. 107). So Harding et al. proposed a broader explanation than Inglehart. Welfare policies in the narrow sense are therefore not the only villain in the piece. Nor is that really Inglehart's contention.

Flanagan (1982, p. 408) argued that "value orientations are changing along four dimensions: (a) from austerity to self-indulgence; (b) from piety and self-discipline to secularism and permissiveness; (c) from conformity to independence; and (d) from devotion to authority, cynicism and self-assertiveness." So Flanagan sees the value priorities changing in the same general direction as Harding et al. But Flanagan explains this value change by a "functional constraint theory" (so that the value systems that best ensure the survival and well-being of the individual and community in a certain socioeconomic context will prevail, and socio-economic development will improve the conditions of physical security, self-sufficiency and affluence. These improved conditions permit value system changes in the direction of weaker moral [austerity, piety] and social [conformity, authoritarianism] constraints). Flanagan therefore does not rely on a specific theory of psychological needs to explain the value shift.

That the broad value systems depicted by Harding et al. and by Flanagan are valid indicators of "religious values" is compatible with the findings of Inglehart that such value systems show a remarkably high degree of structure and coherence, and that a substantial portion of the general public seems to manifest a consistent orientation towards religious and cultural values, extending across a wide range of topics (Inglehart, 1984, pp. 9, 11). As he says, "The unifying element holding this value system together, seems to be the Ten Commandments of the Old Testament, coupled with the belief that these commandments reflect the will of an omnipotent God. If one accepts *that* belief, it is mandatory that one adheres to the entire system."

Thus, one would generally expect indicators of traditional-conservative values to correlate positively, and indicators of radical-secular values to correlate negatively with measures of commitment to the Christian faith.

At the empirical level, suffice it to say that Inglehart has presented massive support for marked and systematic age-group differences in the basic value orientations. Very consistently, younger age-groups score higher on measures of Post-Materialist values and lower on measures of commitment to the Christian faith. However, the general question of adult changes or stability in basic (religious) values among consecutive age cohorts is not yet settled. Therefore, the long-term effects of the age-group differences proposed by Inglehart remain to be established.

Happiness and Psychological Well-being

The term *happiness* has not often been used by empirical social and behavioral scientists. This lack of empirical concern has contributed to flourishing myths about happiness, which hold that modern society is a "sink of unhappiness," that living conditions do not matter, and that happiness is not a significant issue (Veenhoven, 1984, p. 395f). Despite (or maybe because of) such (mis)understandings, the ideal of promoting happiness pervades past and present theology and moral philosophy. But to include the concept of happiness in the vocabulary of the social sciences would help to reveal mythical misunderstandings of modern society and contribute to the mutual exchange between social science, theology, and moral philosophy.

In an extensive social scientific study on "The Conditions of Happiness," happiness is defined as "the degree to which the individual judges the overall quality of his life-as-a-whole favorably" (Veenhoven, 1984, p. 22). There are two aspects or "components" of this overall happiness: (a) *the hedonic level of affect*, as the degree to which the person's experiences are pleasant in character, and (b) *contentment*, or the degree to which an individual judges that his aspirations are being met (Veenhoven, 1984, p. 26f). These definitions evidently relate happiness to such concepts as psychological well-being, quality of life, positive mental health, life satisfaction. The happiness scales referred to show that the present understanding of happiness is close to some meanings of psychological well-being (cf. Veenhoven, 1984, p. 36f).

Value Systems and Happiness

The relationships between individuals' value systems on the one hand, and their experiences of happiness or subjective well-being on the other are undoubtedly complex. For what kinds of individuals, living in what kind of social contexts, are what kinds of value systems related to what kinds of well-being? Irrespective of religious or nonreligious values, there are hardly any clear-cut answers to such questions (Veenhoven, 1984; Spilka, Hood, & Gorsuch, 1985, Chapter 12). However, in the restricted context of the present paper, a few hypotheses have gained at least some empirical support. Inglehart maintains that the "Post-Materialists tend to manifest relatively low levels of satisfaction with many aspects of their lives, despite the fact that they rank above average in income, education, and occupational status" (Inglehart, 1977, p. 122). His explanation of the Post-Materialists' dissatisfaction is straightforward and "rationalistic": "A relatively small minority in predominantly Materialist societies, they are relatively apt to perceive a disparity between their own values and the society that surrounds them" (Inglehart, 1977, p. 143). This level of satisfaction depends on the "fit" between the way individuals perceive their environment, and their values, aspirations, and expectations concerning that environment.

In his study of value systems, Harding reports that dissatisfaction is an affective facet of anti-consensual values and that "those who endorsed traditional-conservative values tended to emerge as somewhat more contented with life than those with more secular-radical views" (Harding et al., 1986, p. 232). The deviant personal and social values of the latter help to account for their lower well-being and discontent. Psychosocial experiences of value-alienation thus explain the somewhat higher dissatisfaction of secular-radicals. Veenhoven (1984, p. 187f) reports a similar view. Thus, minority status (whether ethnic or ideological) is found to be detrimental to experiences of happiness. The explanation is either that, due to discrimination, minorities face worse living conditions, or that the social rejection of minorities is detrimental to the development of self-esteem, a variable firmly related to happiness (Veenhoven, 1984, p. 336f).

Veenhoven (1984, p. 356) further reports the correlations between happiness and ethical values to be mostly small and variable across time and social categories. As for the correlation between religious participation (church-going) and experiences of happiness, three American population studies, repeated at intervals of 10 years, showed steadily declining correlations between overall happiness and church attendance rates. The positive effect of religious participation thus withered as the churches lost ground and supportive power in Western society. "Religious answers to existential questions lost credibility; hence people draw less strength from religious services. As the political power of the churches lessened and their welfare work was largely taken over by the state, attendants' church membership has withered as well" (Veenhoven, 1984, p. 328). Accordingly, the national levels of welfare expenditures and church commitment are assumed to correlate negatively.

Thus, the society in which one lives is an important predictor of the general level of happiness, and of its associated factors. "Differences in happiness *between* Western countries seem greater than differences in happiness *within* them" (Veenhoven, 1984, p. 261). Other studies have shown a close association between personal and national development. The rate of economic development of a nation-state is an important predictor of national levels of authoritarianism (cf. Harding et al., 1986, and Flanagan, 1982 on the relationship between authoritarianism and the traditional-conservative value systems), and the sense of well-being and personal satisfaction (Inkeles & Diamond, 1980). As for the cross-national European differences, it should be mentioned that those in the northern (and Protestant) countries show greater happiness than in the southern (and Catholic) countries, and that small countries show greater happiness than big ones (Veenhoven, 1984, p. 142f; Inkeles & Diamond, 1980, p. 94; Harding et al., 1986, p. 183f).

The relations between value systems and happiness have been examined at the individual-intranational and the macrostructural-international levels of analysis. For the former, a positive relation between religious commitment and traditional-conservative attitudes with happiness is assumed, with a negative relationship between radical-secular values and happiness. Explanations of these relationships are of at least two kinds. A commonsense, straightforwardly "rationalistic" explanation assumes a discrepancy between the contents of value systems and the way society works to cause dissatisfaction. (So Post-Materialists highly value a nonauthoritarian education system and when the education system is perceived to be authoritarian, the Post-Materialists are dissatisfied). A sociopsychological explanation assumes that the dissatisfaction of Post-Materialists is a result of their minority status (Harding et al., 1986, Veenhoven, 1984).

The hypotheses at a macrostructural level attempt to explain social value system changes (towards secularization) by means of lower degrees of psychological benefit obtained from the preceding religious value system. The psychological benefits formerly obtained from religion are then obtained from other sources, such as the welfare policies that produce an enriched institutional environment, which in turn yields enhanced levels of psychological benefit (cf. Inkeles & Diamond, 1980, p. 105). Hence, countries scoring higher on welfare policies should be more secularized and demonstrate lower levels of association between religious involvement and psychological well-being. That hypothesis is the main focus of this paper. In a certain sense, this macrostructural, cross-national study might define the range of applicability of an individual-intranational hypothesis about the relationship between value systems and experiences of happiness mentioned above. The assumed relations between value systems and experiences of happiness can only be expected in certain societal categories, including those relatively low on secularization. It should also be noted that this theoretical approach might involve a kind of exchange theory when, as a behavior pattern, church-going loses the relative strength of its associated rewards because of socioeconomic development, and becomes "extinguished."

It must be emphasized, however, that most hypotheses on the relation between value systems on the one hand and experiences of happiness and subjective well-being on the other, contain strong *ceteris paribus* clauses, and that the empirical support for them is uncertain. Since the reported measures of association seldom control for contaminating factors, they might well be spurious. "No checks having been made, nothing can be said for sure," to quote Veenhoven (1984, p. 327). Experiences of happiness, subjective well-being, and overall satisfaction with life are indeed affected in many ways and any study of experiences of happiness and subjective well-being can only expect statistical analyses to produce modest levels of significance, since they are indeed overdetermined.

Data Sets and Measures of Happiness, Value Systems, and Socioeconomic Status

The Data Sets

For the empirical analyses reported below, the data sets from the comprehensive cross-national study performed by the European Value Systems Study Group (e.g., Harding et al., 1986) have been used. That EVSSG study was designed to explore the possible homogeneity and change of Europeans' religious, moral, and social values and behaviors. During 1981 and 1982 the same questionnaire was distributed to random samples of the general population in more than 20 countries, most belonging to the industrialized Western world. The samples approximated about 1,300 respondents in each country.

In the following analyses, data sets from the following 7 countries are used: Spain (n = 2,303), Italy (n = 1,348), France (n = 1,199), West Germany (n = 1,305, divided into Catholic Germany and Protestant Germany), Great Britain (n = 1,231), Denmark (n = 1,182), and Norway (n = 1,348). The reasons for the selection of these 7 countries are described below.

Measures of Happiness, Value Systems, and Socioeconomic Status

Two measures of happiness were used, which correspond rather well to the criteria outlined by Veenhoven (1984, Chapter 4). As a measure of "Overall Happiness," a single unweighted additive score was derived from three 10-point rating scales of satisfaction (questionnaire items numbered Q129, Q130, Q131; the exact wording of these interview questions being in Harding et al., 1986, Appendix). These scales probed general satisfaction with life "these days," "five years ago," and "in five years' time." This Overall Happiness score corresponds well with Veenhoven's (1984, p. 21) definition of overall happiness with "life-as-a-whole," although a measurement problem not investigated here concerns the rather high rate of omissions for the anticipated life satisfaction rating scale.

As a second measure of happiness, the well-known 10-item Bradburn Affect Balance Scale (Bradburn, 1969), was used. Five items on this scale relate to positive emotional experiences "during the last fortnight" and five relate to negative emotional experiences during the same period. "Numerous studies have shown that a composite index, the Affect Balance Score, derived by subtracting negative scores from positive scores, proves to be a better predictor of well-being and happiness than either of the two scales taken separately" (Harding et al., 1986, p. 189f). Despite some criticism, the Bradburn Affect Balance Score (BAS) could be a valid measure of the "hedonic" component of happiness (Veenhoven, 1984, p. 93f).

As for the validity of the two happiness scales, it can be mentioned that they correlate positively with a 4-point rating scale of self-reported happiness. For the Overall Happiness scale, Pearson correlations for the 7 countries range between .40 and .50; for the Affect Balance Score the correlations range between .35 and .45. Thus, the two happiness scales relate to experiences that people describe in ordinary language as "happy." It should also be mentioned that for every country in this study, each scale of happiness is significantly and negatively related to a scale of alienation (defined as experiences and feelings of being alone, that life is meaningless, and that one does not have a free choice or any control as to the way one's life turns out).

As a measure of "Christian commitment," a single additive 4-point scale was used. Fulfilling each of the following criteria yields 1 point: belief in a personal God (Q166), the importance of God scored 8 or above on a 10-point importance rating scale (Q167), all Ten Commandments rated as "fully applicable" to one-self (Q208), and divine service attendance at least monthly (Q157). These criteria correspond rather well to Inglehart's analysis quoted above.

As measures of the traditional-conservative (T-C) and radical-secular (R-S) value systems, two simple 11-item additive scales were used. The 11 items asked about views on the following issues:

a: whether people should follow a superior's instructions at work (Q144); T-C: "yes"; R-S: "must be convinced first."

b: whether there are clear guidelines about what is good and evil (Q154); T-C: "yes"; R-S: "no."

c: whether marriage is an outdated institution (Q246); T-C: "no"; R-S: "yes."

d: whether individuals could enjoy complete sexual freedom (Q247); T-C: "no"; R-S: "yes."

e: whether children need both father and mother (Q256); T-C: "agree"; R-S: "disagree."

f: whether a woman needs children in order to be fulfilled (Q257); T-C: "needs children"; R-S: "not necessary."

g: whether there are absolute moral sexual rules (Q258); T-C: "agree"; R-S: "disagree."

h: whether children always must love and respect their parents (Q259); T-C: "yes"; R-C: "no."

i–k: confidence in social institutions like the armed forces, the legal system, and the police (Q349); T-C: "a great deal"; R-S: "not very much" or "less."

These 11 items tap the two value systems defined by the work of Inglehart, Harding et al., and Flanagan already referred to.

As indicators of socioeconomic status the items used assessed:

age,
health (self-reported health "these days" on a 5-point rating scale with 1 = *very good*),
income (family income on a 10-point rating scale),
education (age when full-time education was or will be completed), and
employed (whether a member of the labor force or not).

Results

Some Zero-order Correlations

Our theoretical approach assumes a positive correlation between the Christian commitment and the Traditional-Conservative scales and a negative correlation between the Christian commitment and the radical-secular scales. This is also the case for each of the 7 countries. Although statistically significant at the .001 level, the Pearson correlations are, however, not especially strong, since the unweighted mean correlations for the 7 countries are .40 and −.36 respectively. So Christian commitment does not explain more than about 15% of the variance in the two value system scales. The scale of Christian commitment and the two value system scales are therefore retained as separate measures. As expected from the scoring method, the Traditional-Conservative and Radical-Secular value scales show strong, negative correlations with each other (unweighted mean correlation = −.73).

That Christian commitment and the Traditional-Conservative scales would correlate positively with age and negatively with education, and that the Radical-Secular scale would correlate positively with education and negatively with age, are basic assumptions in Inglehart's theory. With two minor exceptions (since education is not significantly related to the Christian commitment scale in France or Great Britain) this is the case. It should, however, be noted that the correlations are not especially strong, since age and education do not explain more than about 10% of the variance in the three value system measures.

The correlations between Overall Happiness and the Affect Balance Score scales range between .29 and .42. So the two measures of happiness are retained as separate scores. The relation of age, education, and employment to the two reported measures of happiness are mostly negligible across the 7 countries. By contrast, self-reported health and the family income cannot be disregarded as significant conditions for each aspect of happiness.

Happiness, Value Systems, and the Social Correlates of Age, Education, Income, and Health

The above results show that regardless of country, the two happiness scales are related to health and income, and that the three value system scales are related to age and education. Furthermore, the measure of income is associated with age and education. In order to establish the non-spurious relations between a value system and the happiness scales, some kind of a multivariate analysis is needed. LISREL (see, for example, Long, 1983; Joreskog & Sörbom, 1986) was chosen for this analysis. To specify the structural equation model for LISREL, an analysis of the theoretical relation between the variables under study is necessary for these cross-national analyses.

A Scheme for Cross-national Comparisons

The hypotheses on value systems and happiness discussed above suggest intra- as well as international analyses. The latter mainly concern the impact of rates of secularization and welfare policies on happiness and its associated factors. Countries rating higher on welfare policies and secularization were expected to demonstrate a weaker association between religious values and happiness as compared to countries rating lower on welfare policies and secularization. However, the national levels of happiness and well-being and their associated factors, and the size of the main denominational contrast (Catholic vs. Protestant) in the countries concerned, were also important. In order to "control" for such contaminating circumstances, the scheme for cross-national comparisons depicted in Figure 14.1 was used.

As indicated in Figure 14.1, Spain and Italy are compared with France and Catholic Germany; Great Britain with Protestant Germany, and Norway with Denmark. Theoretically, these pairwise comparisons should demonstrate stronger positive associations between religious value systems and happiness for Spain and Italy, Great Britain, and Norway, as compared to France and Catholic Germany, Protestant Germany and Denmark, respectively. These comparisons also control for the effect of the size and denomination of the various countries. The obtained pairwise, cross-national differences in the strength of the association between value systems and happiness, would therefore be "explained" by their differing levels of secularization and welfare policies.

The data included in Figure 14.1 justify the categorization of countries as "high" or "low" on secularization. (Note that the "high" and "low" categories for secularization and welfare policy refer only to countries within the same size and denomination category.) The data on secularization rates were computed according to the formula, 100—"folk-

Countries	Comparatively low on secularization and welfare policies	Comparatively high on secularization and welfare policies
Southern, Catholic, large.	Spain secular: 49 welfare: ?	France secular: 67 welfare: 29.
	Italy secular: 52 welfare: 30	Catholic Germany secular: 61 (66) welfare: 32.
Middle European, Protestant, large.	Great Britain secular: 51 welfare: 24	Protestant Germany secular: 61 welfare: 32.
Northern, Protestant, small.	Norway secular: 58 welfare: 27	Denmark secular: 76 welfare: 33.

FIGURE 14.1. Scheme for cross-national comparisons on happiness. (For the measures of secularization rate and welfare policies, see the text.)

religiousness rate" (for the definition of "folk-religiousness rate" see Listhaug, 1983, p. 6). For the Scandinavian countries, this categorization is also based on the analysis of religious change in the Nordic countries during the last 50 years, presented by Gustafsson (1987). The data on welfare policies express welfare expenditure as a percentage of the total national expenditure. Admittedly, these data ought to be richer, and longitudinal welfare policy data would have been preferred (following Inglehart's views on the importance of material conditions during preadult formative years for consecutive age cohorts' religious involvement).

The LISREL Models

Given the theoretical assumptions and empirical findings reported above, a LISREL structural component model for directly observed variables can be specified. This model, shown in Figure 14.2, is a recursive system of the exogenous variables "age" through "radical-secular values" and the jointly dependent variables Overall Happiness and Bradburn Affect Balance Score. To be fully specified, each national LISREL structural component model must be complete regarding the effects of social correlates on happiness (see above), and the effects of value system variables on the happiness variables. For the specification of the latter aspect, the theoretical analyses above are assumed to justify the assumptions that within each set of the pairwise cross-national comparisons according to Figure 14.1, the countries scoring comparatively high on secularization should demonstrate a weaker or nonsignificant impact of the value system

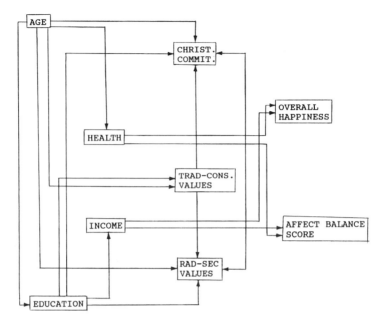

FIGURE 14.2. Basics of a LISREL structural component model, common to all the countries included in the present study, on the predictors of happiness. (For the relations between value systems and indicators of happiness in various countries, see the text.)

variables on the happiness variables in contrast to the countries scoring comparatively low on secularization. A summary of the LISREL analyses (one for each country), is presented in Table 14.1.

The results of the LISREL analyses are compatible with the assumed cross-national variable impact of the value systems. Thus, the following might be noticed:

a) For *Spain*, the Christian commitment scale is positively associated with the Overall Happiness scale, and radical-secular is negatively associated with Overall Happiness and Affect Balance Score, respectively; for *France*, no such statistically significant relationships were found;

b) For *Italy*, the Christian commitment is positively associated with Overall Happiness; for *Catholic Germany*, Christian commitment is negatively related to the Affect Balance Score;

c) For *Great Britain*, the traditional-conservative scale is positively associated with Overall Happiness, and the radical-secular scale negatively related to the Affect Balance Score; for *Protestant Germany*, no such statistically significant relations are found;

d) For *Norway*, Christian commitment and Traditional-Conservative are positively related to Overall Happiness, and the Radical-Secular scale is negatively related to the Affect Balance Score; for *Denmark* only the Traditional-Conservative scale is positively related to Overall Happiness.

It can be concluded that the hypotheses about the cross-national variable impact of value systems on the experiences of happiness have gained empirical support.

TABLE 14.1. Measures of the goodness of fit and significant ($p < .01$) standardized parameter estimates ("gammas"), for the relations between a LISREL Model's exogenous and endogenous variables.

Countries:	Spain		France	
	Overall Happiness	BAS	Overall Happiness	BAS
Exogenous variables:				
Social correlates:				
age	−.08			
health	−.18	−.13	−.13	.25
income	.13	.07	.14	
education			.20	
Value systems				
Christian commitment	.11			
Traditional-Conservative				
Radical-Secular	−.14	−.19		
Total coefficient of				
determination	.12		.17	
GFI	.99		.99	
RMSR	.01		.02	
Chi square	n.s.		n.s.	

Countries:	Italy		Catholic Germany	
	Overall Happiness	BAS	Overall Happiness	BAS
Exogenous variables:				
Social correlates:				
age			.21	
health	−.21	−.20	−.42	−.26
income	.08	.12	.10	
education		.09		
Value systems				
Christian commitment	.18			−.17
Traditional-Conservative				
Radical-Secular				
Total coefficient of				
determination	.16		.26	
GFI	.99		.99	
RMSR	.02		.02	
Chi square	n.s.		n.s.	

(*Continued*)

TABLE 14.1. *Continued*

Countries:	Great Britain		Protestant Germany	
	Overall Happiness	BAS	Overall Happiness	BAS
Exogenous variables:				
Social correlates:				
age	.11		18	
health	−.16	−.21	−.35	−27
income		.14		
education			.20	
Value systems				
Christian commitment				
Traditional-Conservative	.12			
Radical-Secular				
Total coefficient of				
determination	.12		.18	
GFI	.99		.99	
RMSR	.02		.03	
Chi square	n.s.		n.s	

Countries:	Norway		Denmark	
	Overall Happiness	BAS	Overall Happiness	BAS
Exogenous variables:				
Social correlates:				
age				.10
health	−.23	−.18	−.30	−.19
income	.30	.12		.10
education			−.10	
Value systems				
Christian commitment	.06			
Traditional-Conservative	.08		.20	
Radical-Secular		−.09		
Total coefficient of				
determination	.23		.17	
GFI	.99		.99	
RMSR	.01		.01	
Chi square	$p < .05$		n.s.	

Discussion

The results reported above could be critically evaluated as regards to the validity and reliability of the scales used, details of the statistical analyses and their interpretation, the number of omitted but relevant dependent and independent variables, and so on. Being more concerned with the theoretical issues, details of the empirical analyses will not, however, be discussed here.

In the present study, the effect of the social correlates on happiness are of less interest than the cross-nationally consistent impact of the welfare-related variables of health and income. In all the countries studied, good health and a good income are associated with experiences of happiness. We might also note the minor impact of education on happiness, which does not support claims that education, by its personality-developing qualities, enhances experiences of happiness.

Two measures of happiness, closely related to psychological well-being and subjective quality of life, were used in these empirical analyses. The Overall Happiness scale concerns general satisfaction with "life-as-a-whole" and covers evaluations of past, present, and future experiences. In other words, to be happy one must accept one's history, be satisfied with the present, and feel confident about future life satisfactions. Those who experience past, present, and anticipated future value attainment are by definition happy. But to accept one's history, to be satisfied with the present, and to feel confident about future life satisfaction, some standard of judgement is necessary. Personal value systems are almost by definition involved in forming that standard. Thus, the judgement or appreciation of one's life-as-a-whole is mainly cognitive in character and concerns the experienced distance between one's perceived ("objective") environment and the attainment of one's values, aspirations, and expectations concerning that environment. In other words, the experience of overall happiness and general satisfaction with "life-as-a-whole" can be understood as a token of a durable, long-term "fit" between an individual's environment and their values, aspirations, and expectations (Cambell, Converse, & Rodgers, 1976, p. 13ff; Blom & Listhaug, 1988).

The second measure of happiness through the Affect Balance Score is assumed to tap the hedonic, emotional-affective component of experiences of happiness. Thus, besides being related to our long-standing satisfaction, experiences of happiness are also constituted from the transient positive and negative emotions that are part of one's daily life's ordinary as well as extraordinary events (Veenhoven, 1984, p. 91f; Bayelec & Sidenap, 1983). It can, however, hardly be denied that such accidental or fortuitous positive or negative experiences must also be related to personal value systems. So one item on the Bradburn Affect Balance scale asks if things are going "one's way" and another asks whether one is pleased about having "accomplished something." Such questions can scarcely be answered without involving one's personal values and aspirations. If the Overall Happiness scale is sensitive to a long-term or durable fit between a person's perceived environment and their value systems, the Affect Balance Score scale should be sensitive to its short-term, variable fit. Both measures of happiness should in one way or another relate to the long-standing and durable, and the short-term "distance" or "fit" between the perceived environment and one's personal values, aspirations, and expectations concerning that environment.

Given this interpretation of those two measures, it should come as no surprise that such religious values as Christian commitment and traditional-conservative values are associated with experiences of happiness in the comparatively less secularized countries where Christianity is still strong and visible. In societies where the Christian faith is less publicly visible, less publicly noticed and cared about, and less publicly appreciated, there must by definition be a greater distance and "misfit" between the believers' Christian values and their environment. Although important, selective perception cannot itself remake such a "misfit" into a "fit." Societies comparatively high on secularization thus demonstrate a weakened association between Christian commitment or traditional-conservative values and experiences of happiness; comparatively less secularized countries should similarly demonstrate a strengthened association.

As for the psychology of religion, such argument so far discussed indicates that the dynamics of religion and mental health should not be neglected, nor should it be explored without considering the degree of secularization of the social environment. Whether religious commitment and religious value systems are a support or a burden depends on the secularization of their socioreligious context. In heavily Catholic Spain, the religious commitment should side with well-being, while in secularized Denmark that is less likely to be the case. And the same effect should be obtained in different religious and cultural regions *within* those larger socioreligious contexts.

As for the sociology of religion, these findings may relate to theories of secularization, at least with regard to current phases of the secularization process. Admittedly, answers to the question, "Which causes what?" are uncertain. Is a certain level of secularization a cause of the weakened association between a Christian commitment and experiences of happiness, or should a certain level of secularization be explained by such a weakened association? According to the latter view, people will abandon their religious commitment because it is detrimental to their psychological well-being or because it does not contribute to their experiences of happiness. Probably those questions should not be approached as an either/or option, since interpretations of the weakened association as both a cause and a consequence of a process of general secularisation can be made. A weakened association between the religious commitment and their experiences of happiness makes people abandon their religious involvement, which decreases the proportion of the population that is church-involved. This decrease leads to a further weakening of the association between religious commitment and happiness, which makes more people abandon their religious commitment, leading to a further weakening, and so on.

One might note that the theoretical perspective and empirical findings discussed in this paper provide an unexpected view of the relationship between religious commitment and experiences of alienation. In countries comparatively high on secularization, experiences of value-alienation would be a consequence and not a source of religious commitment. The mechanisms discussed above suggest that religious commitment would in some circumstances lead to experiences of unhappiness and value-alienation, although the opposite relationship between religion and alienation is often assumed.

The theoretical approach of this paper can be understood as a kind of cost-benefit model. That people maintain or abandon their Christian commitment and value systems is related to the net advantages of the perceived benefits and costs associated with that commitment. A religious commitment that is not associated with experiences of happiness and well-being is, other things being equal, more likely to be abandoned. And those perceived benefits and costs depend, among other things, on the rate of secularization in one's country. The more secularized the social setting, the higher are these costs and the lower the benefits.

References

Bayelec, O. & Sidenap, K. (1983). *Happiness and Humour: An analysis approach.* Unpublished paper, C.I.S.R. Conference, London.

Blom, S. & Listhaug, O. (1988). Familie og livskvalitet. *Tidskrift for samfunnsforskning* (Family and quality of life). *29,* 291f.

Bradburn, N. (1969). *The structure of psychological well-being.* Chicago: Aldine.

Cambell, A., Converse, P., & Rodgers, W. (1976). *The quality of American life.* New York: Russell Sage Foundation.

Engberg, J. (1986). *Folkrrelserna i vlfrdssamhllet* (Social movements in welfare society). Dissertation, University of Ume, Sweden.

Flanagan, S. (1982). Changing values in advanced industrialized countries. *Comparative Political Studies, 14*(4).

Gustafsson, G. (1987). Religious change in the five Scandinavian countries, 1930–1980. *Comparative Social Research, 10.*

Harding, S., Phillips, D., & Fogarty, M. (1986). *Contrasting values in Western Europe: Unity, diversity and change.* London: Macmillan.

Inglehart, R. (1977). *The silent revolution: Changing values and political styles.* Princeton, NJ: Princeton University Press.

Inglehart, R. (1981). Post-materialism in an environment of insecurity. *American Political Science Review, 75*(4), 880–900.

Inglehart, R. (1982). Changing values in Japan and the West. *Comparative Political Studies, 14*(4), 445f.

Inglehart, R. (1984). *Generational politics and cultural change.* Paper presented at the Conference on Changing Political Culture of Youth in Western Democracies. Lake Como, Italy.

Inglehart, R. (1985). Aggregate stability and individual-level flux in mass belief systems. *The American Political Science Review, 79*(1), 97f.

Inkeles, A. & Diamond, L. (1980). Personal development and national development. In A. Szalai & F. Andrews (Eds.), *The quality of life: Comparative studies.* London: Sage Publications.

Joreskog, K.-G. & Sörbom, D. (1986). *Lisrel VI: Analysis of linear structural relationships by maximum likelihood instrumental variables and least square methods.* Uppsala: Department of Statistics, University of Uppsala.

Listhaug, O. (1983). *Norske verdier i et komparativt perspektiv* (Norwegian values in a comparative perspective). (ISS-rapport nr. 12). Trondheim, Norway: Institutt for sociologi og samfunnsvitenskap, Universitetet i Trondheim.

Long, J.S. (1983). *Covariance structure models. An introduction to LISREL.* London: Sage Publications.

Spilka, B., Hood, R.W., Jr., & Gorsuch, R.L. (1985). *The psychology of religion: An empirical approach.* Englewood Cliffs, NJ: Prentice Hall.

Veenhoven, R. (1984). *Conditions of happiness.* Dordrecht, Holland: Kluwer Boston Academic Publishers.

Wuthnow, R. & Nass, C. (1988). Government activity and civil privatism. *Journal for the Scientific Study of Religion*, *27*(2), 157–174.

15
Conclusion

Laurence B. Brown

These papers have explored various facets of the relationships between religion and mental health. They do not advocate simple or unitary solutions, but recognize cautiously that more work is needed to clarify these relationships. Nevertheless, they all accept that religions can offer preventive and therapeutic resources, most obviously among the poor, homeless, bereaved, and for those who are physically or mentally ill. But not only there.

Current prejudices that surround these controversial issues are heavily influenced by Freud's interpretation of religious ideas as cultural illusions that (might) fulfill primal wishes. Freud also saw religious practices as a residue of neurotic or compulsive obsessions that can help those who are immature to cope with the insecurity that besets most people from time to time. He assumed that this insight removed the "need" for a religion, and that at both societal and individual levels religions involve complex and psychologically adaptive fantasies that can become a focus of mental illness.

Had Freud used depression rather than psychoneurosis as the model for his interpretations of religiousness, he would have produced an analysis closer to the experience of many people, even if it would have been less newsworthy. Although some would blame God for every disaster (Lalljee, Brown, & Hilton, 1990), depression links with a negative self-assessment, despair, hopelessness and helplessness, and the "dark night of the soul." By tradition, these are all aligned with Christian states of mind. Furthermore, since depression can be understood in "bio-psycho-social" terms, it does not as readily invite the destruction of religion as does its interpretation through psychoneurosis.

The role of personality in religion is similarly questionable because, as noted in the Introduction, "One researcher views a worship lifestyle positively in terms of reverence, humility and constructive obedience, as universal moral laws, whereas another researcher views the same lifestyle negatively as self-abasing, unprogressive and blindly conforming" (Bergin, 1983). Similar ambiguities are found in the role of personality traits, although in religion they are naively used to account for religious differences, or they are tied to investigators' often unstated efforts to break up, or support religious phenomena, than to clarify their impact on mental health or on the ways religious attachments are realized.

It is unfortunate that no equivalently powerful account of the links between religion and mental health has replaced Freud's analyses of pathological religious experiences, and of their illusory if obsessional character, or of Jung's or Erikson's accounts of religion in the same broad tradition (cf. Heimbrock, 1991). Williams James's (1902/1985, p. 71ff) analysis of "the religion of healthy-mindedness," which he contrasted against that of the sick soul, was overshadowed by Freud's deconstructions of religious belief and practice, perhaps because it is hard, as James said, to maintain a "tendency which looks on all things and sees that they are good" (p. 78).

Mature Religious Attitudes

This undue prescriptiveness failed to recognize the importance of the variety of religious meanings that can be constructed, and forced religion and mental health into a strait jacket that disregarded the extent to which familiar concepts are constantly reconstrued, so that for example, "God" can become a synonym for both "father" and "nature." Godin (1971) escaped those problems by holding that a neglected goal for our psychological analyses of religion is to help purify religious images of whatever components might be obstacles to a developing maturity. Among those obstacles he included moralism, the intrusion of parental or oedipal symbols, and an inability to transform religious images into a "life of faith" that recognizes "God's plan in history" (1971, pp. 118 and 130).

While most religious people recognize the pathological forms of religion as overzealous or unsanctioned, they also know that "healthy" attitudes to it require some conformity with accepted practices, doctrines, or beliefs, and that a religious identity supports claims on religious experience. But little is known about how to display religiousness in a way that does not seem either habitual or excessively enthusiastic. While attempts have been made to control minority religious groups (and new religious movements) by legal processes, or by attributing a psychosis or neurosis to their members and malevolence to the institution that supports them, differential diagnoses between a keen religiousness and mental illness must depend on agreed, if still poorly specified signs, and not merely on prejudice. Larson et al. (1986) therefore concluded that "psychiatric research (on religious variables) lacks conceptual and methodological sophistication."

The uses of any religion's resources require more careful study than they have received, and sounder evidence is needed to support those who would hold that religions consistently produce mental illness. Although the relationship between religion and mental health has been surrounded by controversy and bias, that is not a reason for disregarding the results of social and psychological research, or for failing to pursue the issues that the papers here have explored.

As a never-to-be-completed product of cultural, social, personal, and perhaps biological processes, religions seem to have been more plausibly aligned with the research traditions of sociology, than with those of psychology. Perhaps this is so because sociologists are able to locate their data socially, more clearly than have psychologists. The hurdles that both disciplines must cross before disputes about the relationships between religion and mental health can be resolved include their oversimplified solutions and a bias toward internal and personal, rather than external and social causes. Personality theories have similarly emphasized individuals rather than their environments, and relatively stable or biological, rather than social explanations of individual differences. Direct comparisons between those who are or are not "religious" have rather selectively guided a search for the subtle effects of religious systems on the characteristics and adjustment of those who are influenced by them.

Despite that, religious doctrines and liturgical practices, at least as they are known through Western Christian traditions, have been adapted to specific cultures and are publicly available. For that reason alone they are able to support the pathologies of an unknown, but probably small number of individuals. Psychiatric and psychoanalytic perspectives have therefore been thought to stand in opposition to religiously committed views about the validity of some (often one's own) religious perspectives.

The attitudes to religion and mental health were contrasted in the work of Bergin (1980), in the claims of Chesen (1972) or Ellis (1976). While Bergin is sympathetic, Ellis adopted an absolute stance against any psychological benefits that a religion might offer. It was, however, noted in the Introduction that Batson and Ventis (1982) emphasized that religious people can be flexible, open, and tolerant, even if some of them are inflexible. Furthermore, unless we assume an explicit commitment, or a defined sequence of religious development (cf. Dykstra & Parkes, 1986), the impact of any religion on individuals, and on the groups to which they belong, should be expected to alter from time to time.

While the validity of any causal hypotheses about the relationships between religion and mental health is yet to be firmly established, there is an increasing consensus that religion is more likely to help solve the problems of those who are mentally ill than to have caused their illness or distress. As social "objects," religions combine their mysteries with the institutional realities and with fantasies of their followers (cf. Rizzuto, 1979, p. 53) to produce a paradoxical complementarity which parallels that between mental health and illness, as it balances social realities against whatever meanings are constructed around those realities.

The Sources of Data

The idiographic, or case study and narrative methods that characterize clinical investigations allow a person's experience to be located within the ongoing biography of their life, as they attempt to capture the meaning of their experiences. But hard cases do not make good science and group comparisons are needed to establish the general relationships between religion and mental health. Nearly all of the papers here contribute directly to this debate through those nomothetic approaches.

It is almost commonplace to align religiousness with an attitudinal or personality trait that mediates between religious systems and a person's health or illness, rather than expecting direct effects of every form of alignment with a religious tradition or denomination, whether in the contrasted modes of religious orientation as intrinsic or extrinsic, committed or consensual, or through end, means, or questing solutions. Equating those processes with personality variables once seemed a simple step in psychological analysis. But religious reactions have not been found to be reliably aligned with particular "kinds" of personality or religious orientation, nor are they necessarily "pathogenic," despite the voluminous literature on religious differences, and (more recently) on cults. As Loevinger (1984, p. 65) said, "I have never heard anyone espouse the doctrine that behaviour is predictable on the basis of personality alone, to the exclusion of situational considerations. Anyone unresponsive to situational demands would be, ipso facto, crazy."

A person's maladjustment, neurosis, or psychosis must be diagnosed with reference to some "clinical" features as "identifiable behavioral signs or symptoms . . . which require a minimal amount of inference on the part of the observer. For some disorders, however, particularly the personality disorders, the criteria require much more inference on the part of the observer" (American Psychiatric Assn., DSM-III-R, 1987, p. xxiii). Furthermore, "for most of the DSM-III-R disorders, the etiology is unknown. Many theories have been advanced and buttressed by evidence—not always convincing—in attempts to explain how these disorders come about" (ibid.). This approach to diagnosis in DSM-III-R is descriptive and atheoretical, not least, as they note, because any other commitment "would be an obstacle to (the) use of the manual by clinicians of varying theoretical orientations, since it would not be possible to present all reasonable etiologic theories for each disorder" (ibid.).

The extent to which theories themselves influence what will be observed is seldom noted in debates about religion and mental health, perhaps because that form of the problem implicates a specific ideology about religion, rather than a balanced approach to the full range of psychological maladjustments. Preferring one explanatory theory, whether in natural or transcendental terms, is as suspect as the arguments about a "choice" of symptoms. A recent news commentator on the crises in Somalia who remarked that "religion is important because the lives of so many [not only there, I suppose] hang by a thread," emphasized the ease with which religion has been understood as an (approved or disapproved) adjustment or coping mechanism.

The search for general causes (which could be "real" or imposed) might also involve an attributional exercise that aims to reduce the variance, and allows specific details to be understood in a broad context. For this reason alone, work is still needed on the attitudes that can support claims about the deleterious effects of religion on mental health, and on the psychological benefits of religion. A better theoretical consensus is needed, not only about religion and mental health but about the comparative efficacy of religiously supported and other therapeutic interventions, and about the particular problems that are encountered. In such analyses it would be important to establish whether any doctrinal system or set of religious practices directly influence physiological reactions, in the immune system for example (Ader & Cohen, 1985), or if they simply draw on one's coping mechanisms to alleviate psychosocial stressors and activate social or other supports.

Religious Attitudes

While heresy can be distinguished from apostasy (and schism) they are all forms of religious defection. But to identify a group or an individual's religious practices and beliefs as psychologically "deviant" rather than theologically heretical, aligns them with the norms standing behind mental health or illness. Current examples of disapproved religious solutions include Jehovah's Witnesses' attitudes to blood transfusions, Catholic attitudes to contraception and to the ordination of women, and the enclosed cults that draw ready criticism. "New religious movements" and the "space" they occupy (Robbins & Anthony, 1982) have been regularly attacked for their effects on mental health, as Barker's (1989) "practical introduction" shows. She notes that while someone might want "the 'right' description, the 'right' explanation or 'right' advice . . . often the truth is that there is no one clear answer" (p. 3). The variety of new religious movements, and the impossibility of distinguishing between "destructive" and "benign cults," led Barker to conclude that, "As individuals, members of NRMs are not so very different from other people" (p. 5). The biased assessments of their organizational practices depend on having "a number of ethical, social and political considerations" weighed by "a small percentage of assessors who are uncompromisingly either for or against any NRM, whatever it is like" (Barker, p. 5).

While those groups are assumed to draw in first-generation followers of charismatic leaders, from those with particular socio-demographic characteristics, attacks on them often focus on the traditions they claim to be aligned with, their techniques of "brainwashing," persuasion, conversion, or the "subliminal suggestion" and "unusual experiences" they are thought to practice. Nevertheless, many in those groups are positively committed to them, and claim improved health or self-development as a result of their membership. Any accounts of deception, and the criminal charges that have been brought against NRMs (Barker, 1989, p. 39ff) should therefore be set against the benefits their members claim (Barker, 1989, p. 53ff). Although the psychiatric literature does not agree about the balance between the good and bad consequences of both the new and older religious movements, as a diagnostic system the DSM-III-R tries to exclude political alignments, and misjudgments of behavior that is "entirely normative for a particular culture" (DSM-III-R, 1987, p. xxvi).

An earlier version of those hostile religious prejudices was examined by Kroll and Bachrach (1982) with reference to pre-Crusade chronicles of the lives of the saints. They found that in only 9 of a set of 57 descriptions "did the sources attribute mental illness to sin or wrongdoing" and that that description was itself used for its "propaganda value against an enemy of their patron saints, their monastery lands, or their religious values." That the care of the sick demands a sympathetic (rather than a moralistic) understanding of the causes of their illnesses (cf. Blackburn, 1988) is a continuing and everyday problem for unconventional life-styles, and for social prototypes (or stereotypes) about the causes of particular illnesses, the characteristics of those who might be subject to them, the care they can expect, and the anticipated consequences of different illnesses themselves (cf. Lalljee, Lamb, & Carnibella, 1993).

The hope that a person's religious beliefs or practice might help to identify what is wrong with them is confounded by the fact that in crisis, some people "naturally" turn to religion in their attempt to cope. Prayer is a widely recognized means of doing this, even if it is not as effective as other help-seeking strategies (Parker, Brown, & Blignault, 1986).

While some religious groups try to constrain the access to secular therapies or advice, consultation with an "approved" counselor or psychiatrist who shares, or is sympathetic to, a religious ideology could therefore activate the practical and other supports that are available through a religion (Jensen & Bergin, 1988). Deciding to conform with particular meditative or dietary practices *might*, however, exacerbate previously undetected predispositions to a psychiatric breakdown. But decisions about whether that is the case are not made easily, and they are unlikely to be independent of what particular groups accept or make available. Reactions to religious traditions and groups seem to overgeneralize easily, especially in the absence of a detailed knowledge about their doctrines, practices, and social controls.

It is important that religious people are able to justify themselves both to other insiders, and to outsiders because, as Bowker suggests, "religions are highly dangerous because they are so important and because they create so much in, and of, human life" (1987, p. 7). But we do not know for whom religions could be hazardous, or what makes them "dangerous," as the continued analyses of Jonestown show (Moore & McGehee, 1989). In protecting their place in society, and transmitting their own traditions, religion could resemble poetry, by controlling boundaries that are to be identified metaphorically (or theologically and aesthetically) rather than literally.

Being or Doing Religion?

The "personality" or character of a religion is therefore found most clearly in talk about the experiences, beliefs, and practices it sanctions (cf. Funder & Colvin, 1991). For an observer to understand such talk could be like making a (psychiatric) diagnosis after translating the language that is used with reference to some form of socially agreed knowledge, and approved conventions. The factors that are expected to implicate a person's style of religiousness might then be like the V-codes of the World Health Organization (WHO) International Classification of Disorders (ICD-9-CM), which are applied to medical conditions that are a focus of attention or treatment, but are not attributable to one of the "mental disorders" (American Psychiatric Assn., DSM-III, 1980, p. 331). These codes include malingering, antisocial behavior, academic or occupational problems, bereavement, noncompliance with treatment, marital, family, and "other interpersonal problems" (DSM-III, 1980). The effects of religion could also be compared with addictions or attachments to sport, where it seems hard for some to abandon really strong commitments. The analogies continue, while the place of religions in culture, their (mysterious) sanctions and the emotions surrounding any defence of a "true" religion all support the social and moral influence they have on individuals.

Emancipating the wide range of social and scientific explanations of the origins or assumed meaning of religion from the constraints of religious systems themselves on thought, reasoning and explanation has itself been a long, slow process that is still incomplete, as Wulff's (1991) account of the major European and North American schools in the psychology of religion shows. This range itself presents problems to those who would criticize religion for its maladaptive effects, although Christopher Smart (1722–1771), whose "madness" compelled him to pray in public, is said to have occasioned Dr. Johnson to say, "I'd as lief pray with Kit Smart as anyone else." Specific social contexts or individuals accept what others would criticize, which means that religious signs, like many psychiatric markers of mental illness, are ambiguous and could necessarily be unclear.

Postscript

An aim of these papers has been to identify some psychological and social reactions to those who rely on religious solutions. Since religions tend to work best for those who can accept them, there is an inherent ambiguity in expecting internal, subjective, or spiritual processes to have priority over the external and institutional features that shape the lives of those who have been brought up within traditions they might hope to transcend. The search for enlightenment, or for new and varied experiences, cannot therefore explain the religiousness of everyone. Many people are likely to be conventionally "religious" until the going gets tough. Even if a religious alignment is part of someone's identity, it can be put on (like a garment) to help a person appear pious or forgiven, rather than super-ficial, or to explain particular events and outcomes.

William James described feelings as private and dumb (1985, p. 341) to emphasize how hard it is to describe them—even metaphorically—through prescribed and sanctioned terms. These feelings can be dismissed as a sign of madness. While scientific explanations, on the other hand, are expected to pass a test of empirical and consensual support, many arguments about religion and mental health are restricted to personal motives that are assumed to operate, or to reasons that are advanced for being actively "religious."

But how do we understand those who experience religion transcen-dentally or identify it as theater, find it in pilgrimages to sacred sites and, as tourists, in visits to ancient cities, or in high ceremonials, and not in terms of doctrines or sacraments? To answer that question requires a detailed knowledge of the demands of specific traditions, the social sanc-tions accepted by individuals, as well as an adequate analytic model.

DSM-III-R (1988) notes that DSM I (1952) consistently used the term "reaction" in its diagnostic descriptions, reflecting "Adolf Meyer's psy-chobiologic view that mental disorders represented reactions of the per-sonality (sic) to psychological, social, and biological factors" (p. xviii). The second edition in 1968 aimed for "neutral terms," that were not theoretically committed. In 1980, DSM-III offered a classification accept-able "to clinicians and researchers of varying theoretical orientations," without breaking with tradition (DSM-III-R, 1987, p. xix). DSM-III-R (1987) itself aimed to avoid identifying any "syndrome or pattern" with an "expectable response to a particular event," which should "be con-sidered a manifestation of a behavioural, psychological or biological dysfunction in the person."

Psychiatric diagnoses now deliberately try to exclude "deviant be-haviour, e.g. political, religious, or sexual," as well as "conflicts that are primarily between the individual and society . . . unless that deviance or conflict is a symptom of dysfunction in the person" (DSM-III-R, 1987, p. xxii). The apparently neutral (but still clinically biased) perspective of DSM-III-R has pushed psychiatric dysfunctions inside individuals. But religious practices can be set at a distance from any reactions that display defined "mental states" because of their claims on external and social traditions. Only when those claims "are uttered like statements about a mental state, that is, with subjective certainty and incorrigible by others" (Spitzer, 1990) can they be called "delusions." So long as we are talking about our own inner mental life, whatever we say need not be delusional.

That psychiatry itself faces those problems with a variety of theories tends to be neglected by those who would stigmatize religion. For example, phobic disorders can be explained "as a displacement of anxiety resulting from the breakdown of defense mechanisms that keep internal conflicts out of consciousness," "on the basis of learned avoidance re-sponses to conditioned anxiety," or as a "dysregulation of basic biological systems mediating separation anxiety" (DSM-III-R, 1987, p. xviii).

Psychiatry changed through the 1980's, identifying the structured cri-teria needed to make differential diagnoses that can be validated against the effects of specific treatments. Agreed estimates of the prevalence of mental illnesses across cultures and other groups are how expected to exclude prejudiced opinions about such social pathologies as alcohol or "substance" abuse. It is also realized that good clinical care involves shared responsibilities with other professionals who are medically trained, giving access to informed advice about how to reinterpret or understand whatever might be wrong.

But religious explanations are unlike the explanations of religion, since they reflect both religious and secular assumptions about what is involved. Our basic question then becomes, "Whose orthodoxy about religion and mental health should prevail, and for which groups?" That form of the problem requires an attitude that questions religious, psychiatric, or psychological conventions, and is not "obsessed" with literalism, be-haviorism, psychoanalysis, biological processes, social psychology, and so on. To advocate prayer or faith healing, psychotherapy or counseling as a solution for practical difficulties demands explicit supporting evidence that might be as weak and circumstantial as that surrounding any placebo treatment.

Systematic studies can clarify these issues, but they do not remove the ambiguity of whatever psychological involvement the orthodox controls of religion itself can have (cf. Shumacher, 1992). We are all influenced by the received traditions of our culture, to which we might conform, or that we try to transcend. In this sense, most people are, as William James suggested, "once" rather than "twice-born." It is those in the latter group who appear to be more at risk to adverse interactions between their religion and their mental health. William James (1985, p. 80) therefore emphasized that "The systematic cultivation of healthy-mindedness as a religious attitude is consonant with important currents in human nature, and is anything but absurd." He saw the "advance of liberalism in Christianity" as a "victory of reality-mindedness . . . over the morbidity with which the old hell-fire theology was more harmoniously related" (p. 81), and the advantages of optimism over pessimism (cf. Taylor, 1989), so that "invasive moral states and passionate enthusiasms . . . can alter how one understands the world" (James, 1985, p. 81). Principles like these are well known to contemporary psychology, and they continue to provide the ground on which the links between religion and positive mental health must stand. And religious attitudes are more likely to be a consequence than a cause of the kinds of social practice to which people become committed, or of which they disapprove.

References

Ader, R. & Cohen, N. (1985). CNS-immune system interactions with conditioning phenomena. *Behavioral and Brain Sciences*, 8, 379–394.

American Psychiatric Association. (1980). *Diagnostic and statistical manual of mental disorders* (3rd ed., [DSM-III]). Washington, DC: Author.

American Psychiatric Association. (1987). *Diagnostic and statistical manual of mental disorders*. (3rd ed., rev. [DSM-III-R]). Washington, DC: Author.

Barker, E. (1989). *New religious movements: A practical introduction*. London: Her Majesty's Stationery Office.

Batson, C.D. & Ventis, W.L. (1982). *The religious experience: A social-psychological perspective*. New York: Oxford University Press.

Bergin, A.E. (1980). Psychotherapy and religious values. *Journal of Consulting and Clinical Psychology*, 48, 95–105.

Bergin, A.E. (1983). Religiosity and mental health: A critical reevaluation and meta-analysis. *Professional Psychology: Research and Practice*, 14(2), 170–184.

Blackburn, R. (1988). On moral judgements and personality disorders: The myth of psychopathic personality revisited. *British Journal of Psychiatry*, 153, 505–512.

Bowker, J. (1987). *Licensed insanities: Religions and belief in God in the contemporary world*. London: Darton, Longman and Todd.

Chesen, E.S. (1972). *Religion may be hazardous to your health*. New York: Peter H. Weyden.

Dykstra, C. & Parkes, S. (Eds.). (1986). *Faith development and Fowler*. Birmingham, AL: Religious Education Press.

Ellis, A. (1976). *The case against religion: A psychotherapist's view*. New York: Institute for Rational Living.

Funder, D.C. & Colvin, C.R. (1991). Explanations in behavioral consistency: Properties of persons, situations, and behaviors. *Journal of Personality and Social Psychology*, 60(5), 773–794.

Godin, A. (1971). Some developmental tasks in Christian education. In M.P. Strommen (Ed.), *Research on religious development: A comprehensive handbook. A project of the Religious Education Association* (pp. 109–154). New York: Hawthorn Books.

Heimbrock, H.-G. (1991). Psychoanalytic understanding of religion. *International Journal for the Psychology of Religion*, *1*(2), 71–89.

James, W. (1902). *The varieties of religious experience*. New York: Collier. Reprinted in Smith, J.E. (Ed.). (1985). *The works of William James* (Vol. 15). Cambridge, MA.: Harvard University Press.

Jensen, J.P. & Bergin, A.E. (1988). Mental health values of professional therapists: A national interdisciplinary survey. *Professional Psychology: Research and Practice*, *19*(3), 290–297.

Kroll, J. & Bachrach, B. (1982). Medieval visions and contemporary hallucinations. *Psychological Medicine*, *12*, 709–721.

Lalljee, M., Brown, L.B., & Hilton, D. (1990). The relationship between images of God, explanations for failure to do one's duty to God, and invoking God's agency. *Journal of Psychology and Theology*, *18*(2), 166–173.

Lalljee, M., Lamb, R., & Carnibella, G. (1993). Lay prototypes of illness: Their content and use. *Psychology and Health*, *8*(1), 33–49.

Larson, D.B., Mansell-Patlison, E., Blazer, D.G., Omran, A.R., Keplan. B.H., et al. (1986). Systematic analysis of research on religious variables in four major psychiatric journals, 1978–1982. *American Journal of Psychiatry*, *143*(3), 329–334.

Loevinger, J. (1984). On the self and predictive behaviour. In R.A. Zucker, J. Aronoff, & A.I. Rabin (Eds.), *Personality and the prediction of behavior* (pp. 43–68). Orlando: Academic Press.

Moore, R. & McGehee, F. (Eds.). (1989). *New religious movements, mass suicide and people's temple*. Lewistin, NY: Edwin Mellon Press.

Parker, G.B., Brown, L.B., & Blignault, I. (1986). Coping behaviors as predictors of the course of clinical depression. *Archives of General Psychiatry*, *43*, 561–565.

Rizzuto, A.M. (1979). *The birth of the living God: A psychoanalytic study*. Chicago: University of Chicago Press.

Robbins, T. & Anthony D. (1982). Deprogramming, brainwashing and the medicalization of new religious movements. *Social Problems*, *29*, 283–297.

Shumacher, J.F. (1992). *Religion and mental health*, New York: Oxford University Press.

Spitzer, M. (1990). On defining delusions. *Comprehensive Psychiatry*, *31*(5), 377–397.

Taylor, S.E. (1989). *Positive illusions: Creative self-deception and the healthy mind*. New York: Basic Books.

World Health Organization. (1978). *Ninth revision of the international classification of diseases* (ICD-9). Geneva: Author.

Wulff, D.M. (1991). *Psychology of religion: Classic and contemporary views*. New York: John Wiley and Sons.

Author Index

Subject Index